The Song is Not the Same: Jews and American Popular Music

The Jewish Role in American Life

An Annual Review

The Song is Not the Same: Jews and American Popular Music

The Jewish Role in American Life

An Annual Review

Volume 8

Bruce Zuckerman, *Editor*
Josh Kun, *Guest Editor*
Lisa Ansell, *Associate Editor*

Published by the Purdue University Press for
the USC Casden Institute for the Study of the
Jewish Role in American Life

© 2011 by the
University of Southern California
Casden Institute for the
Study of the Jewish Role in American Life.
All rights reserved.

Production Editor, Marilyn Lundberg

Cover photo:
Song sheet: "When Mose with his Nose Leads the Band."
Photo by Buyenlarge. Courtesy of Getty Images.

ISBN 978-1-55753-586-3
ISBN 1-5573-586-8
ISSN 1934-7529

Published by Purdue University Press
West Lafayette, Indiana
www.thepress.purdue.edu
pupress@purdue.edu

Printed in the United States of America.

For subscription information,
call 1-800-247-6553

Contents

FOREWORD — vii

Gayle Wald — 1
Dreaming of Michael Jackson: Notes on Jewish Listening

Jody Rosen — 9
"Cohen Owes Me Ninety-Seven Dollars":
Images of Jews from the Jewish Sheet-Music Trade

Peter La Chapelle — 29
"Dances Partake of the Racial Characteristics of the People
Who Dance Them": Nordicism, Antisemitism, and Henry
Ford's Old-Time Music and Dance Revival

Jonathan Z. S. Pollack — 71
"Ovoutie Slanguage is Absolutely Kosher": Yiddish in
Scat-Singing, Jazz Jargon, and Black Music

Josh Kun — 89
"If I Embarrass You, Tell Your Friends": The Musical
Comedy of Bell Barth and Pearl Williams

David Kaufman — 115
"Here's a Foreign Song I Learned in Utah": The Anxiety
of Jewish Influence in the Music of Bob Dylan

Jeff Janeczko — 137
Negotiating Boundaries: Musical Hybridity in
Tzadik's Radical Jewish Culture Series

ABOUT THE CONTRIBUTORS — 169

ABOUT THE USC CASDEN INSTITUTE — 171

Foreword

This volume continues a practice that has proven highly successful in producing the two previous *Annual Review*s, namely, inviting an outstanding cultural critic and scholar to guest-edit a collection of essays that focuses on his/her area of expertise. In particular, we have used these volumes to explore aspects of the Jewish role in American life that at first glance may seem all too familiar but which we have tried to illuminate from a perspective that throws such well-known topics into a different kind of relief. In this instance, the topic is once again ostensibly well-traveled ground: Jews and their relationship to American popular music. But we knew we could count on our guest editor for Volume 8, Josh Kun, Associate Professor of Communication in the Annenberg School of Communication & Journalism at the University of Southern California, to look at this topic with a different sort of attitude than we might conventionally expect.

Kun has built a career out of looking at the cultural aspects of the Jewish role in American music in an offbeat fashion, especially in his role as one of the founders of the Idelsohn Society for Musical Preservation, an organization that has led the way in finding and saving from obscurity essential and utterly fascinating musical voices of note that have a Jewish dimension. He signals his intentions for this *Annual Review* from the outset with the title he has chosen for it: "The Song is not the Same." This title, at least for me, immediately triggers a kind of musical counter-memory that starts to play in my mind and I am time-warped back to the 60s where I imagine I can see lead singer Levi Stubbs rocking back and forth, while being backed by the other three Four Tops, as he croons the "hook" from a classic Motown oldie: "It's the same old song, but with a different meaning since you've been gone."

This song, of course, evokes the enduring memory of a lost love, triggered every time the singer recalls how a "melody keeps haunting me, reminding me how in love we used to be." Times may have changed, lovers may have parted—thereby endowing the melody and lyrics with a different, sadly sentimental meaning—but the song is still the same: it's just everything else that has changed. So likewise we seem to feel about Jews and their contributions to American popular music, as it arose and flourished in the twentieth century.

We recall Berlin, the Gershwins, and the other icons of Tin Pan Alley with affection, remembering the same old songs, heard in recordings and seen in films that still flicker across our TV and computer screens from a time gone by. Granted, times may have changed, as our ears have become attuned to different and ever proliferating genres of music, but somewhere back there we know we can still find an enduring body of popular melodies and lyrics that Jews have contributed to the American songbook. We know these songs; they are our songs, the same ones we've always known.

Or are they? Kun's aim as editor of this *Annual Review* is to play a contrapuntal theme against our musical expectations. You think back and believe you hear the same old song? Listen again. The song is not the same. There is a far greater complexity to those harmonies that shape our memories. When you tune your ear to take in the subtleties, you find a much more enriched and enriching texture to the Jewish role in American popular music. While one can hardly hope to encompass all aspects of this concern in a single volume, Kun has brought together here an eclectic group of essays that run the gamut of Jewish popular music but which all speak to a common theme, how much more there is to learn about a subject we thought was all so familiar—how much the song is not the same as we thought it was or think it ought to be.

One aspect of particular note emphasized herein speaks to this latter point—sometimes people want the song to be the same—especially when they are confronted by a new sound that they feel is simply too shrill. Thus Peter LaChapelle considers how none other than Henry Ford reacted to jazz and the Jazz Age, noting how the perceived threat of this "alien" music fed his anti-Semitism while fostering his desire to maintain and promote more traditional genres from the previous century through what was termed "old-time music." This theme also is a focus of Jeff Janeczko's consideration of an avant-garde extension of klezmer music both in terms of those who wished to break out and hybridize this genre of music-making with other genres, those who celebrated this innovation and those who resisted such post-klezmer music as inimical to taste and tradition.

Other essays in this collection look at aspects of Jewish-American popular music that surprise us, in particular, Jonathan Pollack's exploration of the way Jewish/Yiddish colloquialisms found their way into scat and other forms of jazz singing done by black performers. Jody Rosen's survey of "Jewface" images on songsheets of the early twentieth century (one of which serves as the cover image for this *Annual Review*) seem almost shocking in the casual fashion they project Jewish stereotypes that could be just as easily at home in the most virulent, Nazi anti-Jewish propaganda. Josh Kun celebrates the raw humor of such singing comediennes as Belle Barth and Pearl Williams, who in their late-night cabaret shows staked out a distinctly Jewish territory of raunch and thereby paved the way for both female and male humorists, who continue to push beyond the edges of what is conventionally called good taste. Finally two essays focus on particular personalities and the impact of their music from a Jewish perspective. Thus, David Kaufman takes a close look at the real and imagined Jewish aspects of Bob Dylan's songs while Gayle Wald reminisces on how Michael Jackson shaped an impressionable tween-girl's image of a pop-icon in a distinctly Jewish manner.

Since this volume is all about music, it only makes sense that we give our readers an opportunity to hear and see aspects of this subject matter that are less easily placed in print. So, as is signaled by editorial notes in this volume, we have established a website where our readers can go to listen to relevant musical clips featured in Janeczko's survey of post-klezmer music and have also placed full color versions of the cover sheets featured in Rosen's study of Jew-face images.

As was similarly the case for last year's volume of the *Annual Review*, this volume developed out of a grant from the Casden Institute given to Josh Kun so he could explore in a more systematic manner the ways in which Jewish slang and jargon found their way into the music sung and performed by black musicians primarily during the Jazz Age. This initial research proved so rewarding that it seemed a natural extension of this project to expand the realm of inquiry so that it evolved into this wide-ranging study of Jews and American popular music that constitute this collection of essays. One of the particular pleasures of my role as Myron and Marion Director of the Casden Institute is the opportunity this has afforded me to work with a series of creative guest-editors over an extended period of time. Working with Josh Kun on Volume 8 of the *Annual Review* has proven to be no exception, and I want to take this occasion to thank him for the fine job he has done in making this volume possible.

Lisa Ansell, Associate Director of the Casden Institute has had quite a busy year—especially because she has been occupied by the bringing of her son, Gabriel Hayim Schneider, into the world. First-time mothers are supposed to be overwhelmed by all the added chores and responsibilities, but Lisa must be some kind of super-mom, since she has still managed to keep the Casden Institute on a steady course and done the essential editorial work she needed to do as Associate Editor of this volume. This has also been a difficult and demanding year for my colleague Dr. Marilyn J. Lundberg who has nonetheless done all that needs to be done as Production Editor for this *Annual Review* without missing a dotted "i" or crossed "t." Howard Gillman, Dean of the College of Letters, Arts & Sciences and Susan Wilcox, Associate Dean for College Advancement continue to give the Casden Institute their unreserved support and enthusiasm, so essential to our ongoing success.

Of the many supporters of the Casden Institute, Ruth Ziegler, Carmen Warschaw, Mark and Sam Tarica, and—of course—Alan Casden always take pride of place. Their attentiveness to our needs and aspirations has always played a vital role in our growth.

This is a very exciting time of transition for our home institution, the University of Southern California. The year has witnessed the appointment and inauguration of C. L. Max Nikias as President of USC and Elizabeth Garrett as Provost. They have begun their terms of office by projecting an ambitious vision for our future that makes all of us feel lucky to be here at such a momentous time of opportunity. All of us at the Casden Institute send Max and Beth our warmest congratulations and look forward with enthusiasm to their leadership of USC. As they begin to chart the course for our future, it seems, entirely appropriate on the occasion of their respective appointments, to dedicate this volume in their honor.

Bruce Zuckerman, *Myron and Marian Casden Director*

Dreaming of Michael Jackson: Notes on Jewish Listening

Gayle Wald

It would seem counterintuitive to title a piece on Jewish listening "Dreaming of Michael Jackson." After all, when Jackson died in June 2009, he was remembered for many things: his remarkable career, his magnificent talent, his penchant for bodily self-invention, his role as a groundbreaking African-American musician, and the spectacle of a complex and difficult life lived in public—for many things, in other words, but *not* for his relation to Jewish listeners or to something we might deign to call "Jewish listening practices." Even the post-mortem media gawking that focused on Jackson's sometimes contradictory relationship to Judaism or Jewish people—his close relationship with "Rabbi to the Stars" Shmuley Boteach; the controversy surrounding the lyrics of his 1995 song "They Don't Care about Us"; his apparent attraction to the mystical tradition of Kabbalah—did not connect the late performer to Jewish listeners, let alone listeners who might hear Michael Jackson "Jewishly."

In my own experience, however, Michael Jackson figures prominently, not just as an idol of my youth but also as a popular musician through whom I negotiated Jewish American identity in the 1970s. For me, "Michael Jackson" (in quotes, because I am referring not merely to the performer but to his performances and his persona: in short, to a range of significations that cluster around the artist's name) provided a canvas upon which I came subsequently to write and rewrite my sense of a Jewish self.

It goes without saying that I did not think any of this when I was a third grader listening to Jackson Five records. In fact, I didn't think any of this at all until Michael Jackson died, and I was prompted, like everyone else, to contemplate *my* Michael Jackson. (Clearly, the cultural imperative to think about Michael Jackson in highly personal terms says something about the ways audiences have been taught to engage with pop music stars at the level of identity.) *My* Michael, I realized, was certainly not the relatively recent Michael Jackson of *Bad* (1987), *Dangerous* (1991), or *HIStory* (1995), and it wasn't even the Michael of *Off the Wall* (1979), however much I love that album. Rather, *my* Michael was the boy in the Jackson Five with the ethereally great voice, sweetly radiant face, and diaphanous Afro. He was the teenybopper pop-idol Michael, the indisputable leader of his older brothers, the one looking out of a pin-up photo of a 1972 *Tiger Beat*, reclining, perhaps a tad self-consciously and therefore all the more charmingly, on a patch of grass in front of a rhododendron bush, wearing striped slacks and a striped button-down shirt artfully parted at the hem to provide a peek of a wide brown grommet belt—a hint of grown-up sexuality (see http://www.nowpublic.com/culture/michael-jackson-pinup-tiger-beat-1972).

Given Michael's outfit and hairdo, it's relatively easy to locate the *Tiger Beat* photograph in time, as belonging to the 1970s. It's much harder, however, to locate it in space. Perhaps that patch of browning grass, with the rhododendron bush behind it, was the photographer's backyard? Perhaps Michael was posing in the Jacksons' own backyard? Perhaps the patch of grass beneath him is outside Motown Studios, at the time recently relocated from Detroit to Los Angeles?

What strikes me in retrospect is that the setting in which Michael was pictured could have just as easily been *my* backyard. I was born in Northeast Philadelphia, and in 1972, when I was in second grade, my family (my father and mother, my younger sister) moved to the Philadelphia suburbs. Geographically, this meant moving five or six miles north and a bit west. Architecturally, it meant moving from a brick duplex with cement front steps to what my parents meaningfully referred to as a "stand-alone" house: a four-bedroom Colonial set on a half-acre of property in a brand new subdivision called Wheatfield West. The agrarian metaphor—perhaps a reference to the fields that were home to flocks of pheasants before the bulldozers moved in—was apt, albeit in an unintentionally funny way, since socially speaking, moving to Wheatfield West meant moving from a predominantly Jewish urban neighborhood, within easy driving distance of my small extended family, to what some in my parents' extended circle of Jewish friends considered a non-Jewish wilderness. When we moved, I went from being one of several Jewish kids in class to being the only Jewish kid, from one who could trade her matzoh at lunchtime to one who, in the interest of diversity, had to give a presentation on the Passover story at Easter time. Occasionally at recess, the tough kids would throw pennies at me and once or twice, expressions of anti-Semitism on our street took a rather more violent and alarming turn; but these were for the most part isolated incidents, written off as the mindless pranks of bad kids.

In fact, the larger neighborhood, Ambler, Pennsylvania, was in the early and mid-1970s a multicultural hodgepodge, home, especially around Wheatfield West, to Irish and Italian Americans, whose large Catholic families could comfortably spread out in new housing developments. Although "space" meant different things to us, all of our families ostensibly shared the American dream of claiming it. So the girls, with whom I would have studied the 1972 Michael pin-up from *Tiger Beat* (I don't recall any boys being so interested), were white girls—newly suburban, middle-class white *ethnic* girls. Together and alone, we not only listened and danced to the Jackson Five, but debated which one was cutest and which one we would marry when we grew up. In my memory, matrimonial fantasy was a common fan-practice, a creative way that girls like us, as avid consumers of pop music and pop spectacle, worked out our incipient desires (always heterosexual, always consummated in marriage) even as we worked out status and hierarchy within our own group (the alpha-girls got their first-choice boys; the others took the boys that were left). Of the brothers in the Jackson Five, Michael was hands-down our favorite; Tito, Jermaine, and the others were not as cute, and in any case were too old to fulfill our fantasies. It was Michael, the youngest brother, who possessed, at least in his star persona, the right combination of purity and sexuality, actual and symbolic youth. He was funky and innocent, sure but shy, inexperienced and yet able to sing with authentic emotion about unrequited love. We hadn't yet gone through breakups, let alone "gone out" with boys, but Michael helped us imagine and rehearse these experiences. Such rehearsals were, in turn, fully in line with a conventional trajectory of middle-class Jewish girlhood, in which it was assumed we would date, and then marry, Jewish men before going on to produce Jewish families and reproduce "the Jewish people."

In short, we consumed Jackson Five and Michael Jackson music in ways that our parents and capitalism alike deemed both acceptable and appropriate: by reading fanzines, listening to records, and animatedly discussing our likes and dislikes. Our suburban bedrooms, carpeted sanctuaries, seemed to have been designed expressly for such privatized, domesticated expressions of desire. Dreaming about Michael Jackson, we acted according to the terms of a familiar gendered vocabulary of preadolescent heterosexual eroticism (crushes, dreams of marriage, etc.). Ostensibly, nothing we were doing in those bedrooms conflicted with the expectations governing nice Jewish girls.

Yet in listening to Michael Jackson, we also projected ourselves into futures that our parents would not have recognized and of which they would have almost certainly disapproved. Even as our consumption *practices* conformed to expectation, that is to say, our listening and dreaming abetted points of contact with, and crossover into, forbidden territory. In particular the fantasy of marrying Michael Jackson, which sometimes took the form of imagining that *Michael* would choose one of *us* (from among all the other girls!), took shape in a world in which such sexual and marital unions—had they been real—would have been social anathema. Whispered rumors of parents who sat *shiva* for sons and daughters who married non-Jews, in flagrant acts of refusal to conform to prescribed narratives of Jewish adulthood, were also part of our domestic soundscape in those years. With grandparents living among us who had survived pogroms and the Holocaust, and whose spoken English still bore the sonic imprint of these places of Jewish persecution and genocide, and with the melody and lyrics of "Hatikvah" sounding in our collective Jewish American unconscious, "intermarriage" (the word itself was vaguely obscene, like "intercourse") loomed as a profound offense, not merely to the family but to the community and to history—indeed, to the lost Six Million.

Michael Jackson and his brothers represented a racialized version of such transgression within this economy of exogamy-as-violent-betrayal; they were Black before they were Gentiles, *schwartzes* before they were *goyim*. (I don't think we knew that the Jacksons were Seventh-Day Adventists, and in any case the distinctions among non-Catholic Christians were at best hazy to us.) Our dreams about Michael were thus racially integrated even as we were part of the upwardly mobile demographic of those who left Philadelphia after 1968, thereby helping to create the predominantly brown and black "inner city." Symbolically, these dreams reflected our parents' support of Civil Rights even as they ventured decidedly beyond the limits of their liberalism.

Another boy-band features in my memory of these years, and that is, of course, the Osmonds. The brothers from Ogden, Utah, with their toothy smiles and shaggy dos, had a massive hit in January 1971 with "One Bad Apple," a song that explicitly used the resources of the famous Muscle Shoals Sound Studio Rhythm Section to make Osmonds sound a little blacker and a little funkier—in effect, a lot more like the Jackson Five. At the time, it was not uncommon for listeners to hear "One Bad Apple" on the radio and think it was a

Jackson Five song, but of course such mistakes were precisely the point. Unlike the Jacksons, who like the rest of the Motown acts of the era walked a narrow tightrope when it came to the embodiment of pop sensibilities, with the genre's connotations of innocent and healthy sexuality, the Osmonds laid relatively easy claim to the monikers "wholesome" and "all-American." Indeed, by means of what George Lipsitz has called "the possessive investment in whiteness," the boys from Utah, unlike the boys from Gary, were able to appropriate the sonic signatures of "black" music without relinquishing their claim upon racial normativity (Lipsitz).

As a girl, I would not have described the difference between these boybands in such terms, and yet I listened to the Osmonds in the context of my own social (dis)location. "One Bad Apple" was undeniably a great pop single, but the Osmonds did not appeal to me with the same power of the Jackson Five. In and of itself, there is nothing remarkable about this; I was certainly not alone in judging the brothers from Ogden, Utah as inferior in their singing and dancing to the brothers from Gary, Indiana. But their Mormonism—an important part of their sexually modulated public image— gave my ambivalent regard for them an additional dimension that concerned even as it interpolated me as a *Jewish* girl. That is, the Osmonds' self-representation as Mormons was for me slightly threatening (in my naïveté I didn't imagine that Mormons liked Jews), and their squeaky cleanness struck me as, well, a bit too *Aryan*. They were, in a phrase, *too white* for me as a Jewish girl, even as their whiteness was precisely how they communicated their availability for my pre-adolescent pop fantasies.

Although I can only gesture toward it in these few pages, there is an immensely complicated story to be told here—about Jewish-American assimilationist desires, Jewish-American articulations of racial discourse in the United States, gendered narratives of Jewish-American success, and racialized expressions of gendered desire. The story of *my* Michael Jackson is significant, in other words, not for what it says about *me*, but for what it might tell us about the relation of popular music to the negotiation of gendered Jewish middle-class identities in the 1970s. In closing, then, I want to use it to enumerate four principles for the future study of Jewish listening.

First, my story about dreaming of Michael Jackson from a carpeted bedroom in Wheatfield West circa 1972 implies that *negotiations of Jewishness, and hence theorizations of Jewish listening as a cultural practice through which Jewish identities are calibrated and recalibrated, may be independent of any consideration of Jewish performers or Jewish music.* Although I grew up hearing music

I identified as Jewish—from the choir in my large and prosperous Reform congregation to the Israeli and Hebrew folk songs I encountered in Jewish youth groups and summer camp to the Neil Diamond records that rendered my aunt weak-kneed or to the Alan Sherman comedy LPs that made my father double over with laughter—this story about Michael Jackson is not a story about the ostensible discovery or affirmation of a Jewish self in Jewish sounds, or sounds that are marked or marketed as Jewish. It may well be that sonically speaking, Jewish identities in the post-World War II era of Jewish-American economic advancement and cultural assimilation are primarily negotiated outside the realm of Jewish music per se. This does not make the listeners or the listening practices any less Jewish, but it does mean that we need to be attuned to possibilities of Jewish listening and Jewish sonic self-fashioning staged in ostensibly non-Jewish contexts.

Indeed—and this is the second possibility—*sonic negotiations of Jewish-American identity are necessarily shaped by discourses of Jewish racialization and Jewish otherness in the United States.* The example of Michael Jackson and the Jackson Five introduces the idea that as late twentieth-century American Jews left urban Jewish enclaves such as Philadelphia for the suburbs (sometimes but not always coded as the gentile suburbs), sonic negotiations of Jewish identity were increasingly staged through musical performers or performances that could somehow embody lost urban spaces and urban identities. Perhaps, that is to say, listening to Michael Jackson was for American girls of my age and circumstance a means of negotiating—once again, through the figure of blackness—our explicitly articulated status as ethnic others, once we moved out of the city's Jewish enclaves, which were themselves undergoing rapid transformation.

This is not to say that such fantasies, which exemplify the potential of desire to flout social expectations and norms, necessarily served a transgressive function. *In other words, even if Jews remain outsiders to discourses of normative race, gender, and nationality, there is nothing inherently destabilizing to the social order in listening self-consciously through Jewish ears.* For some of us, dreaming of Michael Jackson was a conventional exercise, a means of imaginatively letting off "steam" to enable an ultimate embrace of social norms. For others, especially those with an incipient desire to break out from social norms, such culturally sanctioned, "appropriately" gendered, heterosexual fan-practices were a means of challenging the racial/ethnic boundaries that we were supposed to occupy. That is, listening and fandom (done mostly in the manner of "good girls") enabled some of us to tolerate the fixed social, cultural, and geographic spaces, within which we were discovering and creating ourselves. In this sense, dreaming of Michael was not only fun, but it was vital to our survival.

This is also the message of the 1987 film *Dirty Dancing*, in which the young, upper-middle-class Jewish female protagonist explores and expresses her desire to distance herself from Jewishness-as-assimilation-and-gendered-containment through an erotic link to a man who represents ethnic and class difference. In a context in which the protagonist has limited outlets for such expression, music and dance are represented as conduits for the creation of explicitly Jewish alternatives to what in her world is normative Jewishness. The film strongly suggests that her boundary-crossing desires, while ambiguously "resolved" within the context of the film, will in the future translate into explicit political investments in social justice. Through music and dance, a Jewish leftist heroine is born.

The example of *Dirty Dancing* brings me to my last point, which is that *Jewish listening is always gendered, and that inquiry into modes of listening "Jewishly" may provide us with key insights into the identity-formation of (Jewish) girls and women*, those subjects who have traditionally been marginalized in studies of (Jewish) popular music. As important as it is for us to study Jewish performers and performance practices, it may only be by expanding our field of inquiry to include Jewish *listening* and *listening practices* that we can fully comes to grips with the experiences of Jewish girls and women, who traditionally have had fewer opportunities, and less enticement, to take up positions of prominence within popular music.

Works Cited

Dirty Dancing. Perf. Jennifer Grey and Patrick Swayze. Great American Films and Vestron Pictures, 1987.

Jackson, Michael. *Bad.* Epic, 1987.

———. *Dangerous.* Epic, 1991.

———. *HIStory.* Epic, 1995.

———. *Off the Wall.* Epic, 1979.

Lipsitz, George. *The Possessive Investment in Whiteness: How White People Profit from Identity Politics.* Philadelphia: Temple UP, 2006.

Michael Jackson Pinup. *Tiger Beat.* 1972. 14 Feb. 2011 <http://www.nowpublic.com/culture/michael-jackson-pinup-tiger-beat-1972>.

The Osmonds. "One Bad Apple." MGM, 1970.

"Cohen Owes Me Ninety-Seven Dollars": Images of Jews from the Jewish Sheet-Music Trade

Jody Rosen

In 1899, the M. Witmark & Sons Company, one of New York's leading popular song firms, published a number called "Oh, Such A Business." The song told the story of a tightfisted Jewish pawnshop owner; its lyrics were composed in a malaprop-heavy parody of Yiddish speech. It was, in other words, a "Jewface" number—a comic dialect song, written for the variety stage's singing-and-shticking specialists in "Hebrew impersonation."

Was "Oh, Such A Business" a hit? We can't be sure. The prolific vocal duo of Arthur Collins and Byron G. Harlan recorded the song in a 1901 Victor Records session, but the disc was never commercially released. No mentions of the song surface in the trade press of the period. Today, "Oh, Such A Business" survives less as a song, and more as an *objet d'art*: the three-page sheet-music folio that rolled off of the Witmark & Sons presses, with striking cover illustration framing an inset photo of the vaudevillian Joe Welch in full Jewface regalia (Fig. 1*).

Song-sheets are the ur-pop musical artifacts. They are remnants of a lost musical age, the period before the rise of radio and the emergence of the 78 rpm disc followed eventually by the LP, when singing stars stalked the vaudeville boards and audiences experienced popular music first and foremost as a participatory activity, belting out the latest Tin Pan Alley offerings

---

* Color versions of the figures can be viewed at http://casdeninstitute.usc.edu/annual.

around the parlor-room piano. For historians of Jewish dialect music, which reached a pinnacle of popularity between the years 1900–1920, song-sheets are the primary documents. Although perhaps a few dozen wax-cylinder and 78 recordings of the songs exist, the bulk of the Jewface repertoire was never recorded and survives today solely as notes on sheet-music staves. But musical notation is not the only language in which the song-sheets speak. Jewface sheet-music covers carry crucial history lessons, bring the song's themes into vivid focus, and preserve the long-forgotten composers and performers who turned Jewish-dialect ditties into Progressive Era pop hits. Gazing at the bright, garish sheet-music cover illustrations, we can sharpen how we hear these century-old songs all the clearer.

American song publishers have always used eye-catching designs to sell sheet music. In the first half of the nineteenth century, song-sheet art was largely text-based—titles splashed across covers in ornamental fonts—but after the Civil War, advances in lithography brought black-and-white illustrations to sheet music. By the turn of the twentieth century, new photographic printing techniques and the development of offset presses made elaborate color illustration ubiquitous among commercial publishers. Whether peddling snappy ragtime songs or sentimental ballads, Tin Pan Alley's song factories delivered their product in seductive packages: graphically arresting, boldly colorful, unmistakably *moderne*.

Judged by contemporary standards, Jewface song-sheet covers strike us, first and foremost, as bizarre. Indeed, to a modern sensibility, Jewish dialect songs are offensive: apparent relics of an earlier pop culture era's taste for coarse ethnic and racial caricature. But Jewface music often reached consumers in elegant packages—beneath *art nouveau* and proto-Deco sheet-music covers that bore little or no relation to the content of the songs themselves.

Songs like "Jake, Jake (The Yiddisha Ball Player)" (Fig. 2), "At that Yiddish Society Ball" (Fig. 3), "Under the Matzos Tree" (Fig. 4), and "Under the Hebrew Moon" (Fig. 5) are broad farces, with lyrics that trade in anti-Semitic imagery and tunes that move through stereotypically "Jewish" intervals over dolorous minor keys. But the sheet-music covers are purely decorative—graceful swoops and swags reminiscent of Viennese Secessionist design. The cover for "Cohen Owes Me Ninety-Seven Dollars" (Fig. 6), Irving Berlin's famous farce about a miserly *shmatte* or rag salesman, features a stylized window topped by floral garlands, a tableau that offers no hint of the song's romping ethnic comedy. These juxtapositions seem odd, but they tell us something important about the contemporary understanding of Jewface genre. In 2010, a song like

"Cohen Owes Me Ninety-Seven Dollars" seems exotic and somewhat offensive, but in 1915 it was mainstream pop and would have been seen by no one—least of all Jews—as occasion for angry responses from the Anti-Defamation League (had the ADL existed). Such a song was so normative that the Waterson, Berlin & Snyder Company saw no need to signal its novelty status, but rather simply packaged it with a generically "pretty" cover.

Sometimes publishers were less coy about advertising their products' Jewishness. "Rosenbaum" (Fig. 7) places an impish Jewish toy soldier against a dichromatic field of red and blue. There are images of embodied Jewish ethnicity that verge on *Shturmer*-style caricature (so-named after the infamous Nazi newspaper that specialized in this type of anti-Semitic imagery): the grotesquely hook-nosed Jewish John Philip Sousa of "When Mose with His Nose Leads the Band" (Fig. 8), and the blackface Jew on the cover of "Jerusalem Rag" (Fig. 9), a reminder that, in the first decades of the century, Jews were still categorized as non-white in the United States Census. The song-sheets for "Oh, Such A Business" (Fig. 1) and "Get A Girl with Lots of Money, Abie" (Fig. 10), feature photographs of Hebrew comedians in the stereotypical garb of their trade: tattered black overcoats, scraggly fake beards, derby caps pulled down tight across the ears.

These song-sheets remind us that Jewish men were almost always the protagonists of Jewface songs, and the butt of their own jokes. The stock-character in Hebrew comedy was "Abie Cohen"—a Jewish refraction of that blackface staple, Sambo. He was an old world Jew, bumbling through the polyglot new world metropolis, mangling the English language, misapprehending American customs, failing spectacularly in romance, punctuating his pratfalls with the stereotypical despairing cries of "oy!"

We still know this Abie-stereotype quite well. He has never really gone away, although perhaps today we would associate him more quickly with other names. Nonetheless, this schlemiel, who has been a staple of popular culture up through Woody Allen, Larry David and Ben Stiller, first penetrated American consciousness in songs like "Oh, Such A Business." Jewface songs often wring broad comedy from the schlemiel-archetype, showing the failures of Jewish men to play heroic American roles: baseball player ("Jake, Jake"), boxer ("There Never Was a White Hope Whose Christian Name Was Cohen" [Fig. 11]), cowboy ("Yonkle, the Cow Boy Jew" [Fig. 12]; "I'm A Yiddish Cowboy" [Fig. 13]), Indian chief ("Big Chief Dynamite" [Fig. 14]). The World War I-era "Yankee Doodle Abie" tells the story of a cowardly Jewish soldier who hides behind the ammunition wagon counting his money while the battles rages.

The sheet-music cover depicts a Jew in a doughboy uniform, with diamonds spilling out of his rifle (not illustrated).

Lyrics that focus on Jewish money-grubbing serve as the perennial punchline of Jewface songs (Figs. 15, 16). The song-sheet for Irving Berlin's "Business is Business, Rosey Cohen" (Fig. 17) makes the theme plain, setting its cover photograph between giant *art nouveau* dollar signs. Some sheet-music covers draw on the nineteenth-century European traditions of anti-Semitic caricature: note the gleaming diamond broaches on the covers of "Big Chief Dynamite" (Fig. 14), "Kleiner Kohen" (Fig. 18), and "Oi Yoi Yoi" (Fig. 19). But in most of the songs, the Jews are depicted as having much humbler origin. They are ghetto strivers, obsessed with petty business matters, which, invariably, they confuse with matters of the heart. "That's Yiddisha Love" (Fig. 20) sums up the comic conflation of finance and romance: "If she's honest and frank/And has money in the bank/Oi, oi!/That's Yiddisha love."

However, Yiddisha love really doesn't stand a chance in the American melting pot. Abie implores his woman to stay with him, but loses her to the lures of modernity and assimilation—to gentile suitors, and to that powerfully sensual, democratizing force, American popular culture, as in Berlin's 1909 hit "Sadie Salome, Go Home" (not illustrated), about a Jewish girl who runs away from her boyfriend to become a star on the burlesque stage. Song-sheet cover art drives the point home, portraying the Jewish female as a sleek post-ethnic "new woman" (Fig. 21). And while Jewish women move fluidly across ethnic lines—even giving birth to "Irisher, Yiddisher boys" ("Moysha Machree [They're Proud of Their Irisher, Yiddisher Boy]"; Fig. 22)—Jewish men invariably flop. As a 1910 song puts it: "It's tough when Izzy Rosenstein loves Genevieve Malone" (Fig. 23).

Of course, Jews were hardly the only group lampooned on Tin Pan Alley. But among the wide variety of turn-of-the-century ethnic and racial dialect music, Jewface songs represent a special case. In its business and creative spheres, the popular song trade was dominated by Jews, and Jewface music was, accordingly, largely a Jewish enterprise: songs by, of, and for Jews.

The sheet-music covers tell the story: nearly every song was either composed by a Jew, or published by a Jewish-owned song firm, or both. Study the cover photos, and you find that songs were introduced by some of the most celebrated Jewish vaudevillians: Sophie Tucker (not illustrated), Al Jolson (not illustrated), Fanny Brice (Fig. 24), Eddie Cantor (not illustrated), to name only the most prominent. Jews have always loved Jewish jokes—and these songs told plenty of them. Sometimes the in-jokes were right there on the sheet-music.

On the song-sheet for one of the earliest published Jewish dialect numbers, "Dot Beautiful Hebrew Girl" (Fig. 25), the title arcs over a single Hebrew word כשר, "kosher," in bold point red lettering—a big wink at the Jewish audience. Here, as elsewhere, you can tell the song is the genuine article by its cover.

Of course, "kosher" signifies different things to different audiences. One of the notable things about the Jewface images we find on these song-sheets (not to mention in their lyrics and music) is how they show the willingness of Jewish entertainers, writers, artists and publishers to sell Jewish clichés to the general public and thereby reinforce the popular assumptions of how Jews ought to be seen. Jews might be sensitive to the mockery and satire that lurk just under the surface of these images, but to the popular sensibilities of those who mostly bought these song-sheets, none of these subtleties would have been so manifest. Indeed, virtually the same image-types could be adopted by the Nazis and other purveyors of anti-Semitic propaganda, without a hint of irony, as *genuine* depictions of Jews—no joking!

To be sure, Jewish songwriters and their fellow travelers on Tin Pan Alley hardly confined themselves to the popularization of Jewish stereotypes. They were just as ready to create and promote blackface music with all the stereotypical mammies and Swanees that went with it. Likewise, they were just as quick to sentimentalize a "White Christmas" (perhaps even with the double-entendre intended) just like the one their Christian audiences used to know. Perhaps the point to be made about all this is that the bright lines we might tend to draw between virulent prejudice and ironic, even innocent, stereotype were hardly so clear at the beginning of the twentieth century. If, when viewed from the perspective of the twenty-first century, the depictions on these song-sheets may seem at best politically incorrect and at worse a self-inflicted wound by Jews on Jews, it is useful to recall that a century or so ago it tweren't necessarily so.

Fig. 1: "Oh, Such a Business"

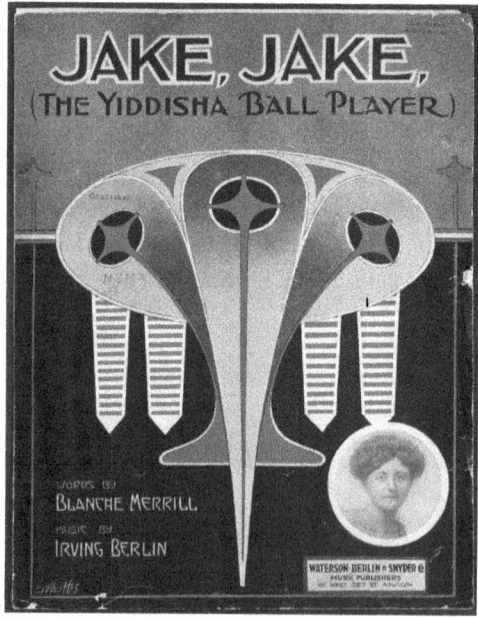

Fig. 2: "Jake, Jake (The Yiddisha Ball Player)"

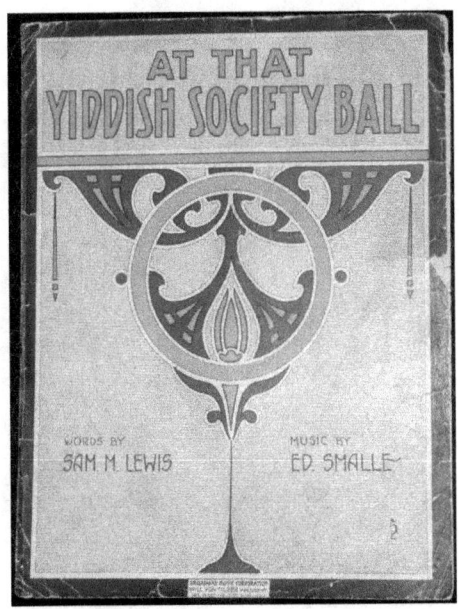

Fig. 3: "At That Yiddish Society Ball"

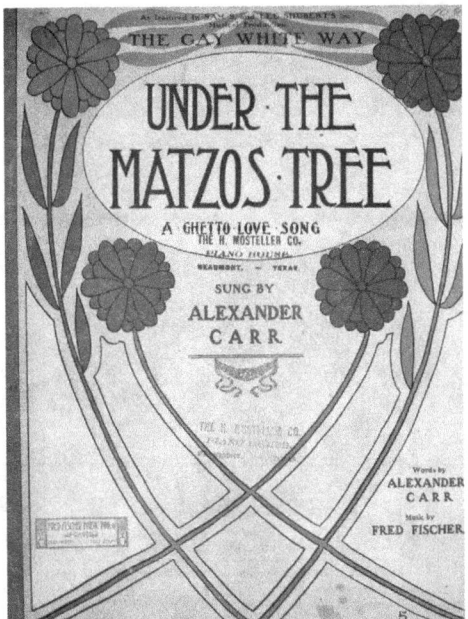

Fig. 4: "Under the Matzos Tree"

Fig. 5: "Under the Hebrew Moon"

Fig. 6: "Cohen Owes Me Ninety Seven Dollars"

Fig. 7: "Rosenbaum"

Fig. 8: "When Mose with His Nose Leads the Band"

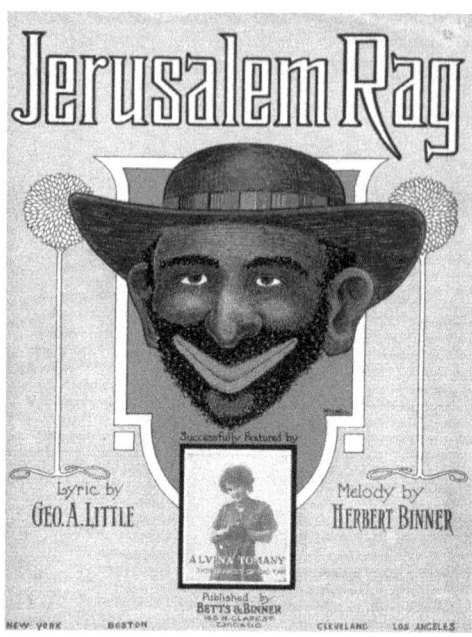

Fig. 9: "Jerusalem Rag"

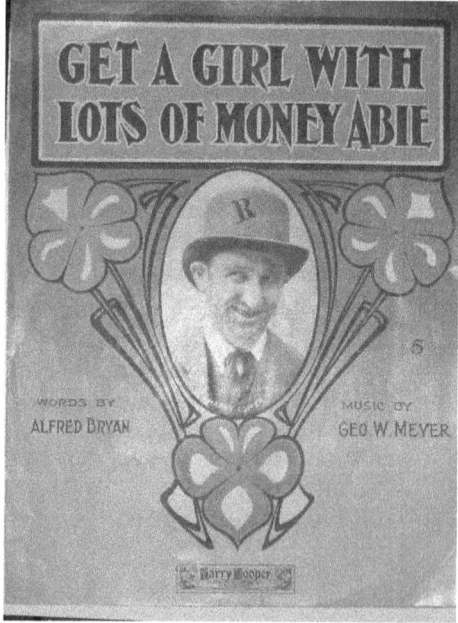

Fig. 10: "Get a Girl with Lots of Money Abie"

Fig. 11: "There Never Was a White Hope Whose Christian Name was Cohen"

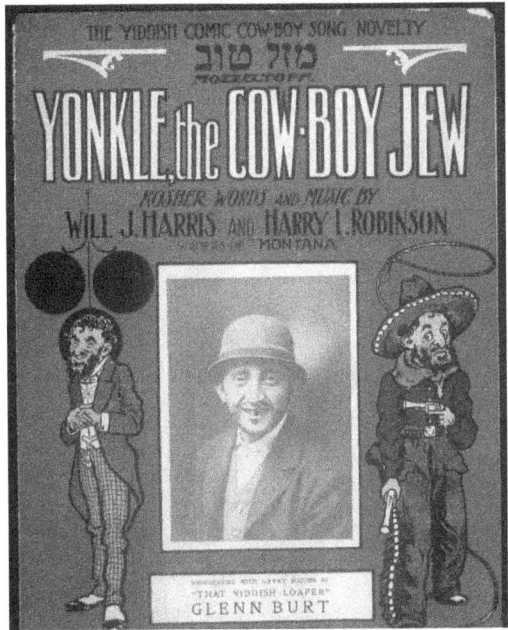

Fig. 12: "Yonkle the Cow-Boy Jew"

Fig. 13: "I'm a Yiddish Cowboy"

Fig. 14: "Big Chief Dynamite"

Fig. 15: "Never Mind the Family Tree, Look at the Business Plant"

Fig. 16: "D-O-U-G-H (Oi, Oi, That's a Bus'ness Proposition)"

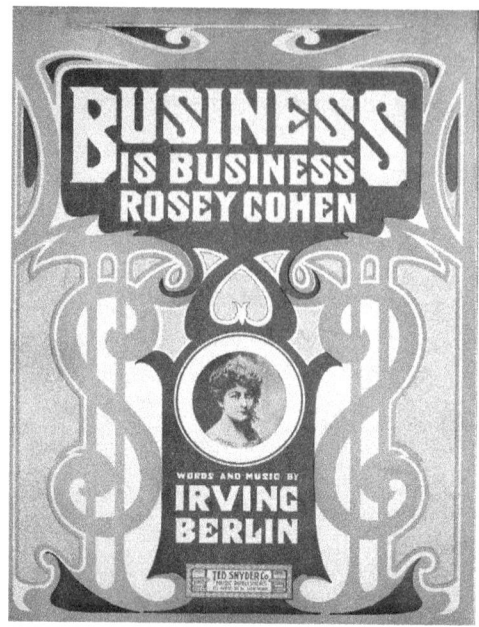

Fig. 17: "Business is Business Rosey Cohen"

Fig. 18: "Kleiner Kohen"

Fig. 19: "Oi, Yoi, Yoi, Yoi (A Hebrew Love Song)"

Fig. 20: "That's Yiddisha Love"

Fig. 21: "Nat'an! Nat'an! Tell Me for What Are You Waitin', Nat'an?"

Fig. 22: "Moysha Machree (They're Proud of Their Irisher, Yiddisher Boy)"

Fig. 23: "It's Tough When Izzy Rosenstein Loves Genevieve Malone

Fig. 24: Fanny Brice on the cover of "Fol de Rol Dol Doi"

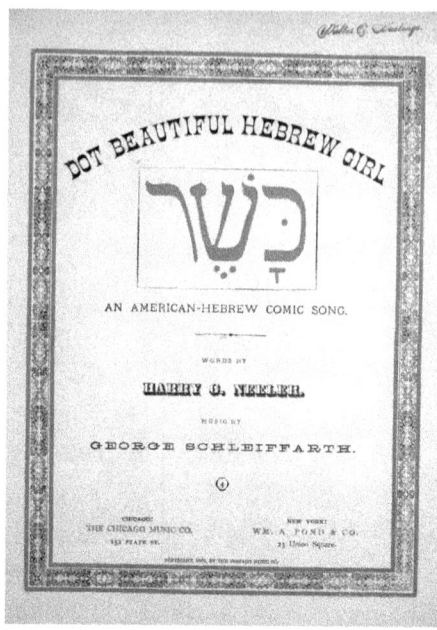

Fig. 25: "Dot Beautiful Hebrew Girl"

Works Cited

Berlin, Irving. Sheet music. "Business is Business, Rosey Cohen." New York: Snyder Music, 1911.

———. Sheet music. "Cohen Owes Me Ninety-Seven Dollars." New York: Waterson, Berlin & Snyder, 1915.

———. Sheet music. "White Christmas." New York: Irving Berlin, 1942.

Branen, Jeff T. and Al Piantadosi. Sheet music. "Big Chief Dynamite." Chicago: Rossiter Music, 1909.

Brockman, James. Sheet music. "Never Mind the Family Tree, Look at the Business Plant." New York: Witmark, 1911.

———. Sheet music. "That's Yiddisha Love." New York: Whitmark, 1910.

Bryan, Alfred and Geo. W. Meyer. Sheet music. "Get A Girl with Lots of Money, Abie." New York: Harry Cooper Music, 1908.

Fischer, Fred. Sheet music. "Rosenbaum." New York: Fischer Music, 1909.

———. Sheet music. "Under the Matzos Tree." New York: Fischer Music, 1907.

Fitzgibbon, Bert, Jack Drislane and Theodore Morse. Sheet music. "When Mose with His Nose Leads the Band." New York: Haviland, 1906.

Gillespie, Arthur and Gus Edwards. Sheet music. "Oh, Such A Business." Perf. Arthur Collins and Byron G. Harlan. Victor Records session, 1901.

Gold, Belle, perf. Sheet music. "D-o-u-g-h (Oi, Oi, That's a Bus'ness Proposition)." Philadelphia: Morris.

Harris, Will J. and Harry I. Robinson. Sheet music. "Yonkle, the Cow Boy Jew." Chicago: Rossiter Music, 1907. Henry, Max. "Kleiner Kohen." Detroit: Daniels & Russell, 1903.

Jardon, Dolly and Edward Madden. Sheet music. "Under the Hebrew Moon." New York: Shapiro, 1909.

Kahn, Gus and Grace Le Boy. Sheet music. "It's Tough when Izzy Rosenstein Loves Genevieve Malone." Chicago: Rossiter Music, 1910.

Kendis, James. Sheet music. "Moysha Machree (They're Proud of Their Irisher, Yiddisher Boy)." New York: Kendis, 1916.

———. Sheet music. "Nat'an! Nat'an! Tell Me for What Are You Waitin', Nat'an?" Kendis, 1906.

Lee, Irving and Phil Schwartz. Sheet music. "There Never Was a White Hope Whose Christian Name Was Cohen." Chicago: Rossiter Music, 1912.

Leslie, Edgar and Irving Berlin. Sheet music. "Sadie Salome, Go Home." New York: Snyder, 1909.

Leslie, Edgar, Al Piantodosi and Halsey K. Mohr. Sheet music. "I'm A Yiddish Cowboy." New York: Barron Music, 1909.

Lewis, Sam M. and Archie Gottler. Sheet music. "At that Yiddish Society Ball." New York: Leo Feist, 1915.

Little, Geo. and Herbert Binner. Sheet music. "Jerusalem Rag." Chicago: Betts & Binner, 1912.

Longbrake, Arthur and Ed. Edwards. Sheet music. "Yankee Doodle Abie." Philadelphia: Longbrake & Edwards, 1911.

Madden, Edward and Jean Schwartz. Sheet music. "Fol de Rol Dol Doi. A Yiddish Seranade." Perf. Fanny Brice. New York: Remick, 1912.

Merrill, Blanche and Irving Berlin. Sheet music. "Jake, Jake (The Yiddisha Ball Player)." New York: Waterson, Berlin & Snyder, 1913.

Neeler, Harry G. and George Schleiffarth. Sheet music. "Dot Beautiful Hebrew Girl." Chicago: Chicago Music, 1881.

Smith, Chris. Sheet music. "Oi ,Yoi, Yoi Yoi (A Hebrew Love Song)." New York: Jacobs, 1904.

"Dances Partake of the Racial Characteristics of the People Who Dance Them": Nordicism, Antisemitism, and Henry Ford's Old-Time Music and Dance Revival

Peter La Chapelle

Jazz is celebrated today as an integral part of our American culture. It would be hard to find anyone at the beginning of the twenty-first century who looks askance at jazz or sees it as alien to American identity and values. Few would demean its origins within black music or view in a negative light its development by music publishers and song writers, many of whom were Jewish, in the artistic milieu popularly known as "Tin Pan Alley." But in the 1920s and 1930s, this was quite another matter. There was a far less welcoming attitude in certain social circles towards jazz. Many questioned just how truly American it was—especially when compared to what was then often called "old-time" music. This could mean anything from squares, quadrilles, reels and rounds, to ballroom (but non-Latin) forms of social dancing to country fiddling and related hillbilly genres—just as long as the music was identifiably white and European in origin (even if the unseen performers at recording sessions were occasionally of another color or if the music itself borrowed significantly from black music traditions). The nostalgia for these forms of music and more broadly, for the nineteenth century life and culture out of which they emerged was often rooted in regional pride, the socioeconomic circumstances of its participants, and a more general anxiety about the modern world, but occasionally had a distinct and sharp aspect of prejudice as its fellow traveler—or perhaps we might better say, its dance partner. If today we tend to view the 1920s and 1930s as a high point of the Jazz Age, there were those at that time who were determined to fight against this cultural and musical shift in popular tastes because they viewed jazz as inimical and alien to American old-time values—values that needed to be preserved against their perceived enemies at all costs. And some turned, in part, to old-time music as a means to entice the American public back to an idealized life founded on nineteenth century values that resonated with what they nostalgically perceived to be the traditional rhythms of traditional music.

One of the leaders of this effort to revive the rhythms of an imagined past was Henry Ford. Carmaker and philanthropist, mechanizer and sermonizer, Ford, in fact, was more than just an occasional naysayer of jazz, he was a leading proponent of re-creating all aspects of nineteenth century culture in 1920s America. Though passionate about collecting antiques—the old-time furniture, machinery, and farm equipment that would eventually fill the halls of his Henry Ford Museum and populate his recreated Greenfield Village (Simonds 153–214; Richards, *Last Billionaire* 161–95)—he also sought to revive forms of "Old American" music and dance that he believed were central to reclaiming the ways of a forgotten but vital Old America, the type of music and dance that "cheered the pioneer race as it moved from coast to coast," as one of Ford's editorial publicist opined. "The music Washington's troops sang," that editorial continued: "and Daniel Boone whistled on strange mountains, and Abraham Lincoln heard, and the people of the 'Covered Wagon' trains loved. It is truly American. It has the pulse of life in it. No 'blues' there."[1]

From 1923 until his death in 1947, Ford poured thousands of dollars into the enterprise, buying and restoring three historic inns to serve in part as dance venues, building an elegant dance hall in Dearborn, and hiring a full-time dance master, who stayed on his payroll for some twenty years. He underwrote the salaries of an old-time dance orchestra, paid for old-time dance education for hundreds of university students and thousands of Michigan school children, and covered the costs for writing and the distributing four separate printings of a dance manual. Ford even extended his reach into the media, financing more than twenty old-time musical recordings, two coast-to-coast radio relay broadcasts, a network radio series, and documentary motion picture shorts of favorite old time fiddlers.[2]

At first, the press reacted to Ford's passion for an earlier generation's sound and footwork with terms associated with leisure or religious fervor: It was a "missionary labor" ("Henry Ford Shakes a Wicket Hoof" 38), a "hobby" (Pope SM4), and a "revival" ("Ford and His Fiddler" 6). Before long, however, the metaphors sounded downright militaristic. The *New York Times* labeled his promotion of old-time music and dance as a "campaign" ("Ford Hires Big Hall" 2) while the *Literary Digest* preferred the less subtle "crusade" ("Fiddling to Henry Ford" 356). The *Los Angeles Times* was more blunt: "Ford Wars on Jazz" (E2). Even the children's press got into the fray. *Youth's Companion*, a 100-year-old magazine that would later merge with *American Boy*, applauded the media blitz that occurred when Ford invited old-time Maine fiddler Mellie Dunham to play for large audiences and intense press scrutiny in Michigan in 1925. Dunham's arrival in Dearborn, the magazine argued, was:

> . . . a step in Mr. Ford's campaign against the ugliness of present-day dances and the tyranny of the jazz band. He (Ford) is for Money Musk against the Blues of whatever tinge; for the dignified Lancers or the romping Portland Fancy, against the acrobatic Charleston; for the jollity of the fiddle against the moan of the saxophone. Mellie Dunham is the first wave of Mr. Ford's shock troops advancing against the entrenched atrocities of Jazz-mania. ("Take Down the Fiddle and the Bow" 10)

The use of so many martial metaphors—the "shock troops" of *Youth's Companion* and the *Los Angeles Times* notion of Ford warring on jazz—over so short a time was odd, seemingly out of character for the billionaire tinkerer and carmaker. To be sure, his factories eventually produced vehicles and airplane engines for the American effort in World War I (Lacey 154–58), but Ford was, after all, best known politically in the 1920s for his pacifism—most notably his support of the League of Nations and his chartering of the ill-planned and much ballyhooed 1915 Peace Ship mission to Europe in an idealistic effort to end that war (Brinkley 194–200; Lacey 137–46).

But, perhaps, the martial language was accurate in a way. Ford's promotion of old-time music and his opposition to jazz in the 1920s were not isolated nor compartmentalized cultural skirmishes. They were closely associated with an ongoing rhetorical war that he and his public relations machine had waged against immigrants, non-northern Europeans, and, most vehemently, Jews. Although other factors—Ford's reformist and agrarian leanings, his love for history, his anti-modernist inclinations, the joys and camaraderie of social dancing, his yearnings for a lost youth—played a role, the xenophobic and antisemitic leanings of Henry Ford and relevant members of his executive staff figured prominently as rationales behind the effort to revive rural what was perceived as traditional American music and dance.

Numerous writers have documented how Ford used his newspaper, *The Dearborn Independent*, in the 1920s to accuse Jews in finance, government, and entertainment of undermining Anglo-Saxon culture (Ribuffo 448, 452–53, 457; Kun 356; Carr 87–90). Less known is how this antisemitic world view permeated important aspects of Ford's attempts to promote old-time fiddling—important in the development of the hillbilly or country music genre—and "traditional American" dances such as reels, rounds, and squares. Although some sources have sought to downplay connections between Ford's antisemitism and this old time revival,³ a full examination of the Ford's publicity efforts and his antisemitic efforts during the full span of the 1920s and of the archival material related to the campaign including oral histories of staff members and unpublished manuscripts, suggests a very direct connection. Ford went to considerable expense to support these nineteenth century art forms as an alternative to dancehalls and mass-produced jazz and Tin Pan Alley, venues and genres the *Independent* claimed were despoiled by Jewish influence.⁴ In fact, substantial evidence supports the conclusion that the author of the old-time dance and music revival's formal *raison d'être*, expressed in the introductory essay in Ford's popular old-time dance manual *Good Morning*, was none other than the same Ford journalist, ghostwriter and editor who spearheaded the *Independent*'s antisemitic campaign on behalf of the carmaker.⁵

This antisemitism was coupled with Nordicism, a belief about the racial destiny of Northern European peoples that drew explicitly from the "scientific" racism and eugenic thought of the era.⁶ Ford and his staff's explanations of why they promoted old-time music and dance often built on antisemitic and Nordicist ideas disseminated in earlier Ford-produced literature, while the overall old-time campaign occurred simultaneously with Ford's ongoing antisemitic publicity campaign. As an early draft of *Good Morning* argued, moral authorities roundly criticized modern forms of popular music and dance, especially those deriving from jazz and Tin Pan Alley, because they were so racially foreign to Protestant, Anglo-Saxon America. "Dances partake of the racial characteristics of the people who dance them," it argued, before moving on to fret about the groundswell of "foreign" musical styles and dances that were being hawked by the American music industry. Nevertheless the manual predicted a resurgence of the "type of dancing which has survived longest amongst the northern peoples."⁷

Ford's old-time campaign deserves scrutiny because of the role it played at a critical juncture in the emergence of major commercial genres of American music such as country and folk in the 1920s (Peterson 59–62; C. K. Wolfe

77–80). Indeed, Ford's efforts denote a circling of the wagons around specific notions of whiteness and American-ness that already were being pushed by the recording industry through the creation of genres that segregated peoples and musical styles by race, region, and socioeconomic status: blues and jazz as black "race music"; hillbilly or old-time as a poor, usually Southern, and almost always white, music. Most accounts of this bifurcation of genres argue that industry figures such as Frank Walker and Ralph Peer invented categories as a way of making artificial distinctions that either mirrored existing racial segregation in the South or fit within existing national patterns of production and consumption—this despite the fact that black and white musicians had long been involved in "a creolized synthesis of European and African influences" (Roy 462; see also Otto and Bums 407–17; Peterson 194–96; Miller 29–32, 223–26; 253–92; Feder 45–73). Ford went a step further than Walker or Peer. He not only hoped to advance one genre (old-time/hillbilly) over another (race music), he further sought to build deeper boundaries around that genre by adding religion and national origin to old-time/hillbilly's existing list of racial, class, and geographic requirements. Ford's promotional efforts, then, are key to understanding how events outside the South and outside of recording industry marketing practices—in this case a large, sustained, national media campaign centered in the northern Midwest—might naturalize notions that old-time/hillbilly music was not only white and American, but also antithetical to groups such as immigrants and particularly Jews. In doing so, Ford's efforts reflect a pointed agenda where promotion of one musical and dance style over another was used to shape the debate about who is or who is not a proper citizen of the American republic.

Ford's first love, his "old-time" or "old American" dances, were for the most part resurrected nineteenth century ballroom dances, some of folk and some of courtly origins, but all of European roots and many with important regionalized American variations. The sources for these dances, Richard Nevell tells us, were not original folk dances but "updated, sophisticated versions of the country dances that really emphasized morality and manners" (65, and more generally, 63–65).[8] Ford began to seek out musicians who could, not only play the old "authentic" music to accompany them,[9] but who could also make phonograph records, thereby "extending the effect of his ideas on dancing," according to one executive close to Ford (Liebold, Reminiscences 1367). This led Ford and the growing portions of his staff charged with maintaining his antiquarian pursuits to venture into what at the time was called "old-time music," an important forerunner of what would later become known as "country" music. Although Ford's influence was somewhat fleeting—the original full-fledged media campaign for old-time dance and music seems to have extended just over three years, from October 1923 to December 1927—his efforts serve as an important link in ensuring the survival and continuity of what has become known as contra-dancing and appear, to a lesser a degree, to have provided impetus for the standardization and popularization of western square dance.[10] Perhaps even more importantly, they helped popularize what would become country music inside and outside of the South by sparking a spate of well-publicized, fiercely-fought fiddling contests in 1926. Although Ford certainly didn't invent the fiddling contest, and was generally uninvolved in these competitions, his promotion of key fiddlers invigorated an interest previously unseen before even in the South.[11]

Ford's promotion of old-time dance and music appears to have started gradually and from within his immediate social circle in Dearborn. Although Ford is reported to have enjoyed social dancing in his youth in the 1880s, specifically at the Joseph Coon Hotel and Tavern outside of Detroit, it is difficult to pin down when the adult Ford first began promoting old-time dancing. Scholarly and journalistic accounts typically date Ford's first forays into the promotion of old time dancing to the mid-1920s, but materials in the Benson Ford Research Center on the grounds of the Henry Ford history and museum complex in Dearborn suggest that he was involved in smaller scale promotion among his immediate social circle in Dearborn as early as 1910. Ford had been a member of a group called the "Greenfield Dancing Club of 1882" and had sponsored a dance for the group at one of his properties in January 1910. According to the invitation, the event was to feature "an Old Time Dancing Party consisting of Square Dances, Virginia Reels, and old fashioned Polkas" and was to take place at the "Old Gulley Homestead," a farmhouse located on the eighty-acre Orin P. Gulley farm in Dearborn that Ford had purchased as a gift for his wife Clara with profits from the Model T.[12]

Ford's first public declaration of interest in traditional music in the national press appears to have occurred nine years later, during eight days of court testimony that would rank among the most humiliating in his life. In summer 1919, Ford took the stand in the libel trial his attorneys had filed against the *Chicago Daily Tribune* after that newspaper criticized Ford's World War I-era pacifism and claimed Ford was an "Anarchist" and "ignorant idealist." His attorneys hoped that putting Ford on the stand would disprove the charge of ignorance, but the plan backfired. Not only were defense attorneys able to make a mockery out of Ford's infamous and until-then-mostly-unknown three-year-old quote in the *Tribune*, "History is more or less bunk," and Ford's testimony that he did not care much for art, history, or music, but Ford appeared woefully ignorant of basic facts of American history (Butterfield 53–66; Brinkley 225–26, 244–48). In his July 15th testimony, Ford could not identify the nations that fought in the War of 1812, and then again on July 16th, misidentified Revolutionary War traitor Benedict Arnold as a writer of some sort ("Henry Ford Still Thinks Soldiers are Murderers" 1; "Odd Definitions" 1).[13] Between these embarrassing and embittering missteps, Ford tried to retract earlier his dismissals of art and music, noting especially his interest in the banjo, a statement that was widely carried by Associated Press wire stories ("History and Art Bunk, Says Ford" I8). Although not matching his later fondness for the fiddle, the cimbalom, and the dulcimer, Ford's early penchant for this instrument, which could be used to play jazz and Tin Pan Alley as well as traditional Appalachian and Euro-American music, would later result in the purchase of historically-significant banjos, especially those related to traditional music traditions, for his growing collection of Americana.[14]

After the *Tribune* trial, the Ford name would not be connected again nationally with traditional music and dancing until October 1923 when the *New York Times* noted that Ford had given a new automobile to Jasper E. "Jep" Bisbee, a traditional fiddler from Paris, Michigan. The article explained that Bisbee, a well-known local fiddler, had played for Ford, inventor Thomas Edison, and tire magnate Harvey Firestone, during a camping trip the three had made to western lower Michigan that summer. The new automobile was simply Ford delivering on a promise ("Ford Keeps a Promise" 2).[15] Ford's patronage of the 88-year-old Bisbee continued to get much press over the next three months with Ford arranging for Bisbee to travel to New Jersey so Edison could record and film him, and with Ford hiring Bisbee to play at a well-publicized "old fashioned house-warming" for Ford's brother-in-law in Traverse City, Michigan ("Ford Brings Old Fiddler" 11; "Edison 'Cans' Music of Old Time Dance Fiddler" 2; "'Jep' Fiddles for Edison" 3). In one article, Traverse City's old-timers reportedly characterized Ford as "mighty spry for a city feller" ("Ford at Oldtime Dance" 3).

Over the next year, Ford quietly sponsored more traditional musicians and made more headlines by organizing well-publicized dances at the Wayside Inn in Sudbury, Mass., the first of three historic tavern-inns he acquired in the 1920s because of his penchant for the past, his of love old-fashioned dancing, and, in this case, the inn's association with poet Henry Wadsworth Longfellow ("Mine Host Ford Fiddler for Dance" E1; "Ford Debt to Longfellow" S6).[16] At the Sudbury functions, Ford occasionally fiddled himself and in August 1924 had hired on a dancing master, Benjamin B. Lovett, to better acquaint himself with the ripple, polkas, the Money Musk, quadrilles, schottisches, reels and Varsovienne (Twork 54).[17] Lovett, who had taught in nearby Hudson, Mass., returned with Ford to Dearborn later that year and stayed on as Ford's personal dancing teacher for some twenty years ("Ford to Learn Oldtime Dances" 1; Richards, *Last Billionaire* 104–05).

By July 1925, the trickle of publicity Ford received for sponsoring Bisbee and the Wayside Inn dances had turned into a veritable tidal wave of coverage that would result in a short-lived but far reaching national old-time fiddling and dancing craze. Ford had ordered a manual of old-time dances to be put together and advance copies of the book, *"Good Morning": Being a Book on the Revival of the Dance,* caught the eye of the press. First, Pulitzer's *New York World*, then *Literary Digest* magazine, and finally the *New York Times* featured lengthy articles on the forth-coming manual, noting Ford's general disdain for jazz and the "modern dances" of commercial dance halls (Richards, "Ford Trips Ripple" S7; "Henry Ford Shakes a Wicked Hoof" 38, 40; Feld SM1–2, SM23). In its press preview, the *Literary Digest* quoted *Good Morning* at length and noted the anti-commercialism of his dance and music revival:

> The characteristics of modern commercial dance is determined by commercial considerations. The older form of dancing requires room. Room in cities, especially in cabarets, is expensive. Hence a form of dancing that has been encouraged that enables the largest possible number of paying couples to dance together in the smallest possible in the smallest possible space. ("Henry Ford Shakes a Wicked Hoof" 40)[18]

Although Lovett reportedly traveled to research the dances, most of the sixty-seven actual dances in the manual were lifted straight out of nineteenth century dance manuals. In fact, Allison Robbins notes that, of the nineteen contra-dances outlined, all but three had a "corresponding melody in Elia Howe's nineteenth-century compilations of dance tunes" (Robbins 4). This does not mean they were not researched or adapted to Ford's tastes. Ford's longtime general secretary recalled:

> Mr. Lovett went into the older types of dances and developed them and applied them in the way that Mr. Ford wanted. They would make changes in the old scheme. Of course, the old-fashioned dances were characteristic of certain localities. For instance, they would dance a

square dance a certain way in certain locations and differently in others. The farther they were away from each other the greater they differed. Mr. Ford's idea was to standardize it to one form of a dance. In doing that he discussed the matter with Lovett, and they decided how they were going to proceed on it.[19]

Lovett, however, was perhaps more direct about the aims of the manual in a later radio interview: "We teach social deportment, poise, carriage, and courteous behavior along with the early American dances."[20] Indeed, according to Lovett's account, it seemed the dances themselves were an afterthought compared to the lessons in proper behavior and instilling an almost-aristocratic set of social mores.

On the heels of *Good Morning*'s release came a second barrage of press attention when Ford began inviting elderly musicians to play for him in Michigan. The first highly-publicized musician to arrive in Detroit to play was Mellie Dunham, a fiddler from Norway, Maine,[21] followed by 71-year-old dulcimer player Jesse Martin of Frewsberg, New York ("Ford to Hear Dulcimer" 21). Dunham's trip to Detroit, however, outshone Martin's. It started with a send-off that drew much fanfare and dozens of Norway's children, including several who held picket signs wishing Dunham, a 77-year-old snow-shoe maker who had recently won the Maine state fiddling championship, a safe return ("Fiddling to Henry Ford" 36). Remarkably, Dunham also drew large crowds when he arrived at the Ford laboratories even though a *New York Times* article noted that thirty-eight other old time fiddlers had already performed for Ford in Dearborn ("Henry Ford Greets New Dance Tune Fiddler" 16).

Ford's championing of the "picturesque, white-haired" Dunham sparked ire and challenges from several other champion fiddlers around the country ("Fiddles as Ford Dances" 1).[22] The most publicized of these, however, involved Uncle Jimmy Thompson of Tennessee. In early January 1926, a Boston newspaper reported that Dunham had not only challenged Thompson, a Southern fiddling champion who performed on the Nashville-based radio barn dance that would become known as the *Grand Ole Opry*, but had bragged openly of his superiority over Southern fiddlers in general (C. K. Wolfe 75–77). Quick to realize the public relations bonanza, both the show's manager and Uncle Jimmy responded ("Fiddler Champ Challenged" 8.). The contest, however, never occurred nor did Thompson ever play for Ford. The publicity drummed up by the episode coupled with the media-fed notion that Ford was anointing national fiddle champions, however, helped increase interest to the point that country music historian C. K. Wolfe has estimated that some 30,000 people took part in local fiddling contests sponsored several weeks later by Ford dealers in Tennessee, Indiana, and Kentucky. The winners of these contests then went on to complete in a regional championship in Louisville (C. K. Wolfe 77–79). Fiddling contests were not new in the South or other regions of the country (Blaustein 53–55), but such widespread interest and enthusiasm was unusual.

Within weeks fiddling contests grew into a national fad. Similar competitions took place in the Pennsylvania, Iowa, New England, and Canada, spurred by the Ford publicity and local boosters' pride in their own musicians (Gifford, *Hammered Dulcimer* 354). The extent to which Ford's fiddling promotion so thoroughly penetrated the consciousness of the nation is perhaps demonstrated by the media coverage and notions of gender equality that surrounded a similar fiddling contest in far away Southern California. Radio station KHJ broadcast the numerous installments of the local contest (Sheedy A5) and a large photo of the nine top finalists—seven men and two women—accompanied a front page story on the *Los Angeles Times* on January 25 ("Fiddling Title at Stake" A1). Loving cups were awarded to the top male competitor—aged 80 or older—and female competitor—aged 70 or older ("Fiddling Title at Stake" A1). "Mellie Dunham please write," opined a later *Los Angeles Times* photo caption accompanying a photo of one of the winners. "Stephen Gilley, 80 years of age, and seven other Southland fiddlers, all Civil War veterans, propose an East-West fiddling match" ("World News" H2).

Broadcasting was also central to the Ford publicity push. In conjunction with dealers who picked up a portion of the costs, Ford Motor Company relayed an "'old time dance' program" to sixteen radio stations nationwide, including San Francisco's powerful KPO. The company's internal organ, the *Ford News*, reported on the reach of KPO rebroadcast:

> [M]any Western dealers' showrooms were crowded with people swaying to good old tunes. In fact, in Carson City, Nevada, twenty-five per cent of the population (400 people) accepted the invitation of the Carson City Garage, and several of the most distinguished state officials and their wives participated. ("West Dances to Ford Orchestra" 4)

Ford repeated the relay broadcast again in 1927, this time to stations in nine states and the District of Columbia and, again, the program was aired in Ford dealer showrooms ("You Are Invited to Hear"; "Dance Music is Radiocast" 1).

Ford's promotion of traditional fiddling and reels, squares, and rounds over other forms of music and dance was consistent with the criticism that his newspaper, *The Dearborn Independent*, had long made of jazz ("Jewish Jazz Becomes Our National Music" 8–9; Harvey 10–11; "A Dance A Week" 29), a criticism Ford himself began to make in his own remarks to the press. Shortly before *Good Morning*'s release in 1925, for instance, he noted that his dancing campaign was seeking to oust jazz, a musical form he argued that had only taken root in the cities ("Ford Wars on Jazz" E2). A year and half later, while promoting old-time dance classes he had financed for several groups of Michigan school children, he noted his distaste again. "In Detroit and surrounding towns," he told a writer on assignment for the *Los Angeles Times*, "there are thousands of school children dancing old-fashioned dances to old-fashioned airs. Jazz has no melody" ("Ford Strong for Coolidge" 1).

Unclear too is when antisemitism became a prevalent aspect of Ford's thought. Much speculation suggests that Ford's thoughts on the matter were cemented by the allegations of two Jewish members of his 1915 Peace Ship mission, who claimed that wealthy Jews in Europe were behind the war (Hapgood 14). Others suggest that Ford was pushed over the line by his loss in the 1918 Michigan Senatorial race to Truman Newberry. Ford reportedly fumed that high placed Jews were behind his defeat (Liebold, Reminiscences 409). Others point as far back as his youth, noting the ways in which Ford's beloved *McGuffey Reader* textbooks naturalized antisemitic notions about Jewish greed (Baldwin 1–7), or to the "Populist anti-Semitism" that might have confronted him as young man in the late nineteenth century or, perhaps, the "pseudo-agrarian" movements that were springing up in the twentieth (Hofstadter 80; Gerber 30). Ford's own political trajectory in the 1920s remained enmeshed in Progressive reform, but seem to have moved stridently to the right without completely breaking with the reformist tradition. A radical-leaning LaFollette Republican who favored women's rights and Wilsonian notions about peace while in his teens, Ford had over time come to the point that he was describing himself publicly as a conservative by 1924 ("Mr. Ford's Page" 5 July 1924, 7; see N 38). Today's political historians might label him an "insurgent" who along with Hiram Johnson, Burton K. Wheeler, and others had moved rapidly from Progressive reformism to—or perhaps blended their Progressivism with—xenophobia, a hatred of labor unions, and an ardent opposition to the New Deal—the difference perhaps being that Ford's transformation occurred much quicker (Hurtigan 30–31; Mulder 5–22; Graham 24–100; Greenbaum).

Whatever the case, Ford and Ford executives, and Ernest G. Liebold, his personal secretary, as well as W. J. Cameron, the *Dearborn Independent*'s editor, clearly were the forces behind the *Dearborn Independent*'s publication of the "International Jew" series. Ford had bought the paper in 1919, filling its pages with light features, ethnocentric travelogues, Western Americana, and editorials preaching hard work and Ford's own unique brand of reform. The "International Jew" series began in 1920 with extravagant claims regarding Jewish economic and political power, continued with attacks on Jews in entertainment and cultural industries, and finally, offered an updated rewritten serialized version of the claims made in conspiratorial antisemitic Tsarist fakery *The Protocols of the Elders of Zion* (Ribuffo 446–53). Each week for twenty-one months, the *Independent* featured a new article on the evil enterprises of the Jews, most of which appeared on the newssheet's front page. Jews were blamed for everything from low harvest prices to smut in movies to corruption in baseball to the lack of religious themes in Christmas cards.[23]

The "International Jew" series was particularly critical of Jews in the music business, blaming Jews for the rise of jazz and arguing that a trust of "Yiddish song manufacturers" on Tin Pan Alley completely controlled the music business. "Jazz is a Jewish creation," the *Independent* opined. "The mush, the slush, the sly suggestion, the abandoned sensuousness of sliding notes, are of Jewish origin." The newspaper went on to quote an unnamed source that described how the "Oriental, especially the Jewish, infection in our music" was more "virulent" than earlier German and French musical influences on the American music culture:

> The insidiousness of the Jewish menace to our artistic integrity is due partly to the speciousness, the superficial charm and persuasiveness of Hebrew art, its brilliance, its violently juxtaposed extremes of passion, its poignant eroticism and pessimism. . . . The Anglo-Saxon group of qualities, the Anglo-Saxon point of view, even though they are so thoroughly disguised in a people descended from every race . . . are nevertheless the vital nucleus of the American temper. And Jewish domination of music, even more than Teutonic or Gallic, threatens to submerge and stultify them at every point.

The article also described how a promising "non-Jewish" song was defeated by a "Jewish manager" who purposefully introduced it to the public with a non-English-speaking singer who was not only overly "Yiddish in appearance" but "sang through his nose" ("Jewish Jazz Becomes Our National Music" 8).

Jewish songsmiths were also accused of delivering smut and repackaging degenerate black music. Irving Berlin's "I Like It," for instance, put "unashamed erotic suggestions" on the lips of children ("Jewish Jazz Becomes Our National Music" 9). A follow-up article noted that, under Jewish control, Tin Pan Alley had been transformed from an entity that emphasized "sentiment" and promoted communal singing to one that promoted showmanship and degenerate "Congo" themes, "seductive" ragtime, and "slimy" jazz ("How the Jewish Song Trust Makes You Sing" 8–9). Indeed, such writing seemed to play on centuries-old notions that Jews were a mongrel race or possessed a heightened sensuality and a "blackness" of the skin that was symptomatic of a potentially infectious disease, usually syphilis (Gilman, *Jew's Body* 150–85; Gilman, *Freud* 19–33).

One might note that Ford and company preferred "unobjectionable" or "clean" songs from the folk tradition and the early "non-Jewish period" of Tin Pan Alley such as "Turkey in the Straw," "Zip Coon" (sung to the same melody), and "After the Ball." Ironically, the first, a fiddle tune from blackface minstrelsy tradition, was often paired in nineteenth century with the highly suggestive lyrics such as "Sugar in the gourd/Honey in the horn/I was never so happy/Since the hour I was born."[24] Charles K. Harris's bestselling hit, "After the Ball," also bristles with what Jon Finson calls "an undercurrent of frustrated sexuality," and, after all, is about an elderly uncle seating a very young niece on his lap and regaling her with stories of his teenage love life.[25]

The "International Jew" series was eventually collected and republished in a four volume set by Ford's Dearborn Publishing Company, the publisher of the *Good Morning* and the *Dearborn Independent*. The book set was then promoted within the pages of the *Independent*. The four volumes were organized into general thematic sections, focusing collectively on Jewish power and cultural influence.[26] Professional historians and other writers have documented the wide reach of the series, both in Europe and America. Hitler was certainly a fan of Ford and the German-language edition of *International Jew*, and he had a large photo of Ford hanging in his private office and also kept a well-stocked collection of Ford's books in his library ("Berlin Hears Ford is Backing Hitler" 2). While the *Independent* often disagreed with Hitler's tactics, it carried generally positive coverage of the nascent National Socialist movement in Germany and of the Italian Fascist Party. A 1923 article by A. R. Pincini praised the Italian Fascist Party and its forced feedings of cod liver oil to Socialists (2); a 1926 editorial criticized some of Mussolini's methods, but praised his purported ability to restore order ("Bark Versus Bite" 11); and finally, a 1927 piece criticized the Fascist role in recent assassinations but argued that Mussolini "lifted

Italy from far down in the rank of nations to the border line of first rank—if Italy afforded the national resources and national temperament to reach this category" (Wilbur 1–2). German National Socialists were likewise justified in "Germany, Prey of Alien, Faces Complete Ruin," an antisemitic 1922 piece that claimed that "alien" Jews controlled Berlin financially but cared little for ordinary Germans, and a 1925 Jew-baiting article, "Anti-Semitism in Germany: Who and Why?" (Wolff, "Germany" 9, 11; Wolff, "Anti-Semitism" 2).

Ultimately, the "International Jew" series came to an end in January 1922, but the newspaper continued to publish antisemitic articles until 1927, when Jewish farm cooperative organizer Aaron Shapiro brought Ford and the newspaper to trial for libel, and successfully brokered a settlement that led to a formal written apology to American Jews, an end of the antisemitic content, and ultimately the end to the *Independent* itself. The settlement also stipulated that Ford fire the newspaper's editor and Ford's personal secretary—conditions that, as we shall see, were never entirely honored (Woeste).

Although the initial first wave of the *Dearborn Independent*'s antisemitic reporting concluded nearly two years before Ford's invitation to Jep Bisbee, the newspaper continued to print articles touting antisemitic stereotypes and, especially, Nordicist content, throughout the span of Ford's old-time music and dancing revival. Nordicism is an early twentieth century race theory contending that northern Europeans formed a master race and that their fall from supremacy would inevitably lead to the crash of civilization. The theory was built on American anthropologist William Z. Ripley's assertions that one could find three distinct European racial groups—Teutons, Mediterraneans, and Alpines—as well as French diplomat Comte Joseph-Arthur de Gobineau's nineteenth century argument that all great civilizations of the past had a northern Teuton, or Aryan, leadership component (Jackson and Weidman 105–07).

Ford and the ghostwriters and executives who staffed his publicity machine, however, were more likely influenced by the Nordicism of eugenicist Madison Grant, as expressed in his 1916 book *The Passing of the Great Race* and by Grant acolyte Lothrop Stoddard in his 1920 book *The Rising Tide of Color Against White World Supremacy*. Grant, in particular, argued that the United States had been founded by Nordics and that it owed much of its success to its Nordic leadership, but he also believed this leadership was being threatened, particularly by blacks and alien Eastern European Jews who retained a "ruthless concentration on self interest" (15–18, 88–91, 167–78).[27] Stoddard, building on Grant's theories, focused on the foreign "Asiatic elements" of American Jews, lumping them in with Mediterraneans and Alpines, whom he argued thrived better than Nordics in the densely populated cities and cramped factories of the modern world (164–65). Nordicist thought seemed especially present in the *Independent*'s original "International Jew" series in that series' argument that Jewish music-makers posed a greater threat to American music than Nordic "Teutons" (German composers) and the Mediterranean-Alpinic "Gauls" (= the French) ("Jewish Jazz Becomes Our National Music" 8).

Music scholar Josh Kun has noted how the *Dearborn Independent* fed upon theories that the Jews who ran Tin Pan Alley were a corrupting "Oriental" menace who were intelligent but incapable of creating their own music (355–56). As historian Jeffrey Melnick notes, Ford's view of music writing unsurprisingly was similarly imbued with traditional American notions about white racial supremacy and the degeneracy of darker races, especially in regard to belief that the Jews had a special ability to "'camouflage' the 'moral filth' of African American music" (Melnick 39). Although both authors' assessments seem to support a basic affinity between Ford's brand of antisemitism and the racial hierarchies inherent in Grant's Nordicism, historian Leo Ribuffo argues that Ford's antisemitism was often closer to the "assimilationist ethnocentrism" of antisemitic Protestant minister Josiah Strong. In contrast to the hardline biological determinism inherent in the Nordicism of Grant, Strong argued that Jews were better viewed as culturally regressive but capable of redemption, if only they conformed to Anglo-Saxon ways. A eugenicist later known as the father of scientific racism, Grant had argued that it would be "fatuous" to assume Jews could be assimilated (Ribuffo 474). While Ribuffo's assertions may have merit, an analysis of materials associated with the old-time revival suggest that they tended to be more Nordicist than in line with assimilationist ethnocentrism.

Even before the old-time campaign, the *Independent*'s ghostwritten editorial column, "Mr. Ford's Page," straddled a fine line between Strong's assimilationism and the hardline Nordicism of Grant and Gobineau. It argued unequivocally that there were "two distinct bloodstreams in the world," a superior "racial element" and an inferior one:

> Human history, checkered with various names, may be but the reappearance of the same bloodstream in various countries at various times, now in Persia as Persians, now in Greece as Greeks, now in Rome as Romans, now in Britain as Britons; now in Babylon, now in Prussia, now in France. Where has the greatness of old nations gone? Did it evaporate into thin air, or did the racial element which created the greatness move out toward the west? . . . We need knowledge

that will give us the racial facts. But we need most of all to learn the obligations of superiority. Every race cannot be assimilated, but every race can assimilate enough to develop a full life for itself. ("Mr. Ford's Page" 17 June 1922, 5)

Another "Mr. Ford's Page" argued that an unstated but existential "White Man's Code," which preached individual accomplishment, was being undermined by ideologically-minded immigrant "orientalists," obviously a thinly-disguised reference to Jews. According to the piece, these orientalists had persuaded workers to look upon dedicated employees as naïve fools and had even convinced doctors and lawyers to refer to their public not as patients and clients, but as customers. At the center of the piece was an enlarged boxed quote that came close to endorsing anti-Jewish vigilantism:

> The enemy has slipped in a great many poisonous seeds, which have sprung up in American thought and borne poisonous fruit. Have you allowed any to grow in your mind? If you have, you are an outpost for the enemy of every nation that is founded on the White Man's Code. According to this Code, a man must be Straight, Fearless of any man, Vigilant. When he fights, it is the enemy not his own kind. ("Mr. Ford's Page" 29 Jan. 1921, 5)

Given this history it is not surprising that antisemitic, Nordicist and racist articles that drew from similar strains of thought continued to run in the *Independent* during Ford's old-time music and dance revival. Such content did not cease with the end of the initial "International Jew" series in January 1922 but continued on, less regularly but no less vehemently, throughout the dance and music craze until Ford's public antisemitic campaign was curtailed with the Shapiro agreement. During 1923 and 1925, two very active years in the old-time music and dancing craze, for instance, the *Independent* ran an article praising the Ku Klux Klan ("When the Ku Klux Klan First Flourished" 4, 13), two articles claiming that "Anglo-Saxon-Celtics" rather than supposedly "Khazar" Jews were the real biblical chosen people ("Are the Jews 'God's Chosen People'?" 12; Tyner 14–15, 27), an article claiming powerful Jews purposefully portrayed themselves as "martyrs" in the media ("Producing Jewish 'Martyrs' by Propaganda" 12), several articles claiming blacks were exploited by Jews (Smith 9; "The Jewish Attempt to Bolshevize the Negro" 12), and an article by one Walter M. Wolff in Berlin who wrote that rising antisemitism in Germany was the result of Jewish control of corporate boards of directors at a supposed ratio of 24-to-1 ("Anti-Semitism in Germany" 2).

Eugenics, a pseudo-scientific field popular with health workers, social scientists, and other researchers in the early twentieth century, was also well represented in the *Independent* during this time period through the writings of University of Minnesota anthropologist Albert Ernest Jenks. At its root, eugenics focused on begetting "well-born," or "eu-genic," children as opposed to "poorly born" hereditarily-deficient offspring, but it also involved attempts to measure skulls and characterize peoples and races by phenotype, leading some eugenicists such as Jenks to seek prohibitions on racial miscegenation and promote sterilizations, and others to advocate for outright racial or ethnic cleansing. Conceived mostly by Americans and British health professionals, eugenic solutions were ultimately enacted in their most extreme by the Nazis.[28] Jenks, an early leader in the fields of racial and physical anthropology, an apologist for British and American white supremacy, and a member of the American Eugenics Society, appears to have written regularly for the *Independent* during the peak years of the old-time revival, producing pieces that preached a doctrine of inferior and superior races and emphasized that individual physical and mental characteristics were determined to a large extent by one's racial stock (Soderstrom 176–204).[29] A two-part series on Slavic racial history penned by Jenks in 1925, for instance, discussed whether Slavs were "broad-headed" Alpines or "long-headed" Teutons and argued that such characteristics made Slavs sensitive and adaptable, but also imitative, brash, emotional, and incapable of ruling themselves. "As to America, we shall profit by the rich heritages our 100,000 Slavic fellow citizens bring, while we guard against being weakened by those of their age-long characteristics which are alien to American institutions" ("How the Slavs Came to Europe" 25–27; "The Slav—Old, Yet Full of Youth" 15–19). By contrast, Jenks described the Anglo-Saxons more flatteringly in a 1927 *Independent* piece, discussing at length their very uniform head sizes and their racial proclivity toward "individual independence" ("Where the Peoples of the British Isles Come From" 6–7, 29). Not coincidentally, historian Mark Soderstrom finds evidence that Jenks argued that "the Jewish race contained 'negro blood' and was 'acquisitive' to the point of participating in 'white slavery'" in a speech before a women's organization in Minneapolis earlier in the century (199).

Often the *Dearborn Independent*'s eugenic, antisemitic and Nordicist reporting appeared more or less simultaneously with new developments in Ford's old-time music and dancing promotions. Less than a month after Bisbee made recordings for Edison and Ford in New Jersey, for instance, the *Independent* ran an article claiming that Jews were attempting to introduce Bolshevism to African Americans ("The Jewish Attempt to Bolshevize the Negro" 12). And two weeks before Ford invited Lovett to teach dance in Detroit, the *Independent*'s "Mr. Ford's Page" editorial made a barely disguised attack on Jews as "money brokers" ("Mr Ford's Page" 16 Aug. 1924, 7). The second of Jenks' racial and biological dissections of the Slavs appeared about a month after the *Independent* printed what would become the official rationale for the dance revival and about month before the official advance release of the *Good Morning* dance manual ("Editorials: The Return of the Dance" 10).[30] A week before the *Independent* began serializing individual old-time dances and sheet music in *Good Morning*, it ran an article titled "Are We a Shylock Nation?" (3; "Waking Up the Old American Dances").

In fact, starting in January 1926, the *Independent* continued to advertise the four volume *International Jew* book series every single week in the very same issues that carried articles promoting old-time dance steps and music, most of which were reprinted from the *Good Morning* manual. In the March 20, 1926 edition of the *Independent*, for instance, an ad for the "International Jew in 4 volumes" appears on page 24 while the "A Dance a Week" feature, focusing on the steps of the "Money Musk" appears on pages 28 and 29. Usually the ad for the *International Jew* volumes was centered amid text within the paper's weekly, "I Read in the Papers that—" digest, a section of abbreviated news blurbs from legitimate news organizations, a placement that would seemingly bolster the credibility of the contents of the book set.

Ford's own comments in the press throughout this period, but particularly at the height of media attention over the fiddling craze in early 1926, included back-handed compliments that perpetuated antisemitic stereotypes and reinforced the *Independent*'s screeds against Jewish songwriters and ruthless manipulative Jewish moneymen, all the while reiterating Nordicistic beliefs about racial competition. In January, Ford was interviewed by the *New York Times* during one of his old-time dance affairs at the Wayside Inn. During that interview, he recanted a bit of his earlier criticisms of jazz, arguing that some jazz was needed in order to compete with traditional music, just as Jewish business acumen was needed to keep non-Jews on their toes:

> And so the conversation went on until it got on the subject of music. Somebody spoke of jazz and somebody else spoke of the impetus Mr. Ford's movement to revive old time dancing and music had gained. "Well, you have to have different movements," said Mr. Ford. "You have to have them to keep things stirred up. You have to have an explosion now and then. It's just like the Jews in this country. We

couldn't get along without them. They keep things stirred up by their business ability." ("Old Time Fiddlers at Wayside Inn" 10)

Fifteen days later, without mentioning music, Ford clarified his statement for the Associated Press arguing that Jews as whole were smarter than many Gentiles and a good social influence because they prompted "the boob Gentiles" to "hustle to keep up"—the implication here being that, if Jews continued to find financial successes, they might inadvertently spur a Nordic resurgence. During the same interview, Ford also repeated early *Independent* diatribes against "international Jewish money power," arguing it was involved in every war ("Ford Kindlier toward Jews" 2).

Although researchers since the 1970s have briefly noted the connections between Ford's distaste for jazz and his antisemitic campaign (Nash 161–63; Blaustein 40; Sutherland 33–37; Menius 26–28; Peterson 59–62), and less regularly the chronological connections and general affinity between Ford's antisemitism and his promotion of old time music,[31] musicologist Allison Robbins has deftly and convincingly argued, in a recent unpublished conference paper, that Ford's antisemitism and his industrial philosophy were primary underlying motivations for Ford's promotion of old-time dance in the *Good Morning* manual. Relying mostly on published materials, Robbins highlights the introductory chapter, "The Return of the Dance," which appears in the widely-distributed, 1926 second edition of the book:

> Denunciation of the dance by the protectors of public morals has usually been occasioned by the importations of dances which are foreign to the expressional needs of our people. With characteristic American judgment, however, the balance is now shifting toward that style of dancing which best fits with the American temperament. There is a revival of that type of dancing which has survived longest amongst the northern peoples. The tide has swung in favor of such dances as are described in this book.

She notes that "'foreign' here could easily be equated with Jewish, or rather, with the black and Latin dances that the Jewish-controlled (Tin Pan Alley) industry marketed and distributed" (10–11).[32] One might add that the introduction's prediction of a renaissance of the forms of dancing "that have survived longest among the northern peoples" invokes the resurgent Nordicism that eugenicist Madison Grant had hoped would stave off a collapse of civilization, while the language of the final sentence "the tide has swung" seems a not-too-veiled homage to the title of Stoddard's Nordicist magnum opus, *The Rising Tide of Color Against White World-Supremacy.*

An analysis of Ford's papers archived at the Benson Ford Research Center and material published in the *Dearborn Independent* demonstrates an even deeper connection between the dance manual and the Nordicism that Ford and his executives professed. An early manuscript for *Good Morning,* in fact contains additional lines (noted below in bold) that were apparently retracted from later published editions:

> Denunciation of the dance by the protectors of public morals has been usually occasioned by the importations of dances which are foreign to the expressional needs of our people. **Dances partake of the racial characteristics of the people who dance them. There have been imported into the United States of recent years dances that originated on the African Congo, dances from the gypsies of the South American pampas, and dances from the hot-blooded races of southern Europe. Wave after wave of foreign importations in dancing styles have swept the country. The result is a reaction against the character of the dances themselves.** With characteristic American judgment, however, the balance is now shifting toward that style of dancing which best fits the American temperament. There is a revival of dancing which has survived longest amongst the northern peoples. The tide has swung in favor of such dances as are described in this book. (Mr. and Mrs. Henry Ford, *Good Morning* [1925])

This version of the text, in fact, appears to be the same text that was released to the press in July 1925 and quoted verbatim in widely-circulated publications such as the popular Sunday edition of the New York *World* and the *Literary Digest* (albeit in the *Digest,* with variations in spelling: "African Kongo" (with a "k"), "gipsies" (with an "i"), "Southern" (in Southern Europe," uppercase) (Richards, "Ford Trips Ripple" S7; "Ford Shakes a Wicked Hoof" 3, 40).[33]

The *World,* the new daily incarnation of Joseph Pulitzer's popular weekly newssheet, the *New York World,* in particular, emphasized the racial component of *Good Morning*'s text, titling the first subheading of its copyrighted press preview "A Nordic," and noting that the manual stemmed from:

> Mr. Ford's belief in the permanent value of things American. Or, to make it broader, things Nordic. Modern dances of devious origin which specialize in equatorial wriggling and leaping, may suit the

Congo or the South American gypsies, but Ford holds they are not native to the minds of Americans. (Richards, "Ford Trips Ripple" S7)

Despite the early coverage, this elongated and much publicized version of the introduction, apparently, did not make it into the first edition of *Good Morning* in 1925, the widely-distributed 1926 second edition, nor subsequent printings of the book.[34]

By mentioning specific geographic regions, this early manuscript not only set *Good Morning* up as a possible opponent to such South American, southern European, and African American dances as the tango, the tarantella, the fandango, the bolero, the Black Bottom and the Charleston,[35] but put forward Nordicist notions about racial hierarchy. To use Madison Grant's language, placed at the bottom were dances of "Negroid" racial origins ("dances that originated in the African Congo"), followed next by those originated from the mixed "race bastards" and "suspiciously swarthy" Mediterranean-Alpinic peoples of Argentina ("dances from the gypsies of the South American pampas"), and finally, those created by the sub-European "Mediterraneans" ("dances from the hot-blooded races of Southern Europe") (Grant 33, 76–78, 111, 148–66).[36] Furthermore, the use of the term "Congo" alluded to an assertion made in the "International Jew" series that Tin Pan Alley's new Jewish songsmiths had introduced a "jungle motif, the so-called 'Congo' stuff into popular pieces" that "swiftly degenerated into a rather more bestial type than the beasts themselves arrive at" ("How the Jewish Song Trust Makes You Sing" 8).

The line about dances partaking "of the racial characteristics of the people who dance them" now takes on new urgency. By promoting tangos and the Charleston, it would appear, Nordics, and even Alpines, might be downgrading themselves within the racial hierarchy. The notion that undesirable racial characteristics might "rub off" onto a superior race via cultural absorption also seemed to have some precedence in Nordicist literature. Although cognizant of the differences between language and race, Grant himself made little distinction between race and culture, arguing that "higher cultures" had been "threatened" periodically throughout history with "absorption by a lower civilization" (58–59). Ford, reportedly, was so appalled by Latin dances that his dancing master Benjamin Lovett had to secretly steal away just to learn them from Doris Easton Travis, a former *Zeigfeld Follies* dancer who had trained under prominent ballroom dance teacher Arthur Murray (Travis 191).

There were inconsistencies in all this. Despite the original manuscript's disdain "for the hot blooded races of Southern Europe," among Ford's featured dances was the Sicilian Circle, a contra-dance that in fact probably does not have any real connection to Sicily (Shaw 378), but which *Good Morning* and the later *Independent* serialization made no effort to clarify (*Good Morning*, 1926 edition 109; "A Dance A Week: Sicilian Circle" 28–29). One might also presume a Nordicist worldview might entertain anti-Slavism,[37] but both *Good Morning* and the *Dearborn Independent* promoted Slavic-origin dances such as polkas (Ford, *Good Morning*, 1926 edition 7, 141; "A Dance a Week: Polka" 28–29). Indeed, *Good Morning* waxed poetically, if also not a bit pejoratively, about the dance originating with a "Bohemian servant girl's joyous steps, artlessly executed, upon receiving good news of her lover" (Ford, *Good Morning*, 1926 edition 7).

The fact that *Good Morning* would employ Nordicist language was perhaps not surprising given the most likely author of the introductory portions of the text was Ford's chief antisemitic journalist, William J. Cameron. Although no smoking-gun document survives to verify this, it is almost certain that the author of the important ideological portions of the text including the "dances partake" portion of "The Return of the Dance" was Cameron. At first glance *Good Morning* seems to have a simple authorship: the "Mr. and Mrs. Henry Ford" mentioned on the frontispieces of the first edition and in the subtitle of the second. The deeper one goes into the sources, however, the more *Good Morning* seems to be the product of a collective effort. Although some six books appeared under his name, Ford rarely, if ever, wrote his own published work (Lewis 215–16). Over the years, most of Ford-attributed literature was the result of the others' pens, either as ghostwriters such as Cameron, who wrote the *Independent*'s "Mr. Ford's Page," which was edited and reprinted in a volume titled *Ford Ideals*[38] or as officially-recognized collaborators such as Samuel Crowther, who is credited as such on Ford's *My Life and Work, Today and Tomorrow,* and *Moving Forward*. Standard music sources such as Richard Nevell's *A Time to Dance* acknowledge this in arguing that the dance manual was coauthored by the Fords and Ford's hired dance master Benjamin Lovett (63).

Lovett indeed seems to have been very involved in the publication of the book. Although he strangely does not mention the publication of *Good Morning* in his reminiscences archived at the Benson Ford Research Center (1–18), Lovett appears to have served as the central compiler and editor for several editions of the book. His correspondence with music publisher Otto Zimmermann & Son Co., regarding a new edition in 1931, depicts a very active presence. In his correspondence with the Cincinnati-based firm, which the

Ford Motor Company apparently hired out to print copies of the book under the Dearborn Publishing Co. name, Lovett approved dummies, corrected typography, grammar, and layout, and forwarded photographs (Otto Zimmerman materials). Other contributors were Clayton Perry, leader of Ford's old-fashioned dance orchestra, who assisted Lovett in traveling and researching the dance steps, and Alfred Hards, a draftsman who was paid to learn and teach the dances and who sketched illustrations for *Good Morning* (Twork 122–26). Lovett's correspondence with Otto Zimmermann representatives also notes an unnamed writer and a "Mr. Robinson" being involved in some of the editing in the 1931 edition.[39]

In light of what is known about the division of duties at the *Independent*, Cameron's authorship of the introductory text of *Good Morning* in 1925 is extremely likely. As editor-in-chief of the *Independent*, Cameron not only solicited and edited articles but served as the un-bylined ghost author of the staff "Editorials" page and of a weekly feature of "Ford" ideas titled first "Mr. Ford's Own Page" and then later simply "Mr. Ford's Page."[40] Generally speaking, Cameron talked with Ford, gleaning what Ford Motor Company production manager Charles E. Sorenson would later call Ford's "sudden flashes of intuition." He would then sit down and clothe them in "words (he) believed were Henry Ford's thoughts" before finally getting the OK from Liebold, Ford's general secretary.[41] Much of the language of "The Return of the Dance" section of *Good Morning*, in fact, first appeared in an official staff editorial in the *Independent* in June 1925, just prior to release of advanced manuscript copy to the press and the subsequent media blitz that followed ("Editorials: The Return of the Dance" 10) Cameron, in fact, appears to have had some history of working with, and ghostwriting for, Lovett on endeavors related to Ford's promotion of old-time dance and music. He wrote Lovett's dialogue, for instance, when Lovett appeared on the Ford-sponsored *Early American Dance Music* program on radio's Blue Network (formerly the NBC Blue Network) in 1944.[42]

A Canadian by birth, Cameron had grown up in Hamilton, Ontario, and later in Detroit. College educated, he had some background as a lay preacher, but was never ordained. In 1904, he began writing for the *Detroit News* and had moved up to the rank of columnist. In 1918, he left the *Detroit News* following his boss, managing editor E. G. Pipp, over to Henry Ford's newly-purchased *Dearborn* Independent (Bryan, *Henry's Lieutenants* 53–54). When Pipp left the *Independent* in 1920 over a dispute with Ford about whether to print the "International Jew" series, Cameron was named editor (Pipp 8–16; Lewis 139). Pipp, Liebold, Ford executive Fred L. Black and most other sources agree that

Cameron wrote most of the articles in the "International Jew" series, likely under the direction of Liebold, who was known for harboring a rather ardent anti-Semitism (Pipp 16; Liebold 479; F. L. Black 144).[43]

Although there is considerable debate about whether it was Cameron or Liebold who first persuaded Ford to engage in the antisemitic newspaper campaign or whether it was Ford's own idea (Lewis 138; Lacey 208), early researcher Leo Ribuffo (455) and more recently political scientist Michael Barkan have argued that Cameron became independently aligned by the 1930s with an antisemitic faction of British-Israelism, a Protestant theological strain that viewed the Anglo-Saxons as direct descendants of the ancient Israelites. While some early British-Israelites and American Anglo-Israelites practiced a philo-Semitism, Cameron aligned himself with the Nordicist-leaning antisemitic Anglo-Saxon Federation, making speeches about Anglo-Israelism at a Dearborn church as early 1933. Barkan argues that Cameron later wrote that an evil "Esau race" had "amalgamated with the Jews, and began the terrible work of corrupting the Jewish religion from within." Barkan postulates that Cameron's exposure to Anglo-Israelism was much earlier and that he was mixing British-Israel theology with antisemitism as early as the "International Jew" series in the early 1920s (Barkan 37–39). Cameron's later writing for Ford on "Mr. Ford's Page" bears witness to this. As late as July 1926, while ghostwriting for Ford on "Mr. Ford's Page," Cameron invoked the old antisemitic chimera again, criticizing the human "parasite" who persuaded those with "Old American names" into "business practices that are the antithesis of American" ("Mr. Ford's Page" 24 July 1926, 9).

Cameron was close to Ford, one of the few executives who lunched daily in Ford's private dining room at the Dearborn Engineering Building (Sorenson 176). Liebold notes that Ford talked to Cameron "almost daily" about publication matters (Reminiscences 451). The two seemed to especially share an affinity for the old-time music Ford preferred. Cameron recalled in his official company reminiscence:

> I've heard him (Ford) play the fiddle. He would play some of the old tunes in my office. Of course, he had a very great, fine, valuable collection of violins but he would take a fiddle from any of the old orchestra men from his little orchestra that he kept there, tune it up and play it. (Reminiscences 207)

Furthermore, Ford protected Cameron, refusing to send him a pink slip even after he had agreed to fire him as part of the Shapiro settlement (Cameron,

"Dances Partake of the Racial Characteristics of the People Who Dance Them"   53

Reminiscence 34). Cameron would stay on to serve as an interpreter of Ford to the press and to write for, and deliver, a weekly sermon-like talk on the music-oriented *Ford Sunday Evening Hour* on the national CBS radio network in the 1930s (Cameron, Reminiscences 38; *Ford Sunday Evening Hour* Folders 6, 8).

Cameron was also involved in promoting the old-time dance as editor of the *Independent*. The *World*'s 1925 press preview of *Good Morning* noted the close emotional and, in this case, physical proximity between Ford's dancing efforts and his antisemitic newspaper:

> So down with the fence of canvas in the laboratory, the pirouetting of other days being done again. It is an amazing environment. Liberty airplanes motors piled high on the waxed floor, printing presses exhaling the next issue of the Dearborn Independent, a wooden dirigible, men bent over blueprints—and twenty-five yards away an orchestra playing music to the Badger gavotte or the Varsovienne for an afternoon class of children. (Richards, "Ford Trips Ripple" S7)[44]

At the very least, Cameron edited the *Independent*'s serialized article versions of the manual content that began appearing in January 1926 as "A Dance of the Week." In that feature's inaugural release, the newspaper ran a three-color lithograph cover illustration of an earnest yet modern-looking group of young white people (four men in suits and bow ties and one modestly-dressed woman, all approximately in their twenties) trying to wake a white-mustached elderly fiddler, an apparent relic of the frontier, who sits snoozing, propped back on a chair in western riding boots, a simple cravat, and plain black lapel-less vest. The fiddler sleeps below a simple nineteenth century wooden mantel clock whose hands signal three o'clock—it is unclear whether it is 3 p.m. or 3 a.m.—a reference perhaps to the tendency of Ford's to run actual dances into the early morning (Cover illustration and "A Dance a Week for Beginners" 32–33). The clock is emblazoned with an oak tree, a favorite symbol among eugenicists for hereditary wellness ("Eugenics tree logo"). The four youths all seem to possess what Madison Grant would have identified as Nordic traits: "wavy brown or blond hair," "fair skin," and high and narrow "aquiline noses" (Grant 31, 167). The text inside is also instructive:

> The word "dance," when seen in print, conveys different things to different people. Some think of it as a jazzy rout from which they would themselves shrink and from which they would protect their children if possible. Others think of it as a monotonous round of steps, endlessly the same.

But those who know the old American dances, the dances which were part of the life of the pioneers from the Atlantic to the Pacific, have an entirely different conception of the dance. ("A Dance a Week" 16 Jan. 1926, 32)

Here we see Cameron, as editor, forging a marriage of convenience between Grant's Nordicism and Frederick Jackson Turner's mythologizing about the special properties of the frontier and the uniqueness of the American character. Indeed the illustration seems a visual representation of *Good Morning*'s assertion that there "is a revival of dancing which has survived longest amongst the northern peoples," coupled with the concerns of the text inside about restoring the hardiness and character that had once stemmed from frontier life.

Although Cameron's role in promoting dance was essential to Ford's efforts, Liebold, as the other Ford executive most closely linked with Ford's antisemitic efforts, was also heavily involved in promoting old-time music and dance in variety of ways. In his company reminiscence, Liebold not only explained how he was the one who arranged for *Good Morning* to be printed for distribution, but also relayed how Lovett was having trouble meeting Ford's expectation that some recordings of the old-time orchestra be made. Lovett asked Liebold to take over this enterprise, especially the technology, and Liebold agreed. "It was very, very trying work and it was very monotonous," he recalled. "We eventually produced twenty or twenty-four records, or something of that number" (1367–69). In 1942, Liebold appears to have taken over outright the editing of the final galleys of the 1943 edition of *Good Morning* (Correspondence).

After 1927, Ford's efforts to publicize old-time music and dance fell out of the national limelight, perhaps stunted by the grim economic news or Ford's labor troubles during the Depression.[45] Old-time music did occasionally get some play on CBS's *Ford Sunday Evening Hour* in the 1930s, and Lovett and other Ford employees continued to work on various new editions of *Good Morning* until 1943 (Lovett, Correspondence [1931]; Liebold, Correspondence). Surviving documents in the Benson Ford Research Center suggest that Lovett and key staff members also put together an *Early American Dance* program on the Blue Network in 1943 and 1944, but with Ford's death in 1947, and little interest among his heirs, promotional efforts effectively ended.

While Ford's support for old-time music and dance may have spoken of nostalgia and an agrarian philosophy, his attempts to resurrect tradition were definitely tinged with a modernistic streak. Nationwide relay broadcasts of old-time music broadcasts were one area in which Ford appears something of a pioneer. Robinson notes, too, that, in his dance manual, Ford "approached old time dances as he did his successful automobiles" by standardizing them (Robbins 2). Even his dance floor was subject to technological innovation. The aging floor in the ballroom at Sudbury Inn was supported with two large automobile springs and sliding wainscoting to give dancers an extra bounce ("Ford Debt to Longfellow" S6). In much the same way, the antisemitism and Nordicism that seemed to undergird Ford's favorite pastime were modernist inventions, which drew on antiquarian prejudices but were thoroughly up-to-date in their ruthlessness. Race theory, eugenics, anthropology, the study and measurements of human phenotypes—all the touchstones of Madison Grant's Nordicism and scientific racism—were fairly recent developments, often considered at the time to be on the cutting edge.

So what to make of the old-time music revival? Writers and historians have offered widely varying assessments regarding Ford's promotion of old-time music and the kinds of Nordicist arguments one finds in *Good Morning* and the *Independent*. Writing for *Sing Out!* magazine in the 1970s, Estelle Scheider and Bob Norman argued that Ford's revival coupled with his racism and antisemitism was "nothing less than a historical and cultural blueprint for a native American Fascism" (27). Leo Ribuffo, as mentioned earlier, argued that Ford's antisemitic muckraking was closer to Protestant minister Josiah Strong's "assimilationist ethnocentrism," which promoted the idea that Jews would be fine Americans if only they learned to adapt Anglo-Saxon ways, than it was to Grant's hardline "biological determinism." Certainly, there is no evidence from Ford's dance and music revival that he or any of his writers or interpreters favored the sustained eliminationist approach that Grant seems to favor: "the sterilization . . . of the criminal, the diseased and the insane and extending gradually to types which may be called weaklings rather than defectives and perhaps ultimately to worthless race types."[46] Furthermore, the evidence on Ford directly supporting European Fascism, at least so far, seems inconclusive,[47] although the very real feelers Ford put out for the presidency in 1922 (Liebold, Reminiscences 520–25)—just after the publication of the "International Jew" and just before the old-time revival—makes one wonder about the potentiality for the kind of nightmare scenario that novelist Philip Roth depicts, a *Plot Against America* only with lots of moralistic sermonizing, fiddling, and quadrille dancing.

Though several sources convincingly argue that the *Dearborn Independent* series and the Dearborn Press's four volume *International Jew* set influenced the Nazis or at least were used in support of Nazi racial ideology, the influence of Ford's promotion of old-time music and nineteenth century folk and social dances on the Nazis remains less certain. Although folk music and folk dance fit with Nazi concerns about *Völkisch*-ness, dance historian Marion Kant and dancer Lillian Karina argue that the Nazi state primarily used German folk dancing essentially for show or rhetorical benefit, providing irregular support or commitment outside of a few specific instances such as annual harvest festival at Bückeburg or as, Joshua Hagen argues, the *Shäfertanz* (Shepherd Dance) (Karina and Kant 87, 209; "Does Five O'Clock Tea Suit Our Time" 50).[48] And though the Nazis shared Ford's distaste for jazz music and dance and at times followed the *Dearborn Independent*'s lead in claiming that American jazz was a degenerate Jewish creation, the Nazis embraced modern dance, a form for which Ford apparently had little use (Karina and Kant 34, 73–77, 167–68.).[49]

Similarly, there seems to be little evidence that the American Far Right has ever used folk and social dance or traditional music to much success. In an important recent work, Patrick Huber has explained how early country recording star Fiddlin' John Carson composed antisemitic lyrics that help spur the scapegoating and, possibly, even the lynching of Jewish factory superintendant Leo Frank; but the populist Carson seems to have had about as much affinity for the local Klan as he did for the Communists (Huber 58–94). Certainly, what has become known as country music has had dalliances with a variety of conservatisms and populisms, and the occasional outburst of antisemitism, but it has also been equally associated with New Deal liberalism, municipal reform, and a consensus-seeking political and social center. Ultimately, it was countercultural youths often associated with the New Left, a group that would have sent Ford and Liebold clamoring for an aspirin and frequently-inebriated Cameron searching for his highball glass, that truly launched a full-fledged second revival in the 1960s of folk and roots music (Cohen 157–263) and, perhaps less well known, of contra dancing (Matthews 293–96).

What Ford's old-time revival does suggest is that Nordicism—to be sure, a more adaptable non-eliminationist sort, but a definite type of Nordicism nonetheless—was more a part of Ford and company's thinking than Ribuffo's and other analyses suggest. Had the antisemitic trifecta of Ford, Cameron and Liebold not ardently believed in Grant's Nordicist race theory, it seems unlikely that they would have stamped them so prominently on *Good Morning*, the capstone of their cherished revival project.

The question that arises, then, is one of reception. Did readers of *Good Morning* and the *Independent*'s "A Dance a Week" feature, dancers at Ford-sponsored affairs, and listeners of the radio relay broadcasts necessarily understand the underlying Nordicist premise? Did they understand that the revival might be a way of trimming back the supposed Jewish cultural influence? It seems unlikely that all, or even most, participants consciously made the connections, but some did as evidenced by a folder of fan letters in the Ford family's Fair Lane papers. One fan writer from Whitinsville, Massachusetts, for example, wrote to thank Ford personally for *Good Morning,* imbuing his missive with the same coded antisemitism that often passed for copy on "Mr. Ford's Page": "The American people will take this work up in no uncertain way. Under your great leadership, the styles of the heathen horde will disappear from the country" (Fan letter).

The Ford revival introduced the notion of a special relationship between the elderly and country music, helped set the stage for country music's rise in nationwide popularity following World War II, and spurred a short-lived revival of contra and squares that helped those forms live on to be revived again in 1950s and 1960s, but it also left other, darker legacies. It added fuel to an already existing campaign of violent stereotyping that fed the fears of racial and antisemitic extremists and justified quotas against Jews among the greater mainstream. It introduced the idea that supposed Jewish cultural hegemony might be overcome with the proper dose of strenuous activity and "clean" Nordic culture. It helped further codify the idea that hillbilly and country music was part and parcel of "white" culture. And, finally, it validated a lot of grumbling about jazz—a kind of kvetching that was replayed in the second half of the twentieth century with the rise of Rock 'n' Roll.

Notes

1. Quoted section is from the last entry of "The Essence of This Issue." This entry and the one before it officially announced the intent of Ford's editors to print descriptions, sheet music, and articles about "old-time dance" and "old American music."
2. Details about old time dance and music expenses have been mostly gleaned from materials in the Benson Ford Research Center, the Henry Ford, Dearborn, MI, especially the reminiscences of Ernest G. Liebold and Benjamin B. Lovett. An important secondary source is Twork. Although it is difficult to set an exact price tag, Ford's expenses were considerable. In addition to the cost of transporting and paying more than forty visiting musicians (some of whom were transported across country in Ford's private car), hiring dancing venues, and paying printing costs associated with Ford's dance manual, Ford also purchased and expensively-refurbished the historic Wayside, Botsford, and Clinton inns (the first in Massachusetts and the second and third in Michigan) primarily as ballroom spaces, devoted factory space to dancing, financed the recording and distribution of some twenty phonograph records, financed old time dancing lessons of Michigan school children and students at various universities across the nation, paid for promotional exhibitions of old time dancing at thirty-four colleges and universities, purchased at least one gold cup for a Michigan fiddling contest, hired members of a permanent old time orchestra, and salaried a full-time dancing-master, who remained in his employ and whom he housed until the 1940s. Ford also gave automobiles as gifts to at least some of his favored fiddlers. In 1937, he built an elegant ballroom, Lovett Hall, in Greenfield Village, specifically for this form of dancing. One should also add to this, the cost of executive and clerical staff time devoted to promoting dance and music, and the printing and distribution costs of the *Dearborn Independent* which in January 1926 began heavily promoting old time dances with its "A Dance a Week" feature. As noted by Foust (421), the *Dearborn Independent* generally operated at a loss, as much as $350,000 a year.
3. These arguments were made most notably, just as this chapter was going to press, in Gifford, "Henry Ford's Dance Revival." Although offering excellent insight into personnel involved, this article wants to read the dance revival as though it was removed from Ford's wider cultural efforts, failing to acknowledge that Ford's anti-semitic campaign in the *Dearborn Independent* continued throughout the old time revival well into 1927 and missing the significant publicity that release of the Ford's old time dance manual garnered for certain Nordicist and scientific racist ideas about music and dance.
4. Ford's distaste for jazz, Tin Pan Alley, and dancehalls are especially evident in the anonymously-penned articles in his newspaper "Jewish Jazz Becomes Our National Music" (8–9), and "How the Jewish Song Trust Makes You Sing" (8–9). Ford

mentions old time music and dancing as an alternative to these forms in the aforementioned "Ford Wars on Jazz" (E2) and Feld (SM2).
5. Details of this will be discussed in the final portion of this chapter.
6. My definitions of, and use of, the terms "Nordicism" and "Nordicist" are borrowed from Gregor's arguments in "Nordicism Revisited." Ford's antisemitism seems to have been influenced by wider scientific racism of his day, but Nordicism seems to best reflect specific type of scientific racism that he and his staff espoused.
7. Manuscript of text portions of "Good Morning" including introductory chapter, "The Return of the Dance," ca. 1925, are found in Miscellaneous Papers, Benson Ford Research Center.
8. Robbins, "Henry Ford's Old Time Dance Revival," an unpublished conference paper provided by Robbins to the author, is perhaps the best analyses of these dances to date, providing a strong foundation for future studies of the Ford revival.
9. Authenticity seems to have been an important goal in much of Ford's antiquarian pursuits. Henry Ford's Early American Orchestra, which was put together in the 1920s, for instance, is described as "an authentic early American combination of violin, dulcimer, cybalom and bass viol" on a script for the Blue Network's Ford-backed *Early American Dance* program, 22 Jan. 1944: 2. The Blue Network was originally a holding of NBC, but was spun off in 1943 and became known as the American Broadcasting Company (ABC) in 1945.
10. On Ford's important role in temporarily reviving and preserving what would become known as contra-dance, see Nevell 63–65, 74; O'Neill 50–53; Matthews 101–35. For more on Ford's impact on the revival of the western square dance, see Everette S. Wolfe. Ford did not champion the western-style squares that would go through a major revival in the 1950s but favored nineteenth century ballroom forms—which included a variety of forms of both social and stylized folk dancing. E. S. Wolfe, however, claims that pivotal western square dance revivalist Lloyd Shaw was summoned to meet Ford and demonstrate some of his Colorado group's old-time dances at some point in 1930s or 1940s and that Ford's campaign to collect and preserve these nineteenth century forms of dance inspired Shaw to do the same with western square dance. One study that argues for a more direct connection, although probably incorrectly, between Ford's efforts and the western square dancing craze sparked by Shaw in the 1950s is "Swing Your Partner."
11. C. K. Wolfe's *A Good Natured Riot* (77–79) is perhaps the best secondary source on the effect of Ford's promotion on the old time, or hillbilly, music audience. See also Peterson 60–62.
12. Invitation and club member listing, 27 Jan. 1910. Bryan, *Friends* (13–15) reproduces the invitation and mentions the 1910 dance, which attracted forty people, but this dance engagement is generally left out of most attempts to mine Ford's dance history.

13. Ironically, Ford's newspaper would claim that Benedict Arnold was a figure involved in various traitorous alliances with Jews.
14. See for instance, the 1890s-era S. S. Stewart banjo noted in the Henry Ford's "Music and Sound" online exhibit.
15. Relying on the Evart, MI, farmer Stewart Carmichael's recollections, Paul Gifford has argued that Ford, Edison and Firestone had come across Bisbee on an annual camping trip in the area after Ford's brother-in-law Milton D. Bryant, a Ford dealer north in Traverse City, north of Paris, had recommended Bisbee as a skilled fiddler; cf. Gifford, "Jasper E. 'Jep' Bisbee."
16. For details about Ford patronage of traditional musicians during this time period, see Gifford, *The Hammered Dulcimer* 352–58.
17. Relying on the remembrances of Lovett's niece, Twork dates the Ford-Lovett encounter as early as October 1923, but Lovett's own reminiscences and corresponding press coverage seem to contradict this.
18. Ford reiterated the main points of this passage in his interview with the *New York Times*: "This is an age of commercialism. With floor space so valuable one can see why owners of restaurants and dance halls can make more profit in dances which require a small space for a large number of people. I suppose we could get seventy-five couples to dance square dances in this hall. Three hundred could get in to dance the fox-trot. It wouldn't pay a commercial agent to encourage the square dance" (Feld SM2).
19. This is hinted at in Ford executive Liebold's reminiscences (1367).
20. Lovett quoted in a script for the Blue Network's *Early American Dance* program (2).
21. "Ford Greets Dunham at Dearborn Home" 14. A helpful secondary source on the Dunham fanfare is Wells.
22. On sparking ire, see, for instance, coverage of challenges to Dunham raised by championship winners in Rhode Island, New England, and California: "71-year-old Fiddler Wins" 8; "Old-Timer Wins Fiddle Title Glory" 7; "Fiddling Title at Stake" A1.
23. This is based on my examination of a run of the *Dearborn Independent* from May 20, 1920 to Jan. 14, 1922. The article on Christmas cards appears after the series, but during a period of ongoing but less frequent antisemitic material: "How Christmas Cards Have Been Degraded" 3.
24. "Turkey in the Straw" was frequently requested and played by old time fiddlers Ford entertained in the mid-1920s. See for instance, "Old-Time Fiddlers at Wayside Inn" 10. This version of the lyrics is drawn from Marling 145. For discussion of "Turkey in the Straw" and other bawdy versions see Cray 238, 253–55, and Titon 183.
25. "After the Ball" is mentioned favorably in "How the Jewish Song Trust Makes You Sing" 8. For lyrics and analysis, see Finson 67–72.
26. The four volumes are *The International Jew, Jewish Activities in the United States, Jewish Influences in American Life,* and *Aspects of Jewish Power in the United States,*

all published by the Dearborn Publishing Company 1920–22.
27. I opted for the fourth revised edition of *Passing* for these passages because it was the most current edition available during Ford's music and dance promotion.
28. Edwin Black discusses the rise and consequences of American eugenics in *War Against the Weak: Eugenics and America's Campaign to Create a Master*, esp. chapters 4–6, 9, 10, 13. Also see Kevles 3–19, 64; Larson 18, 19; Roberts 56–103.
29. Jenks published two articles in the *Independent* in 1925 about racial history of the Slavs, one article in 1926 on the effects World War I seemed to have on children's physical development in Munich, and two in 1927 on the racial history of the British Isles.
30. On the advance release of *Good Morning* to the press, see Richards S7; and "Ford Shakes a Wicked Hoof" 3, 40.
31. Perhaps most explicit in making connections between the old-time revival and Ford's antisemitism is Schneider and Norman 24–25, 27.
32. Robbins' transcription of the "denunciation of the dance" paragraph matches that of the second edition that I viewed at the Benson Ford Research Center. The same phrasing is also used the 1925 first edition. See N 34 for explanation of the various editions.
33. The latter piece drew extensively from the former.
34. *"Good Morning"* (1925) as located in the Fair Lane Papers. The Fair Lane Paper's copy of the published manual does include some pencil-mark edits regarding margins, orphans, and other layout but no editor's comments. Compare with the more widely available *"Good Morning": After a Sleep of Twenty-five Years, Old-fashioned Dancing is Being Revived by Mr. and Mrs. Henry Ford* which carries the inscription "Mr. and Mrs. Benjamin B. Lovett, masters of dancing, assisted in arranging the dance descriptions herein given." The 1941 and 1943 editions of the book are both titled *"Good Morning": Music, Calls, and Directions for Old-time Dancing as Revived by Mr. and Mrs. Henry Ford*. These editions bear the Dearborn Publishing name, but were produced by Cincinnati music publisher Otto Zimmerman & Sons.
35. The dances I list were South American and southern European-origin dances popular during the 1910s and 1920s. See for instance, Elson 355. This early manuscript also seems to draw from the popular notion of the time that African-American culture stemmed directly and primarily from the Congo, rather than from more diffused and reinvented cultural continuances and the larger West African region that historians point to today.
36. Although later Nordicists would deem them undesirable, Grant makes no mention of gypsies.
37. See the general anti-Slavic arguments of Grant 64–65. Grant did not consider Slavs a distinct race, but rather feared they were slightly Nordified Alpinics, whose mixing with Mongolian conquerors had left them "checked in development and warped in culture."

38. Longtime production and development chief Charles E. Sorenson describes how writers such as Cameron and Crowther served as Ford's public mouthpieces in *My Forty Years with Ford* 3, 142–43. Most if not all of secondary sources credit Cameron with writing "Mr. Ford's Page." Cameron admitted his authorship of the column during the Shapiro trial and mentions it in his own Ford Motor Company reminiscences (35). Cameron's authorship is corroborated by Fred L. Black's reminiscences, final draft (21). Cameron states that he wrote the original content of *Ford Ideals* in the form of "Mr. Ford's Page," but was not involved with the selection or editing of the pieces in the aforementioned reminiscence (35).
39. This was probably not Bernard Robinson, an attorney who headed up a Ford-financed investigation of Michigan Senate opponent Truman Newberry.
40. Cameron's authorship of the editorials and "Mr. Ford's Page" is mention in his own Ford Motor Company reminiscences (35), in Black's reminiscences, final draft (21), and in Liebold reminiscences (442). Nearly all the other major sources concur that Cameron did the bulk of the writing for these sections of the paper including Lacey 196; Brinkley 258; Lewis 135.
41. Quoted sections are from Sorenson 3, 176, referring to both Cameron and Crowther's duties of interpreting Ford to the public. The specific process is outlined in Black reminiscences (15–16); Liebold reminiscences (444); Lewis 135; and Brinkley 258. Liebold notes that Cameron and Ford talked almost daily about publication matters in his reminiscences (451).
42. Lovett, handwritten note to W. J. Cameron, with accompanying radio script and materials. On the Blue Network, see N 9.
43. Liebold's antisemitism is documented by many sources, but perhaps the most revealing are his own reminiscences. See for instance, his comments on 447, 458, 518.
44. It should be noted however that some of the Dearborn Publishing Company's printing did take place with contractors off the Ford property.
45. One exception being a 1928 old-time ball he seems to have sponsored in Rutland, Vermont, in 1928; cf. Lhjehlolm 1–2.
46. On Ford's general lack of eliminationist rhetoric see Baldwin 174. The quote is from Grant 51.
47. Max Wallace's *The American Axis; Henry Ford, Charles Lindbergh and the Rise of the Third Reich* and Baldwin's *Henry Ford and the Jews* do not find a smoking gun, but do uncover several possible leads.
48. On Nazi support for the *Shäfertanz*, see Hagen 209.
49. Ford was indifferent to modern dance pioneer Isadora Duncan, ignoring her requests for support. Apparently the feeling was mutual as she was ardently critical of what she saw as the overt sexuality that formed the basis of courtly dances Ford preferred. See Richards, *Last Billionaire* 112; Duncan 342.

Works Cited

"71-year-old Fiddler Wins." *New York Times* 6 Jan. 1926: 8.
"A Dance a Week." *Dearborn Independent* 20 Feb. 1926: 29.
"A Dance a Week for Beginners." *Dearborn Independent* 16 Jan. 1926: 32–33.
"A Dance a Week: Polka." *Dearborn Independent* 1 May 1926: 28–29.
"A Dance a Week: Sicilian Circle." *Dearborn Independent* 27 March 1926: 28–29.
"Are the Jews 'God's Chosen People'?" *Dearborn Independent* 22 Sept. 1923: 12.
"Are We a Shylock Nation?" *Dearborn Independent* 9 Jan. 1926: 3.
Aspects of Jewish Power in the United States. Dearborn: Dearborn, 1922. Vol. 4 of *The International Jew: The World's Foremost Problem.* 4 vols. 1920–22.
Baldwin, Neil. *Henry Ford and the Jews: The Mass Production of Hate.* New York: Public Affairs, 2001.
"Bark Versus Bite," editorial. *Dearborn Independent* 9 Jan. 1926: 11.
Barkan, Michael. *Religion and the Racist Right: The Origins of the Christian Identity Movement.* Chapel Hill: U of North Carolina P, 1994.
"Berlin Hears Ford is Backing Hitler." *New York Times* 20 Dec. 1922: 2.
Black, Edwin. *War against the Weak: Eugenics and America's Campaign to Create a Master Race.* New York: Four Walls Eight Windows, 2003.
Black, Fred L. Reminiscences, draft version. Acc. 65, Box 6, Folder 7. Benson Ford Research Center, the Henry Ford, Dearborn, MI.
———. Reminiscences, final draft. Acc. 65, Box 6, Folder 7. Benson Ford Research Center, the Henry Ford, Dearborn, MI.
Blaustein, Richard Jason. "Traditional Music and Social Change: Old Time Fiddlers Association Movement in the United States." Diss. Indiana U, 1975.
Brinkley, Douglas. *Wheels for the World: Henry Ford, His Company and a Century of Progress.* New York: Penguin, 2003.
Bryan, Ford R. *Friends, Families, and Forays: Scenes from the Life and Times of Henry Ford.* Detroit: Wayne State UP, 2002.
———. *Henry's Lieutenants.* Detroit: Wayne State UP, 1993.
Cameron, William J. *Ford Ideals: Being a Selection from Mr. Ford's Page in the Dearborn Independent.* Dearborn: Dearborn, 1926.
———. Reminiscences. Acc. 65, Box 11, Folder 1. Benson Ford Research Center, the Henry Ford, Dearborn, MI.
Carr, Steve Allen. *Hollywood and Anti-Semitism: A Cultural History Up to World War II.* Cambridge: Cambridge UP, 2001.
Cohen, Ronald D. *Rainbow Quest: The Folk Music Revival and American Society, 1940–1970.* Amherst: U of Massachusetts P, 2002.
Cover illustration. *Dearborn Independent* 16 Jan. 1926: 32–33.
Cray, Ed. *The Erotic Muse; American Bawdy Songs.* 2nd ed. Champaign: U of Illinois P, 1999.

"Dance Music is Radiocast." *Ford News* 15 Jan. 1927: 1.

"Does Five O'Clock Tea Suit Our Time?" *Nazi Culture: Intellectual, Cultural and Social Life in the Third Reich*. Trans. and ed. George L. Mosse. Madison: U of Wisconsin P, 1966. 47–53.

Duncan, Isadora. *My Life*. New York: Liveright, 1955.

Early American Dance. Blue Network. "Radio—Early American Dance Music—1944" folder, Acc. 1, Box 135. Benson Ford Research Center, the Henry Ford, Dearborn, MI.

———. Blue Network. 22 Jan. 1944. Script. "Radio—Early American Dance Music—1944" folder, Acc. 1, Box 135. Benson Ford Research Center, the Henry Ford, Dearborn, MI.

———. Blue Network. 11 March 1944. Script. "Radio—Early American Dance Music—1944" folder, Acc. 1, Box 135. Benson Ford Research Center, the Henry Ford, Dearborn, MI.

"Edison 'Cans' Music of Old Time Dance Fiddler." *New York Times* 22 Nov. 1923: 2.

"Editorials: The Return of the Dance." *Dearborn Independent* 6 June 1925: 10.

Elson, Arthur. *The Book of Musical Knowledge*. Boston: Houghton Mifflin, 1925.

"The Essence of This Issue." *The Dearborn Independent* 9 Jan. 1926: 1.

"Eugenics tree logo." American Philosophical Society, image #233. Ca. 1925. Image Archive of the American Eugenics Movement. 14 Sept. 2010 <http://www.eugenicsarchive.org/html/eugenics/index2.html?tag=233>.

Fan letter to Henry Ford. 11 Nov. 1925. Acc. 1, Box 134, Folder 17. Fair Lane Papers. Benson Ford Research Center, the Henry Ford, Dearborn, MI.

Feder, Lester. "'Song of the South': Country Music, Race, Region, and the Politics of Culture, 1920–1974." Diss. U of California, Los Angeles, 2006.

Feld, Rose C. "Ford Revives the Old Dances." *New York Times* 16 Aug. 1924: SM2.

"Fiddler Champ Challenged." *Los Angeles Times* 4 Jan. 1926: 8.

"Fiddles as Ford Dances." *Los Angeles Times* 12 Dec. 1925: 1.

"Fiddling Title at Stake." *Los Angeles Times* 25 Jan. 1926: A1.

"Fiddling to Henry Ford." *Literary Digest* 88.1 (2 Jan. 1926): 36.

Finson, Jon W. *The Voices That Are Gone: Themes in Nineteenth Century Popular Song* Oxford: Oxford UP, 1994.

Ford, Henry, in collaboration with Samuel Crowther. *Moving Forward*. Garden City, NY: Doubleday, Page, 1930.

———. *My Life and Work*. Garden City, NY: Doubleday, Page, 1922.

———. *Today and Tomorrow*. Garden City, NY: Doubleday, Page, 1926.

Ford, Mr. and Mrs. Henry. *"Good Morning": Being a Book on the Revival of the Dance*. Ca. 1925. Folders 1, 3–5; Box 1, Accession 356, Ford, Henry. Miscellaneous Papers. Benson Ford Research Center, the Henry Ford, Dearborn, MI.

———. "*Good Morning*": *Being a Book on the Revival of the Dance*. Dearborn: Dearborn, 1925. Acc. 1, Box 134, Folder 17. Fair Lane Papers. Benson Ford Research Center, the Henry Ford, Dearborn, MI.

———. "*Good Morning*"; *After a Sleep of Twenty-five Years, Old-fashioned Dancing is Being Revived by Mr. and Mrs. Henry Ford*. 2nd rev. ed. Dearborn: Dearborn, 1926.

———. "*Good Morning*": *Music, Calls, and Directions for Old-time Dancing as Revived by Mr. and Mrs. Henry Ford*. Cincinnati: Dearborn/Zimmerman, 1941.

———. "*Good Morning*": *Music, Calls, and Directions for Old-time Dancing as Revived by Mr. and Mrs. Henry Ford*. Cincinnati: Dearborn/Zimmerman, 1943.

———. "The Return of the Dance." "*Good Morning*": *Being a Book on the Revival of the Dance*. Ca. 1925. Folders 1, 3–5; Box 1, Accession 356, Ford, Henry. Miscellaneous Papers. Benson Ford Research Center, the Henry Ford, Dearborn, MI.

"Ford and His Fiddler Move on Detroit: Will Seek to Convert Local Devotees of Terpischore with Old-fashioned Dances." *New York Times* 13 Dec. 1925: 6.

"Ford at Oldtime Dance." *New York Times* 5 Jan. 1924: 3.

"Ford Brings Old Fiddler." *New York Times* 22 Nov. 1923: 11.

"Ford Debt to Longfellow." *New York Times* 17 Feb.1924: S6.

"Ford Greets Dunham at Dearborn Home." *New York Times* 9 Dec. 1925: 14.

"Ford Hires Big Hall for Old Time Dance." *New York Times* 14 Dec. 1925: 2.

"Ford Keeps a Promise." *New York Times* 13 Oct. 1923: 2.

"Ford Kindlier toward Jews." *Los Angeles Times* 25 Jan. 1926: 2.

"Ford Strong for Coolidge." *Los Angeles Times* 11 Feb. 1927: 1.

Ford Sunday Evening Hour. Acc. 1, Box 165, Folders 1–8. Fair Lane Papers. Benson Ford Research Center, the Henry Ford, Dearborn, MI.

"Ford to Hear Dulcimer." *Los Angeles Times* 13 Dec.1925: 21.

"Ford Wars on Jazz." *Los Angeles Times* 12 July 1925: E2.

Foust, James C. "Mass-Produced Reform: Henry Ford's *Dearborn Independent*." *American Journalism* 14.3–4 (Summer/Fall 1997).

Gerber, David A. "Anti-Semitism and Jewish-Gentile Relations in American Historiography and the American Past." *Anti-Semitism in American History*. Ed. D. Gerber. Urbana: U of Illinois P, 1986. 3–54.

Gifford, Paul M. *The Hammered Dulcimer: A History*. Lanham, MD: Scarecrow, 2001.

———. "Henry Ford's Dance Revival and Fiddle Contests: Myth and Reality." *Journal of the Society for American Music* 4.3 (August 2010): 307–38.

———. "Jasper E. 'Jep' Bisbee: Old-Time Michigan Dance Fiddler." *The Old Time Herald* 9.6. 15 Dec. 2009 <http://www.oldtimeherald.org/archive/back_issues/volume-9/9-6/jasper-bisbee.html>.

Gilman, Sander. *Freud, Race, and Gender*. Princeton: Princeton UP, 1993.

———. *The Jew's Body*. New York: Routledge, 1991.

Graham Jr., Otis. *An Encore for Reform: The Old Progressives and the New Deal*. New York: Oxford UP, 1967.

Grant, Madison. *The Passing of the Great Race: Or, the Racial Basis of European History.* 4th rev. ed. New York: Scribner's, 1922.

Greenbaum, Fred. *Men Against Myths: The Progressive Response.* Westport, CT: Praeger, 2000.

Gregor, A. James. "Nordicism Revisited." *Phylon* 22.4 (1961): 351–60.

Hagen, Joshua. *Preservation, Tourism and Nationalism: The Jewel of the German Past.* Hampshire, UK: Ashgate, 2006.

Hapgood, Norman. "The Inside Story of Henry Ford's Jew-Mania." *Hearst's International* 42 (July 1922): 14.

Harvey, Rexford. "Perpetuating Ideals of Idiocy and Depravity." *Dearborn Independent* 14 Jan. 1922: 10–11.

"Henry Ford Greets New Dance Tune Fiddler." *New York Times* 10 Dec. 1925: 16.

"Henry Ford Shakes a Wicked Hoof." *The Literary Digest* 86.7 (15 Aug.1925): 38.

"Henry Ford Still Thinks Soldiers Are Murderers." *New York Times* 16 July 1919: 1.

"History and Art Bunk, Says Ford." *Los Angeles Times* 16 July 1919: I8.

Hofstadter, Richard. *Age of Reform: From Bryan to FDR.* New York: Vintage, 1960.

"How Christmas Cards Have Been Degraded." *Dearborn Independent* 17 Dec. 1923: 3.

"How the Jewish Song Trust Makes Your Sing." *Dearborn Independent* 13 Aug. 1921: 8–9.

Huber, Patrick. *Linthead Stomp: The Creation of Country Music in the Piedmont South.* Chapel Hill: U of North Carolina P, 2008.

Hurtigan, James. *The Divided Mind of American Liberalism.* Lanham, MD: Lexington Books, 2002.

The International Jew: The World's Foremost Problem. Dearborn: Dearborn, 1920. Vol. 1 of *The International Jew: The World's Foremost Problem.* 4 vols. 1920–22.

Invitation and Club Member Listing. 27 Jan. 1910. "Ford, Henry—Dancing" folder, Vertical File. Benson Ford Archive. Benson Ford Research Center, the Henry Ford, Dearborn, MI.

Jackson, Jr., John and Nadine W. Weidman. *Race, Racism, and Science: Social Impact and Interaction.* Santa Barbara: ABC CLIO, 2004. 105–07.

Jenks, Albert Ernest. "How the Slavs Came to Europe." *Dearborn Independent* 20 June 1925: 25–27.

———. "The Slav—Old, Yet Full of Youth: A Paradoxical People Whose Fluid Nature is Apt to Overflow." *Dearborn Independent* 4 July 1925: 15–19.

———. "Where the Peoples of the British Isles Come From." *Dearborn Independent* 4 March 1927: 6–7, 29.

"'Jep' Fiddles for Edison." *New York Times* 22 Nov. 1923: 3.

Jewish Activities in the United State. Dearborn: Dearborn, 1921. Vol. 2 of *The International Jew: The World's Foremost Problem.* 4 vols. 1920–22.

"The Jewish Attempt to Bolshevize the Negro." *Dearborn Independent* 22 Dec. 1923: 12.

Jewish Influences in American Life. Dearborn: Dearborn, 1921. Vol. 3 of *The International*

Jew: The World's Foremost Problem. 4 vols. 1920–22.

"Jewish Jazz Becomes Our National Music." *Dearborn Independent* 6 Aug. 1921: 8–9.

Karina, Lillian and Marion Kant. *Hitler's Dancers: German Modern Dance and Third Reich.* Trans. Jonathan Steinberg. New York: Berghahn, 2003.

Kevles, Daniel J. *In the Name of Eugenics: Genetics and Uses of Human Heredity.* New York: Knopf, 1985.

Kun, Josh. "The Yiddish Are Coming: Mickey Katz, Antic-Semitism, and the Sound of Jewish Difference." *American Jewish History* 87.4 (December 1999): 356.

Lacey, Robert. *Ford: The Men and the Machine.* Boston: Little, Brown, 1986.

Larson, Edward J. *Sex, Race, and Science: Eugenics in the Deep South.* Baltimore: Johns Hopkins UP, 1995.

Lewis, David L. *The Public Image of Henry Ford: An American Folk Hero and His Company.* Detroit: Wayne State UP, 1976.

Lhjehlolm, Henry E. "Henry Ford Forgets Motors for Stately Rhythms." *Albany Evening News* 14 Aug. 1928: 1–2.

Liebold, Ernest G. Correspondence with Otto Zimmerman and Son representatives. 1942–1943. "The Otto Zimmerman and Son Co. LTD. Inc. 1942–1943" folder, Acc. 285, Box 2786. Benson Ford Research Center, the Henry Ford, Dearborn, MI.

———. Reminiscences. Acc. 65, Vol. 6. Benson Ford Research Center, the Henry Ford, Dearborn, MI.

Lovett, Benjamin B. Correspondence with Otto Zimmerman and Son. Undated (ca. summer 1931). Acc. 285, Box 1405, Folder 1291a. Benson Ford Research Center, the Henry Ford, Dearborn, MI.

———. Correspondence with Otto Zimmerman and Son Company representatives. 1931. Acc. 285, Box 1405, Folder 1291a. Benson Ford Research Center, the Henry Ford, Dearborn, MI.

———. Handwritten note to W. J. Cameron, with accompanying radio script and materials. Ca. June 1924. Acc. 1, Box 135. Benson Ford Research Center. Dearborn, MI.

———. Otto Zimmerman Materials. Acc. 285, Box 1405, Folder 1291a. Henry Ford Office Files. Benson Ford Research Center, the Henry Ford, Dearborn, MI.

———. Reminiscences. Acc. 1, Box 134. Benson Ford Research Center, the Henry Ford, Dearborn, MI.

Marling, Karal Ann. *Designs of the Heart: The Homemade Art of Grandma Moses.* Cambridge: Harvard UP, 2006.

Matthews, Mark. "Promenading Toward Democracy: The History of Squares, Contras, and Waltzes." Unpublished book manuscript, 2009.

Melnick, Jeffrey. "Tin Pan Alley and the Black-Jewish Nation." *American Popular Music: New Approaches to the Twentieth Century.* Ed. Rachel Rubin and Jeffrey Melnick. Amherst: U of Massachusetts P, 2001.

Menius, Art. *Bluegrass Unlimited* 26.8 (February 1992): 26–28.

Miller, Karl Hagstrom. "Segregating Sound: Folklore, Phonographs, and the

Transformation of Southern Music, 1888–1935." Diss. New York U, 2002.

"Mine Host Ford Fiddler for Dance." *New York Times* 10 Feb. 1924: E1.

"Mr. Ford's Page." *Dearborn Independent* 29 Jan. 1921: 5.

———. *Dearborn Independent* 17 June 1922: 5.

———. *Dearborn Independent* 5 July 1924: 7.

———. *Dearborn Independent* 16 Aug. 1924: 7.

———. *Dearborn Independent* 24 July 1926: 9.

Mulder, Ronald A. "Reluctant New Dealers: The Progressive Insurgents in the United States Senate, 1933–1934." *Capitol Studies* 2.2 (1974): 5–22.

"Music and Sound" online exhibit. *The Henry Ford*. 2002. 27 Nov. 2010 <http://www.thehenryford.org/exhibits/collections/Collections/music/instruments/banjo.asp>.

Nash, Roderick. *The Nervous Generation: American Thought, 1917–1930*. 1970. Chicago: Elephant, 1990.

Nevell, Richard. *A Time to Dance: American Country Dancing from Hornpipes to Hot Hash*. New York: St. Martin's, 1977.

"Odd Definitions Given By Ford in Libel Suit." *New York Times* 17 July 1919: 1.

"Old-Time Fiddlers at Wayside Inn." *New York Times* 10 Jan. 1926: 10.

"Old-Timer Wins Fiddle Title Glory." *Los Angeles Times* 8 Jan. 1926: 7.

O'Neill, Kate. "Henry Ford and the Revival of Country Dancing." *Dance Magazine* 71.8 (Aug. 1997): 50–53.

Otto, John S. and Augustus M. Burns. "Black and White Cultural Interaction in the Early Twentieth Century South: Race and Hillbilly Music." *Phylon* 35.4 (Dec. 1974): 407–17.

Peterson, Richard A. *Creating Country Music: Fabricating Authenticity*. Chicago: U of Chicago P, 1997.

Pincini, R. "Fascism as New Cure for Demagogy." *Dearborn Independent* 17 Feb. 1923: 2.

Pipp, E. G. Speech transcript. "Special File and reports—Address by E.G. Pipp on Henry Ford." Acc. 6, Box 1. Edsel Ford Papers. Benson Ford Research Center, the Henry Ford, Dearborn, MI.

Pope, Virginia. "Maine's Champion Fiddler Finds Fame at His Door." *New York Times* 13 Nov. 1925: SM4.

"Producing Jewish 'Martyrs' by Propaganda." *Dearborn Independent* 3 Feb. 1923: 12.

Ribuffo, Leo. "Henry Ford and *The International Jew*." *American Jewish History* 69 (June 1980): 448; 452–53, 457.

Richards, William C. "Ford Trips Ripple as Lizzies Look On." *New York World* 2 Aug. 1925: S7.

———. *The Last Billionaire: Henry Ford*. New York: Scribner's, 1950.

Robbins, Allison. "Henry Ford's Old Time Dance Revival." Unpublished conference paper. Society for American Music's 32nd Annual Conference in Chicago, March 16, 2006.

Roberts, Dorothy. *Killing the Black Body: Race, Reproduction, and the Meaning of Liberty.* New York: Pantheon, 1997.
Roth, Philip. *Plot Against America.* New York: Houghton Mifflin, 2004.
Roy, William G. "Aesthetic Identity, Race, and American Folk Music." *Qualitative Sociology* 25.3 (Fall 2002): 459–69.
Schneider, Estelle and Bob Norman, "The Ford Dance Movement: Fiddling While the Crosses Burned." *Sing Out!* 25.4 (Nov./Dec. 1977): 24–25, 27.
Shaw, Lloyd. *Round Dance Book: A Century of Dancing.* Caldwell, ID: Caxton, 1950.
Sheedy, Paul. "Los Angeles In Fiddle Contest." *Los Angeles Times* 23 Jan. 1926: A5.
Simonds, William Adam. *Henry Ford and Greenfield Village.* New York: Stokes, 1938.
Smith, Llewellyn. "Negroes of Harlem Exploited by Jews." *Dearborn Independent* 29 Dec. 1923: 9.
Soderstrom, Mark. "Family Trees and Timber Rights: Albert E. Jenks, Americanization, and the Rise of Anthropology at the University of Minnesota." *The Journal of the Gilded Age and Progressive Era* 3.2 (April 2004): 176–204.
Sorenson, Charles E. *My Forty Years with Ford.* New York: Norton, 1956.
Stoddard, Lothrop. *The Rising Tide of Color against White World-Supremacy.* New York: Scribner's, 1920.
Sutherland, Pete. "Beware of Old-time Music Revivals! The Henry Ford Story." *Old Time Herald* 2.7 (Feb.–April 1991): 33–37.
"Swing Your Partner." *Inside Michigan* Sept. 1951. Clipping in "Ford, Henry—Dancing" folder, Vertical File. Benson Ford Research Center, the Henry Ford, Dearborn, MI.
"Take Down the Fiddle and the Bow." *The Youth's Companion* 100.1 (7 Jan. 1926): 10.
Titon, Jeff Todd. *Old Time Kentucky Fiddle Tunes.* Lexington: U of Kentucky P, 2001.
Travis, Doris Eaton. *The Days We Danced: The Study of My Theatrical Family from Florenz Ziegfeld to Arthur Murray and Beyond.* Seattle: Marquant, 2003.
Twork, Eva O'Neal. *Henry Ford and Benjamin B. Lovett: The Dancing Billionaire and the Dancing Master.* Detroit: Harlo, 1982.
Tyner, Paul. "Where Are Israel's Lost Tribes?" *Dearborn Independent* 23 May 1925: 14–15, 27.
"Waking Up the Old American Dances." *Dearborn Independent* 16 Jan. 1926: cover issue.
Wallace, Max. *The American Axis: Henry Ford, Charles Lindbergh and the Rise of the Third Reich.* New York: St. Martin's, 2003.
Wells, Paul F. "Mellie Dunham: Maine's Champion Fiddler." *John Edwards Memorial Foundation Quarterly* 12.43 (Autumn 1976).
"West Dances to Ford Orchestra." *Ford News* March 1926: 4.
"When the Ku Klux Klan First Flourished." *Dearborn Independent* 1 Dec. 1923: 4, 13.
Wilbur, James. "Mussolini as Arbiter of Fate in Italy." *Dearborn Independent* 8 Jan. 1927: 1–2.
Woeste, Victoria Saker. "Insecure Equality: Louis Marshall, Henry Ford, and the

Problem of Defamatory Antisemitism, 1920–1929." *Journal of American History* (December 2004): 877–905.

Wolfe, Charles K. *A Good Natured Riot: The Birth of the Grand Ole Opry.* Nashville: Country Music Foundation/Vanderbilt UP, 1999.

Wolfe, Everette S. Letter to H. E. Edmunds, director, Ford Archives. 14 July 1969. Small Acc. 1040. Everette S. Wolfe Papers. Benson Ford Research Center, the Henry Ford, Dearborn, MI.

Wolff, Walter M. "Anti-Semitism in Germany: Where and Why?" *Dearborn Independent* 17 Jan. 1925: 2.

———. "Germany, Prey of Alien, Faces Complete Ruin." *Dearborn Independent* 9 Sept. 1922: 9, 11.

"World News" photo editorial. *Los Angeles Times* 7 Feb. 1926: H2.

"You Are Invited to Hear Henry Ford's Old Fashioned Dance Orchestra." 1927, radio program, Concerts no. 92.150, 9453. Program Collections, Behind the Barriers Program. Benson Ford Research Center, the Henry Ford, Dearborn, MI.

"Ovoutie Slanguage is Absolutely Kosher": Yiddish in Scat-Singing, Jazz Jargon, and Black Music

Jonathan Z. S. Pollack

I'm hinky-dink, a solid sender
A very good friend to Mrs. Bender
Bender, schmender, a bee gezindt!
I'm the cat that's in the know. (Nemo and Mills)

Dan [Burley]'s jive parodies of famous pieces like "The Night Before Christmas" and other poems will remind some readers of the parodies done by Milt Gross in his series "Nize Boy" in the old World many years ago. Gross' language was English as it was handled with the twist of Yiddish dialect, and it stemmed from the imperfect speech of recent Yiddish immigrants . . . (Conrad)

Being "in the know" has always been an essential element of any slang language, especially within African-American culture. Slang has always been used to identify members of an in-group, and often further serves to hide secret knowledge from outsiders. Scholars who have studied the development of Black-English have paid particular attention to slang, since this patois arose during slavery as a way of concealing one's true thoughts and intentions. In addition to drawing upon European languages such as English, French, and Spanish, Black-English has incorporated words from the languages of West Africa, such as "cool," meaning "fast" in Mandingo, or "hip" from the Wolof "hepi" or "hipi," meaning "to see" or "to open one's eyes" (Major 111, 234).

The growth of American cities in the early twentieth century, and the resulting urbanization of American culture, brought African-Americans into contact with newly-arrived immigrants from southern and eastern Europe. In particular, in neighborhoods from Harlem, to Chicago's West Side, to Boyle Heights in Los Angeles, Blacks and immigrant Jews established personal and economic relationships. As Jews learned about American culture through their Black neighbors, so did Blacks learn about American-Jewish culture as it developed in these and other neighborhoods. Along with the sounds of the Yiddish language, Jewish foods became part of the urban landscape. The popularity of delicatessens among entertainers in New York, Los Angeles, and elsewhere ensured that millions of Americans, without personal connections to pastrami, matzo ball soup, and corned-beef sandwiches, would hear about them through their being so often featured in entertainment news.[1]

Scat-singing, jazz jargon, and Black music also incorporated Yiddish words and phrases as the sounds of "hipness"— a vocal code that would be known to musicians and their hangers-on but not to the uninitiated. Yiddish sounds appeared in Black music of this era because of their novelty and their association with Jews, who, to Blacks familiar with Jews as club owners, managers, agents, attorneys, and fans, represented success and power. Other scholars have dealt with the image of Jews among the Black intelligentsia (Lewis 543–64) but slang and song, with their potential for multiple, slippery meanings, have not drawn the same attention. Nonetheless, a considerable body of jazz recordings that used included Yiddish words during the late 1930s and 1940s demonstrates how Yiddish served as a form of "jive" among Black musicians in this period. Like other forms of slang, Yiddish was employed as a secret code, for those "in the know" to deploy in the presence of unknowing "squares." The use of Yiddish in the music of Louis Armstrong, Cab Calloway, and Slim Gaillard, in particular, delineates the multiple images of Jews in Black communities during the 1930s. Yiddish presented new and exciting sounds and words to blend with the existing mélange of Black slang. Yiddish was also the "cash language" (Christensen 36–40) in many Black communities, due to the preponderance of Jewish merchants there. Blacks who sang in Yiddish, as part of a broader "hip" jargon, could thus demonstrate their aspiration to Jewish prosperity while mocking Jewish speech. Black musicians who employed Yiddish in their lyrics and scat-singing brought a humorous double-edge to their take on the popular culture of two out-groups in American society by emphasizing their points of connection as well as their emerging rivalries.

The aim of this essay is to take a closer look at Yiddish lyrics in music by Black musicians as both parody and tribute to the multiple expressions of Jewish-Black relations in the interwar and World War II years. Within the entertainment business, scholars like Michael Paul Rogin, Jeffrey Melnick, and Michael Alexander have provided important background on Jewish entertainers' use of stage Black dialect in vaudeville, Tin Pan Alley, and early Hollywood films. Eric Goldstein has tackled the broader issue of Jewish racial identity, and contrasted Jews and Blacks and similar-yet-different "others" in the interwar years. Cheryl Lynn Greenberg, Hasia Diner, Joe Trotter, and Winston McDowell have discussed Jewish-Black relations in the business world of this era. What I'm calling "ovoutie slanguage" in mid-century American music has its roots in these other forms of popular entertainment plus the broader contexts of "whiteness," "blackness," and business (Rogin; Melnick; Alexander 131–83; Goldstein; Greenberg; Diner, *In The Almost Promised Land*).[2] And, as is so often the case, any story of American popular music in the twentieth century must begin with Louis Armstrong.

LOUIS ARMSTRONG: JEWISH CONNECTIONS AND POSSIBLE INSPIRATIONS

Louis Armstrong (1901–1971) is widely acclaimed as the first superstar of jazz. From the earliest days of jazz recording, in the 1920s, Armstrong's records were recognized as masterworks. In 1926, Armstrong recorded one of the first sides to feature what was called "oofin'" and what later became known as "scatting." Armstrong allegedly dropped the lyric sheet for a song called "Heebie Jeebies" and sang nonsense syllables to fill the space. The song became a hit (Bergreen 266–67; Edwards 627–36).

Although the phrase "heebie jeebies" would seem to indicate some connection to actual Hebrews, the term's origin appears to be a Barney Google comic strip from 1923. Nonetheless, in a later conversation with his friend and Queens neighbor Phoebe Jacobs, Armstrong claimed that his approach to scat singing was an effort to imitate what he called, "the Jews rockin'," or praying, in the storefront synagogues of his native New Orleans (Bergreen 266–67; Edwards 627–36).

For that matter, Armstrong also enjoyed close relations with individual Jews, Jewish families, and Jewish institutions throughout his life. As a child, Armstrong had an early job with the scrap-collecting Karnofsky family in New Orleans. In his autobiographical writings, Armstrong credits the Karnofsky family with helping him buy his first horn, feeding him when he was out late peddling with them, and singing the Irving Berlin tune, "Russian Lullaby," which he remembered fondly years later. Once Armstrong had become a star, he hired Jewish managers Mezz Mezzrow (who also supplied him with marijuana) and Joe Glazer. Armstrong lived in the integrated neighborhood of Corona, Queens, and while recuperating at Beth Israel Hospital near the end of his life, wrote tributes to the Jewish doctor who had saved his life, as well as the aforementioned Jews he had been happy to work with. Armstrong, a man who watched what he ate, praised matzos as a healthful food that he always kept on hand at home (Armstrong 3–36; Mezzrow and Wolfe 244–46).

JEWS EMULATING BLACKS: MINSTRELSY AND POPULAR MUSIC

Recent scholarship has devoted a great deal of time to examining the image of Blacks in Jewish culture. Jewish songwriters, like Irving Berlin, and performers, like Sophie Tucker, incorporated rhythms from ragtime and other Black influences into the popular music they created in the 1910s and 1920s. In his study of this era, Jeffrey Melnick describes music as one of "the languages of Black-Jewish relations" (Melnick 1–15). Specifically, the career of Al Jolson, in particular his film *The Jazz Singer*, has been the focus of much critical work. The basic argument describes how Blackness and blackface minstrelsy represented "Americanness" to first- and second-generation American Jews; so aspiring Jewish entertainers learned the conventions of minstrelsy and blackface more generally (see Rogin; Alexander 133–79; Goldstein 74–82).

Jolson's most famous starring role, as Jakie Rabinowitz/Jack Robin in *The Jazz Singer* (1927) is a perfect illustration of this idea. Rabinowitz, the protagonist, is descended from a long line of cantors, but loves the jazz world and secretly performs as "Jack Robin," a singer in blackface. In *Blackface, White Noise*, the most thorough examination of this topic, Michael Paul Rogin writes that in *The Jazz Singer*, "blackface as American national culture Americanized the son of the immigrant Jew" (6). Although his father disowns his son for his career choice, when the elder Cantor Rabinowitz is on his deathbed, too sick to chant the Kol Nidre prayer that begins the Yom Kippur service, Jakie abandons an opening-night performance to chant Kol Nidre at his father's synagogue.

BLACKS EMULATING JEWS: ENTREPRENEURSHIP, DIASPORIC UNITY, AND CIVIL RIGHTS

At the same time that Louis Armstrong popularized the heebie-jeebies and George Gershwin and Al Jolson embodied Black-Jewish connections in musical composition and performance, there existed a broader undercurrent of voices who emulated Jews and Jewish history in Black communities. Black leaders, from Booker T. Washington, who held up Jewish entrepreneurship as a model for Blacks to follow, to W. E. B. DuBois, who saw the Zionist movement at the time of the Balfour Declaration as a model for a pan-African movement, urged their followers to adapt Jewish ideas for the purposes of Black advancement (Melnick 10; Williams 356). Marcus Garvey's Universal Negro Improvement Association often used Zionist imagery to describe Garvey's plan for reuniting the African diaspora in a new African kingdom. Garvey and his followers also sought to emulate Jewish economic self-sufficiency and, like Zionists, he desired to reunite peoples of African descent in their historic homeland. As Garvey put it, "Our obsession is like that of the Jews. They are working for Palestine. We are working for Africa" (Garvey 10, quoted in Williams 357; UCLA). On a different aspect of Black society, leaders of the NAACP sought out Jewish support for their cause, and looked to Jewish defense organizations for examples of how to wage their legal battles (Lewis 543–64). Howard University Dean Kelly Miller used the term "Black Sanhedrin" for a meeting of Black leaders in 1924 (Lewis 563).

Black emulation of the Zionist movement, Jewish solidarity, and the financial success of some Jews was not without its darker flipside, however. Garvey's description of his movement in Zionist terms was overshadowed by his venomous allegations against Jewish members of the jury that convicted him, as well as by a more general rising pro-Fascist sympathy during the 1930s. Conversations between Black activists and Jewish patrons of the NAACP and Urban League often proved awkward, with Black leaders feeling patronized by comparisons of their experiences to those of Israelites in ancient Egypt (UCLA; Lewis).

Tensions between Blacks and Jews came to a head in 1935. That year, a race riot pitted Black residents of Harlem against Jewish shop-owners. Rumors of a Puerto Rican teenager being assaulted over the theft of a penknife exploded into a conflict that exposed deep fissures between Blacks and Jews in Harlem. Although Harlem had had a sizeable Jewish community in the early twentieth century, as Blacks moved into the neighborhood in the 1920s, Jews began to move out to the Bronx and Brooklyn. Jewish "white flight" from Harlem was not complete, though; many Jewish business owners kept their stores in Harlem even if they lived in a different borough or suburb. To Jewish entrepreneurs, this decision was, to a great extent, an example of Jewish tolerance and embrace of their Black customers; in an age when chain-stores rarely opened in Black neighborhoods, Jewish merchants remained in Black neighborhoods, extending credit and respect to their customers (Gurock 146–51; Greenberg 3–6).

Many Black residents of Harlem saw Jewish merchants in a different light. Rather than family businesses that catered to a Black clientele, Blacks in Harlem saw stores that charged premium prices for discount goods. Furthermore, relatively few Blacks in Harlem worked in Jewish-owned stores, which prompted a "Don't Buy Where You Can't Work" campaign from local activists the year before the riots broke out. The Harlem riots of 1935 represented a major rift between Blacks and Jews, two groups that had had a strong identification with each other, and that prompted strong associations in popular culture, from the blackface careers and well-known Jewish identities of Al Jolson, Fanny Brice, Eddie Cantor, and Sophie Tucker, to the "Jewish jazz" reviled by Henry Ford and others (Greenberg 114–39; Melnick 108–14).

"BAY MIR BISTU SHEYN"

Mirroring the complex interplay between Blacks and Jews, a 1937 live performance set these tensions to music and paved the way for a series of songs with Yiddish lyrics sung by Black performers. Johnny Macklin and George MacLean, a Black song-and-dance team who performed under the name "Johnnie and George," performed a Yiddish song at Grossinger's resort in the Catskills, and at the Yacht Club, a club featuring Jewish entertainers like Henny Youngman, Jerry Lester, and Frances Faye, located on New York's 52nd Street. Titled "Bay Mir Bistu Sheyn" in its original formulation, and originally backing a big production number in a Yiddish musical, the song, as performed by Macklin and MacLean, represented both a hilarious juxtaposition of Black performance in Yiddish—when tensions between Blacks and Jews had been running high—as well as a reminder of the connections between these two groups. From a Black perspective, the song is especially mysterious: is it a further emulation of Jewish culture, or some sort of mockery, akin to Jewish performers who sang in blackface?[3] It is still unclear how Johnnie and George came to perform Shalom Secunda's song "Bay Mir Bistu Sheyn," from his 1932 musical *Men Ken Lebn Nor Men Lost Nisht* (literally: *You Could Live but They Don't Let You*; its producers translated it as "I Would if I Could"). However they came across it, their performance turned lots of heads, and the song took off. Clearly, the public was ready for Black entertainers singing in Yiddish.[4]

CANTOR CAB CALLOWAY?

The set of mixed reactions to Jewish culture also found its way into other jazz records of the 1930s. In the early years of that decade, Calloway's performances, especially of his biggest hit, "Minnie the Moocher," were said to be based on cantorial singing. Cab Calloway actually starred in 1936 with Al Jolson in *The Singing Kid*. Calloway had other connections to Jewish figures in the entertainment business, including some of his songwriters. By the late 1930s, Jewish songwriters had provided Calloway with several Yiddish-inflected songs that became part of his repertoire. His song "A Bee Gezindt," written by Henry Nemo, uses Yiddish to demonstrate that that the singer is "the cat who's in the know," a mission entirely in line with Calloway's "hipster" image that he cultivated throughout the 1930s. Calloway followed "A Bee Gezint" with "Utt-Da-Zay," Buck Ram and Irving Mills' composition that covers an actual Yiddish song, "Ot azoy neyt a shnayder," in which Calloway keeps the subject of the original song, but completely inverts its message (Calloway and Rollins 110–11).

The original dates from the 1880s, when factories and the twelve-hour workday made it harder for tailors to earn a living. "Ot azoy . . ." contains the refrain, "Ot azoy neyt a shnayder/ Ot azoy neyt er doch," which translates to "This is how the tailor stitches/ This is how he really sews." The chorus is intended ironically, though; the song goes on to describe how the tailor does all his work for very little money, and eventually his hard work, long hours, and chronic poverty lead him to, "fardint kadokhes, nit kayn broyt (earn a fever, not any bread)" (Rubin 86–87). This sad, sarcastic tale of a tailor's label undergoes a radical change in Calloway's treatment:

> "Utt da zay," sings the tailor,
> As he fashions pretty clothes;
> "Utt da zay," sings the tailor,
> As he sews, sews, sews.
> He's as busy as a bee,
> Making lovely finery,
> Things my baby loves to wear
> When I take her to the fair.
> "Utt da zay," sings the tailor; all it means is "That's the way."
> When I buy the things he made her, says the tailor, "Utt da zay."

In Calloway's version, the subject of the song is not the producer (the tailor), but the customer. Rather than focusing on the rigors of the tailor's work day, "Utt-Da-Zay" looks at the tailor's output—beautiful clothes that the singer buys for his "baby." The song symbolizes how the Jewish socialist movement, centered in tailors' unions (and often led by one-time tailors) had faded away and become replaced by the magic of American consumerism. Given the original song's use of physical illness as an example of the tailor's suffering, one could say that "consumption" had been replaced by "consuming."

In 1940, Calloway recorded a tribute of sorts to violinist Yehudi Menuhin. Titled "Who's Yehoodi," the song had its origins on a Bob Hope radio show, where Menuhin was scheduled to make a guest appearance as part of his tour of the United States. Hope sidekick Jerry Colonna, forgetting a line, ad-libbed, "Who's Yehudi?" and got big laughs from the studio audience. On that show, and later, the phrase "who's Yehudi" became a catch-phrase to fill space; eventually, the word "Yehudi" came to mean "the man who wasn't there."

Of course, in actual Hebrew, "Yehudi" translates to "Jew." Although "who's Yehoodi" was understood as a joke in this era, the phrase has a set of odd associations, and would have had these even at this time. As anti-Semitism became more prevalent, and more respectable, in Europe and the United States, Jews went to greater lengths to change their names, obtain plastic surgery, and undertake other measures to avoid being seen as "Yehudim." So, a song with lyrics that run,

> G-man Hoover's getting moody
> Got his men on double duty

> Trying to find out—
> Who's Yehoodi!

could stand in for a bunch of Jewish anxieties about not being able to "pass" in American society at a tense time. A "soundie" (a short 16-millimeter film played on special jukeboxes; a precursor to music video) of the Kay Kyser version of the song, featured a stage-Jew character, with black hat, fake beard, and open prayer book, leering at Lane Truesdale, the singer with Kyser's band. Clearly, although Colonna's original joke had no direct connection with anything Jewish beyond Menuhin's first name, subsequent interpreters saw a clear connection. Although Cab Calloway employed cantorial vocalizations on some of his earlier hits, none of those appear in his rendition of "Who's Yehoodi?"

SLIM GAILLARD: YIDDISH AND THE POLYLINGUAL SOUND OF CITIES

Slim Gaillard, a contemporary of Calloway's, had a deliberately obscure background that leaves his interest in Yiddish lyrics hard to trace. Gaillard's place of birth has been claimed as Santa Clara, Cuba, Detroit, Michigan, and Pensacola, Florida. He was said to speak multiple languages—at different times, the list included Greek, Arabic, Hebrew, Portuguese, Turkish, Bulgarian, Spanish, Chinese, Italian, Finnish, and "Syrian." He claimed to have been left on the Greek island of Crete by his father, a worker on a cruise ship. He claimed to have been a driver for Detroit's Purple Gang of Jewish bootleggers. He claimed to have been a professional shoemaker. At various times during his career, he went into long periods of inactivity because he joined the Army, or the Air Force, or entered the ministry, or bought a chicken farm, or began composing symphonic music, or ran a motel, or bought an apple orchard. Given all the random information that he gave to a credulous press, is it any wonder that he worked bits of Yiddish (and Spanish, and Arabic) into his songs?[5]

Gaillard's first "Yiddish" song did not actually contain Yiddish. With bassist Slam Stewart, he released a song entitled, "Vol Vist du Gaily Star." Although this song is built on the chord progressions of "Yosl, Yosl," a popular Yiddish tune from 1922, and the lyrics were mistaken for Yiddish, the phrasing is mostly fake-Spanish and gibberish. The words that close each verse ("laam baylo"), according to Gaillard, were allegedly "the voodoo god of chance," and the whole song was based on a "prayer" uttered by numbers-players in Harlem (Doudna 6; Sapoznik 139). Perhaps this mistake inspired Gaillard to cover the most famous Yiddish song of that era, yet adding another distinctive twist to it:

> Bei mir bist du spaghetti
> Bei mir bist du beef stew
> Bei mir bist du pork chops
> With plenty gravy.
> Bei mir bist du mashed potatoes
> Bei mir bist du scrambled eggs
> Bei mir bist du toast
> With French fries too.
> I could say "gefilte fish"
> But I'll take some orange stew
> Bring me some ice cream pie
> With plenty dough good
> Baked potato pie.

Gaillard's rendition of "Bei Mir Bistu Shayn," which an unknown announcer introduces as "the Hungarian version . . . strictly from Hungary," takes the different words for expressing love and substitutes words related to food, including Jewish foods and imaginary foods (orange stew) with American standards like pork chops.

The concept seemed to click. After his version of "Bei Mir," two of Gaillard's best-known "Yiddish" songs focused entirely on the musical qualities of Jewish foods: "Matzo Balls" and "Dunkin' Bagel." Both really just consist of iconic Jewish foods sung to a basic jump-blues progression:

> Ah, well, ah, matzo balls
> Gefilte fish
> Best old dish I ever, ever had
> Now matzo balls
> And gefilte fish
> Makes you order up a extra dish.
> Matzo balls
> Gefilte fish
> Really, really, really very fine
> Now you put a little horseradish on it
> And make it very mellow
> Because it really knocks you right on out.

The verse of "Dunkin' Bagel" features a call-and-response from Gaillard's bassist, "Bam" Brown:

> Dunkin' bagel
> Dunkin' bagel
> Dunkin' bagel
> Splash! In the coffee.
> Matzo balls (matzo balls a-reeney)
> Gefilte fish (gefilte fish o-vootie)
> Pickled herring (pickled herring vootie)
> Lox-a-rooney (lox-a-rooney)

Several aspects of the relationship between Black and Jewish culture are highlighted in these songs. The whole Jewish content is food itself, without any of the contexts in which those foods are eaten. The foods in "Matzo Balls" are all customarily eaten on Passover, but the song just lists the items and does not mention what time of year the foods might be eaten. Gaillard's songs also juxtapose foods that are not commonly eaten together; matzo balls are not served with horseradish, and bagels are not dunked in coffee like donuts.

In addition to the names of foods, Gaillard built songs around the names of other Yiddish words and phrases. His song, "Drei Six Cents" is probably an approximation of "draysik cents," Yiddish for "thirty cents." Like "Matzo Balls" and "Dunkin' Bagel," "Drei Six Cents" references foods, but this time as a starting point for scatting. In the song's verse, Gaillard and Brown sing:

> Shish kebab (shish kebab shishke vootie)
> Lox a reeney (lox a voutie now oh-ho-wow)
> Shish kebab (shish kebab wowie a-bo)
> Pickled herring (pickle herring pickle picky a one a skimoutie)

Gaillard would have likely heard peddlers calling that sum out, as they sold vegetables, bakery goods, and bought scrap paper and metals. One of Gaillard's later songs, "Mishugana Mambo," is a straightforward song about how to do the dance in the title; although "meshuganner" is Yiddish for "crazy," that word is the only Yiddish in the lyric. Perhaps Gaillard was aware of postwar American Jews' great love for mambos and other Latin dances (Kun 50–68).

After World War II, Gaillard moved to Los Angeles, where he became the leader of one of the regular house bands at Billy Berg's nightclub. Berg, a Jew who had grown up in Harlem, wanted to start a Hollywood nightclub that would feature Black musicians playing to an integrated crowd. Aside from the clubs along Central Avenue, then the heart of Black Los Angeles, black performers were shut out of the city's nightlife, as patrons and often as performers. Berg's associate in this venture, promoter Norman Granz, wanted to use jazz as a force for integration as Café Society had done in Manhattan. Gaillard's biggest fame, then, came in an environment that was hoping to bring audiences together as Gaillard's music brought different languages together (DeVeaux 386–89, 396–98).[6]

In 1947, Gaillard and the other members of his trio, bassist Bam Brown and drummer Scatman Crothers, teamed up with director/producer Jack Rieger to make a short film, "O'Voutie O'Rooney," released by Astor Pictures, a low-budget film company that made films targeted to theaters in Black neighborhoods. Like his better-known contemporary, Edgar Ulmer, Rieger had directed Yiddish-language films and all-Black-cast films in the 1930s and 1940s. The film presents a Gaillard performance at Billy Berg's nightclub in Los Angeles, where the Gaillard trio plays six songs, including "Dunkin' Bagel." Title cards announce each song as it begins. The card that precedes "Dunkin' Bagel" reads, "Ovoutie Slanguage is Absolutely Kosher," reaffirming the song's tie to Jewishness for those viewers too unhip to know for themselves.

A final entry in the Jewish food swing sweepstakes was Cab Calloway's recording of "Everybody Eats When They Come to My House," recorded in 1947. Calloway's song, like Frank Sinatra's recording of Lewis Allan and Earl Robinson's "The House I Live In," two years prior, used "house" as a metaphor for an integrated, peaceful, postwar United States. In Calloway's song, bagels, knishes, and latkes share the table with chili con carne, cacciatore, and pancakes. Among the guests are "Irvy, Fagel, Nishe, and Macky." Jewish foods, by the start of the postwar era, had become part of the American table, thanks in part to hipsters like Calloway and Gaillard.

For their efforts to bring Yiddishisms into jazz, Calloway and Gaillard won fans in American Jewish communities. Even though the end of the big-band era prompted Calloway to cut back his touring and perform in musical comedies, he still managed to thrill Jewish audiences in the Catskills well into the 1950s. Gaillard had fans in the New York chapter of the Shomrim Society, a fraternal group of Jewish policemen. After a private performance, the group awarded Gaillard an honorary gold star, which he tried to use to talk his way out of paying multiple delinquent parking tickets. The badge, of course, invested Gaillard with no actual police power, but the Shomrim Society's awarding it to him shows that Jewish audiences appreciated his contributions ("Slim Gaillard Loses Police Badge—Fined").

CONCLUSIONS

From the beginning of scat-singing on record through the early 1950s, Yiddish words and references in jazz have served as aural reminders of the modern city. If words from many languages help us define "high-modernism" in literature and poetry, perhaps Yiddish and other languages in scat-singing and jive talk represent a kind of "low-modernism"—a modernism of the streets, in which people acknowledge, vocalize, and celebrate the sounds of Los Angeles and New York. Yiddish, the fading mother tongue of "rootless cosmopolitan" American Jews in mid-century America, nonetheless served as an emblem of all that was urban and modern.

Other scholars have drawn the links between Jewishness and Blackness at this time, and described how Jewish entertainers often "blacked up" by imitating Black speech patterns and wearing burnt-cork makeup. For Jewish entertainers, blackness signified Americanness, at the same time that mocking Blacks signified whiteness. Black entertainers like Louis Armstrong, Cab Calloway, and Slim Gaillard demonstrated, in the songs and performances documented here, that using Yiddish established the performer as someone who was hip to information that not everyone knew. Like Yehudi, the mysterious "man who wasn't there," deploying Yiddish allowed the singer a kind of backstage access beyond what the ordinary jazz fan or musician could have. By deploying Yiddish in their songs, singers could demonstrate that they could speak the "cash language" of the music-business milieu, and thus "pass" for Jewish in an aural sense. Yiddish brought some Black musicians closer to their managers and audiences.

The use of Yiddish and other languages by Black singers in the 1940s prefigures the multilingual quality of hip-hop and other popular music influenced by hip-hop. Shortly before his death in 1991, Slim Gaillard made a guest appearance on a song by Toronto rappers Dream Warriors. One of the most popular songs of 2009, Black Eyed Peas' "I've Got a Feeling," features the phrases "mazel tov" and "l'chaim" as part of its tribute to having fun. The descendants of ovoutie slanguage are still kosher, at least in the sense of the Jewish-influenced, kosher-style nature of the contemporary music business and American culture more generally.[7] And their use of Yiddish and Hebrew is not about the cross-cultural connections of the 1930s but certainly more about the Jewishness of the music biz, right? Or at least, the mainstreaming of Jewish phrases through the entertainment industry?

Notes

1. For Harlem, see Gurock 146–56; Greenberg 116–27. For the history of delicatessens, see Moore and Gebler 192–212; Joselit 201–14; Diner, *Hungering for America* 200–04.
2. An important conference volume for understanding Black-Jewish relations is Franklin et al. Trotter and McDowell, both in this volume, are especially relevant.
3. Most sources for this story lack full names for the two singer/dancers; they are identified as Macklin and MacLean in Yates 20. *Life* 31 Jan. 1938: 39, is devoted to the history of the then-current pop hit, "Bei Mir Bist Du Shon." The *Life* account mentions that Johnnie and George learned the song from Jennie Grossinger, performed the song at the Yacht Club, and that Jewish songwriters Sammy Cahn and Saul Chaplin saw this performance. This primary source contrasts with the standard retelling of the story, described in Chaplin 35–38. For more, including the song's greatest popularity as sung by the Andrews Sisters, see Sapoznik 134–37. For evidence that the Yacht Club featured white, Jewish entertainers, see night-club columns in the *New York Times* 25 April 1936: 20; 13 Feb. 1937: 8; 27 Feb. 1937: 8; 17 Oct. 1937: 184. These and subsequent newspaper citations came through use of the ProQuest Historical Newspapers and NewspaperArchive.com subscription databases.
4. It was their main source of fame among Black audiences for years after they debuted it; see also "McClean And Mack [sic] In Hot Spot In East"; "Baby Face Macklin and Geo. MacLean Triumph."
5. For a representative sample, see Doudna 6; "Slim Gaillard, Trio to Begin at Johnny Brown's"; Herndon 26; Kilgallen 20; "Slim Gaillard to Blue Note Nov. 27"; Voce 20–21; "Slim Gaillard, 74."
6. For more on Café Society, see Josephson with Trilling-Josephson; for segregation in Los Angeles at this time, see Himes.
7. A shorter version of this article appeared as "Who's Yehoodi? Scat, Jive, and Yiddish, 1938–1953," *Guilt and Pleasure* 7 (2007): 166–69. Thanks to Josh Kun for encouraging me to revise and expand it. Thanks also to Susan Stafford Friedman, David Goldstein, Kristina Kosnick, Tony Michels, and Norm Pollack.

Works Cited

Alexander, Michael. *Jazz Age Jews*. Princeton: Princeton UP, 2001.

Armstrong, Louis. "Louis Armstrong and the Jewish Family in New Orleans, La., the Year of 1907." *Louis Armstrong, in His Own Words*. Ed. Thomas Brothers. New York: Oxford Univ., 1999. 3–36.

"Baby Face Macklin and Geo. MacLean Triumph." *Chicago Defender* 12 April 1941: 21.

Bergreen, Lawrence. *Louis Armstrong: An Extravagant Life*. New York: Broadway Books, 1997.

Black Eyed Peas, perf. "I've Got a Feeling." *The Beginning*. Interscope Records, 2009.

Calloway, Cab, perf. *The Singing Kid*. Perf. Al Jolson. Warner Bros., 1936.

———, perf. "Who's Yehoodi." Comp. Bill Seckler and Matt Dennis. 1940.

———, comp. "Everybody Eats When They Come to My House." 1947.

Calloway, Cab, and Bryant Rollins. *Of Minnie the Moocher and Me*. New York: Crowell, 1976.

Chaplin, Saul. *The Golden Age of Movie Musicals and Me*. Norman: U of Oklahoma P, 1994.

Christensen, Linda. "Teaching Standard English: Whose Standard." *English Journal* 79:2 (Feb. 1990): 36–40.

Conrad, Earl. Foreword. *Dan Burley's Original Handbook of Harlem Jive*. Dan Burley. illus. Melvin Tapley. 1944.

DeVeaux, Scott. *The Birth of Bebop: A Social and Musical History*. Berkeley: U of California P, 1997.

Diner, Hasia. *Hungering For America: Italian, Irish, and Jewish Foodways in the Age of Migration*. Cambridge, MA: Harvard UP, 2001.

———. *In The Almost Promised Land: American Jews and Blacks, 1915–1935*. Westport, CT: Greenwood, 1977.

Doudna, William L. "Notes To You. . . ." *Wisconsin State Journal* 8 Nov. 1939: 6.

Edwards, Brent Hayes. "Louis Armstrong and the Syntax of Scat." *Critical Inquiry* 28:3 (Spring, 2002): 627–36.

Franklin, V. P., Nancy L. Grant, Harold M. Kletnick, and Genna Rae McNeil, eds. *African Americans and Jews in the Twentieth Century: Studies in Convergence and Conflict*. Columbia: U of Missouri P, 1998.

Gaillard, Slim, perf. "Drei Six Cents." Slim Galliard Quartette. Atomic, 1945.

———. "Dunkin' Bagel." Slim Galliard Quartette. Bee-Bee, 1945.

———. "Mishugana Mambo." Clef, 1953.

Gaillard, Slim, perf., with bassist Slam Stewart. "Bei Mir Bistu Shayn." *The Rudy Vallee Show*. Broadcast 7 July 1938.

———. "Vol Vist du Gaily Star." Vocalion, 1938.

Garvey, Marcus. Editorial. *The Black Man* 3:10 (1938): 10.

Goldstein, Eric L. *The Price of Whiteness: Jews, Race, and American Identity*. Princeton; Princeton UP, 2006.

Greenberg, Cheryl Lynn. *Or Does It Explode? Black Harlem in the Great Depression*. New York: Oxford UP, 1991.

Gurock, Jeffrey. *When Harlem Was Jewish, 1870–1930*. New York: Columbia UP, 1979.

Herndon, Charles. "Slim Gaillard Coins New Jazz Language and Turns to Composition of Symphony." *New York Amsterdam News* 20 Sept. 1952: 26.

Himes, Chester. *If He Hollers, Let Him Go*. Garden City, NY: Doubleday, Doran, 1946.

Jolson, Al, perf. *The Jazz Singer*. Warner Bros., 1927.

Joselit, Jenna Weissman. *The Wonders of America: Reinventing Jewish Culture, 1880–1950*. New York: Hill and Wang, 1994.

Josephson, Barney, with Terry Trilling-Josephson. *Café Society: The Wrong Place for the Right People*. Urbana: U of Illinois P, 2009.

Kilgallen, Dorothy. Syndicated column *Oneonta Star* 1 April 1954: 20.

Kun, Josh. "Bagels, Bongos, and Yiddishe Mambos, or the Other History of Jews in America." *Shofar* 23:4 (Summer, 2005): 50–68.

Lewis, David Levering. "Parallels and Divergences: Assimilationist Strategies of Afro-American and Jewish Elites from 1910 to the Early 1930s." *Journal of American History* 71:3 (Dec., 1984): 543–64.

Life. 31 Jan. 1938: 39.

Major, Clarence, ed. *Juba to Jive: The Dictionary of African-American Slang*. New York, Penguin, 1994.

"McClean And Mack [sic] In Hot Spot In East." *Chicago Defender* 19 Oct. 1940: 21.

McDowell, Winston C. "Keeping Them 'In The Same Boat Together'? Sufi Abdul Hamid, African Americans, Jews, and the Harlem Jobs Boycotts." *African Americans and Jews in the Twentieth Century: Studies in Convergence and Conflict*. Ed. V. P. Franklin, Nancy L. Grant, Harold M. Kletnick, and Genna Rae McNeil. Columbia: U of Missouri P, 1998. 208–36.

Melnick, Jeffrey. *A Right to Sing the Blues: African Americans, Jews, and American Popular Song*. Cambridge: Harvard UP, 1999.

Mezzrow, Mezz, and Bernard Wolfe. *Really the Blues*. Garden City, NY; Anchor, 1972.

Moore, Deborah Dash and Dan Gebler. "The Ta'am of Tourism." *Pacific Historical Review* 68:2 (May, 1999): 192–212.

New York Times. 25 April 1936: 20; 13 Feb. 1937: 8; 27 Feb. 1937: 8; 27 Oct. 1937: 184.

O'Voutie O'Rooney. Perf. Slim Gaillard, Bam Brown, Scatman Crothers. Prod. Jack Rieger. Astor Pictures, 1947.

Pollack, Jonathan Z. S. "Who's Yehoodi? Scat, Jive, and Yiddish, 1938–1953." *Guilt and Pleasure* 7 (2007): 166–69.

Ram, Buck and Irving Mills, comp. "Utt-Da-Zay." 1939.

Rogin, Michael Paul. *Blackface, White Noise: Jewish Immigrants in the Hollywood Melting Pot*. Berkeley: U of California P, 1996.

Rubin, Ruth, ed. *A Treasury of Jewish Folksong*. New York: Schocken, 1950.
Sapoznik, Henry. *Klezmer! Jewish Music from Old World to Our World*. New York: Schirmer, 1999.
Seckler, Bill and Matt Dennis. "Who's Yehoodi." 1940.
Sinatra, Frank, perf. "The House I Live In." Comp. Lewis Allan and Earl Robinson. Rec. 1946. *Early Encores: 1943–'46 (aka Unheard Frank Sinatra, Vol. 2)*. Vintage Jazz Classics.
"Slim Gaillard, 74, a Jazz Pianist And Composer of 30's Hit Songs." *New York Times* 28 Feb., 1991: B16.
"Slim Gaillard Loses Police Badge—Fined." *Amsterdam News* (New York) 26 Sept. 1953: 1.
"Slim Gaillard to Blue Note Nov. 27." *Chicago Defender* 30 Nov. 1957: 18.
"Slim Gaillard, Trio to Begin at Johnny Brown's, Nov. 17." *Pittsburgh Courier* 11 Nov. 1950: 22.
Trotter, Jr., Joe W. "African Americans, Jews, and the City: Perspectives from the Industrial Era, 1900–1950." *African Americans and Jews in the Twentieth Century: Studies in Convergence and Conflict*. Ed. V. P. Franklin, Nancy L. Grant, Harold M. Kletnick, and Genna Rae McNeil. Columbia: U of Missouri P, 1998. 193–207.
UCLA African Studies Center. "Marcus Garvey: Life and Lessons Introduction." 25 March 2010 <http://www.international.ucla.edu/Africa/mgpp/lifeintr.asp>.
Voce, Steve. "Slim Gaillard." *Jazz Journal International* 35:10 (Oct. 1982): 20–21.
Williams, Michael W. "Pan-Africanism and Zionism: The Delusion of Comparability." *Journal of Black Studies* 21:3 (March 1991): 356.
Yates, Ted. "Originated Song Hit; At Famous Door." Pittsburgh *Courier* 12 Feb. 1938: 20.

"If I Embarrass You, Tell Your Friends": The Musical Comedy of Belle Barth and Pearl Williams

Josh Kun

She must shine in ev'ry detail / like a ring you're buying retail/ be a standard size that fits a standard dress. (Merrill and Styne, "If A Girl Isn't Pretty")

Somebody sent me a book of songs and on the first page was [singing] "She'll be comin' round the mountain when she comes, she'll be drivin' six white horses when she comes." Sounds like a freaky broad to me. (Barth, *Bell Barth at Las Vegas*)

I got no talent. I got nuts, big balls, get used to me. (Williams, *A Trip Around The World*)

1. A TRIP AROUND THE WORLD IS NOT A CRUISE

There is little that is known for sure about the night in 1961 when Pearl Williams took the stage at The Cabaret nightclub in Miami Beach. It was most likely a Friday or Saturday; it was sometime well after midnight when it was safe to play blue to a packed room of clinking glasses, cigarette smoke, and perfume, brought south from the Bergdorf's counter; and most everybody sitting on the barstools and nestled elbow-to-elbow in the puckered leather booths were American Jews enjoying a night on the town—some of them on vacation from colder climates up North, others seasonal snowbirds on temporary leave from far-away winters. Pearl Williams squeezed the body that her Russian immigrant parents most definitely would have called *zaftig* into a brocade, red evening gown sprinkled with costume diamonds; fastened her gold bracelets around her wrists; slid her gold hoop earrings into her ears; penciled on her arching black eyebrows; did last one *shpritz* of hair spray over her black coif; wrapped her round shoulders inside an auburn mink; and then grabbed the microphone:

> *Pearl*: Good morning Mr. Gray. Good morning Mrs. Gray. Oh, I like my new name. Don't get used to it girlie, we're checking out of this motel in two hours.
>
> [Band plays opening jazz fanfare.]
>
> *Announcer*: Miss Pearl Williams!
>
> *Pearl*: Thank you. You *mishuganah*, it's me in person. I wish my mother was here. You know my mother, dear, Belle Barth, and she is a mother honey! What we two could do to this joint. We could make a garage outta this. She and I are going on television, would you believe this? We're doing The Tonight Show. We really are, don't get hysterical. We're gonna blow the whole network. She'll take one end and I'll take the other end. We'll bring back radio, what are you worried about?
>
> *Voice in the audience*: What about Patsy Abbott?
>
> *Pearl*: What Patsy Abbott? She's not in our class; what are you crazy? Where she belong with us? She's a nice girl.

The show would be the first that Williams—who was forty-seven years old at the time— would ever record, two full long-playing sides of live material that the raunchy Los Angeles party label Laff Records would release later that year as *A Trip Around The World Is Not A Cruise,* allowing this one time Brooklyn secretary who cut her chops opening for Louis Prima to join a foul-mouthed roster that also included Richard Pryor, LaWanda Page, Red Foxx, George Carlin, Booty Greene, Buzzy Greene, Shecky Greene, and the black ventriloquist act Richard & Willie (best not remembered for their 1976 collaboration with Pryor on the comedy album *Richard Pryor Meets Richard and Willie and the Symbionese Liberation Army*). As it was Williams' first release, her opening minutes worked hard to establish her shtick as another bawdy broad telling jokes and singing songs at the piano in between drags on her "Jewish cigarettes with the gefilte tips." Williams' people were cheating husbands, their mistresses, and their prude wives; she could be a corny rim-shot comic, a cheeky piano belter, and a Yiddish nostalgia machine, but she could also be a bullish aggressor—any woman who walked out of her show was called a "whore"; women who talked during the show got, "Shut your hole and let mine make a little money." If men talked back to her, she threatened to choke them to the death with her thighs or sit on their face until they suffocated. Her medium was the club stage and the adults-only "party record" LP, not the domesticated family-friendly living rooms of television's suburbs.

No matter how many times she claimed to blow the network she never did appear on *The Tonight Show*. She used Yiddish as a punch line and her audience, old enough to know something about the rowdy aisles of the Yiddish theater and the vaudeville hall, was constantly talking back. That same night at The Cabaret she reprised a bit of "Joe and Paul," an old Yiddish radio jingle for a Brooklyn clothing store that was turned into a dirty parody—the first million-selling Yiddish party record—by The Barton Brothers in 1949 ("Joe and Paul, Parts 1 & 2"). "You know, some Jewish words sound terrible," Williams told the audience, "and they are perfectly clean. Like, [sings and plays piano] Joe and Paul, so *fukn nign*. That means pleasure, joy, happiness, in Jewish. It's the only chance I get."

As a big Jewish girl with a big Jewish mouth, Williams was also quick to establish her place among her trash-talking contemporaries. She wanted the audience to know that she knew she wasn't alone. There was, for example, the queen of double-entendre, Ruth Wallis, who started as a novelty songstress performing songs like "Boobs," "Drill 'Em All," "He'd Rather Be A Girl," and "It's A Scream How Levine Does The Rhumba" with fully orchestrated big bands and ended up doing records with titles like *Here's Looking Up Your Hatch*.[1] And there was the much younger pianist and comic Rusty Warren putting her *Knockers Up!* and singing *Songs for Sinners*; but as Warren herself has pointed out, she avoided anything explicitly Jewish and found her biggest audiences in the mid-West. "I didn't do anything ethnic," she has said. "I wanted to talk about sex, and being Jewish had nothing to do with it" (Interview).

Also playing Jewish audiences was Patsy Abbott, the former Goldie Schwartz who dabbled in sexual innuendo in clubs in Miami Beach and Vegas and on LPs like *Suck Up You're Behind* and *Have I Had You Before?*; but who was also wholesome enough to star on Broadway in Mickey Katz's cute 1950s Yinglish revue *Borscht Capades*, and as a result was too much of a nice girl for

Williams' taste. In 1947, Abbott was already heralded by Billboard as "a heftyish lass with a big pair of pipes" whose material was "mostly pops" ("Nightclub Reviews").

Perhaps the most successful of all the bawdy broads of the 1950s and 1960s was Totie Fields, who might have been roughly the same size as Williams, but she was also too nice of a girl. Fields, who got her start as a *tummler* (= emcee) in Boston strip clubs, rarely did material that was sexually explicit; she stopped at her body and its weight, just safe enough to make her a regular on *The Ed Sullivan Show*, where she appeared over twenty times throughout the 1960s. There was nothing "nice girl," or as Fields liked to joke about herself "adooooorable," about Williams, which is in large part why she never appeared on a single TV talk show. TV was where decency reigned and Williams was an architect of the indecent. Or as she liked to say, "If it's long enough, hard enough, in far enough, it's in decent."

But Williams started her Miami Beach show with a nod to the woman who is probably best known of all the bawdy broads of the 1950s and 1960s, her "mother," Belle Barth, who was only three years older than Williams but had helped blaze the trail that made Williams' career possible. By the time Williams records *A Trip Around the World is Not a Cruise*, Barth—who grew up in East Harlem as Annabelle Salzman—was already notorious as not just the dirtiest "freaky broad" around, but as possibly the dirtiest comic, period. Lenny Bruce, who became synonymous with sick and dirty humor, opened for Barth early in his career and is rumored to have complained that while everyone was talking about how dirty and sick he was, it was *really* Barth who was the sickest of them all. Barth, who Walter Winchell dubbed the "Hildegard of the Underworld," was a self-awarded MD, "a maven on dreck," an expert on excrement, and as a result, was arrested and fined on lewdness charges in 1953, and was sued numerous times, including a million dollar lawsuit by two schoolteachers (the claim: Barth's routine damaged their mental and sexual health). No surprise that she was banned from radio and TV. Like Williams and Abbott, she cut her chops in the Sour Cream Sierras of the Borscht Belt vacation hotel circuit, but eventually found a home in the 1950s and 1960s in what can be labeled "the Dreck Circuit," the chair and banquette stuffed nightclubs and cabarets (where as Barth liked to joke, the bar was often the stage). From Las Vegas to NY to Miami Beach, these clubs were a home-away-from-home for Barth and Williams: The Roundtable, The Thunderbird, Nero's Lounge, Harry's American Showroom, The Red Room, Joe's Lounge for Lovers, The Sans Souci. Barth recorded nine albums over the course of five husbands, and all of them were recorded live at various clubs on the Dreck Circuit.[2]

The crew of freaky broads may not have reached the commercial peaks of their mainstream male contemporaries (Jack Benny, Milton Berle, Mort Sahl, Shelley Berman), but they certainly enjoyed relatively successful careers. Barth reputedly sold over two million albums and even once played Carnegie Hall. Williams allegedly sold over a million, took home an average salary of $7,500 per week, and enjoyed an eighteen-year run as the main attraction at the Place Pigalle. "I don't mean to be vulgar," Barth quipped in one of her LP titles, "but it's profitable." In fact, when she wasn't vulgar, she wasn't as profitable (*I Don't Mean To Be Vulgar*). In a 1961 live review of one of her shows at the Roundtable, *Billboard* worried that a cleaned-up act would mean lower sales:

> Belle Barth is a curious anomaly in the disk business. She has sold close to 300,000 records on the After-Hour label but has yet to appear on any best-selling record chart. Her material is blue, and in many towns district attorneys or vice squads have raided her act or kept her records out of stores, or removed them from under the counter. This may be the reason why in her first New York appearance in 10 years . . . she is playing it so Snow-Whiteish . . . that she hasn't any act all. . . . Someone has pulled her claws. . . . You could bring your 13-year-old daughter and not worry about Belle making her blush. . . . Belle, where is thy sting? (Rolondtz)

What was the nature and draw of Barth's comic sting? Who were these non-Snow-Whiteish women, these middle-aged comic "Jewesses" with a mike in one hand and a drink in the other, and why have their contributions to post-WWII popular culture and Jewish American entertainment gone so unheralded? Perhaps one reason is that Barth and Williams challenged available genre expectations. They were neither fully comics nor fully singers. As women who talked and joked openly about sex, who made their weight and size central parts of their routines, and who portrayed themselves as unassimilated Jews still connected to their immigrant pasts, they challenged the accepted expectations of Jewish female civility. They were neither the stereotypical "Jewish wife" nor were they the "Jewish mother," let alone "the Jewish-American princess." They were, to borrow Kathleen Rowe's helpful framework, "unruly women," working-class architects of the piano bar grotesque and yet also the acknowledged queens of the cabaret carnivalesque, who translated the classic comic grotesque realism of "the lower stratum of the body, the life of the belly and reproductive organs" into the domestic lexicons and relationship dramas of post-Word War II Jewish life (Rowe; Bakhtin 21). "Have I got big *baytzim*?" Williams asked her audience at The Cabaret (referring to her breasts as balls). "The knish (her vagina), that I'll never see." Or as Barth said of a former husband, "I divorced him because he was indifferent—I didn't know which way to turn."

Nancy Walker and Zita A. Dresner have suggested that it was male stand-up comics like Lenny Bruce who moved comedy away from the safe and antiseptic "domestic humor"—housewives, suburbia, kids, in-laws—that dominated American comedy of the 1950s, but it was actually female comics like Barth and Williams who were breaking open these comic molds of domesticity and replacing them with new models of Jewish female performance, all done under the radar of mass cultural visibility (Walker and Dresner). It was something Bruce himself was even aware of, claiming in his autobiography *How To Talk Dirty and Influence People* to have learned all of his dirtiness, all of his appetite for sexual humor and commentary, not from any male father figures but from his neighbor Mrs. Janesky, a middle-aged widow who was friends with his mother and who always had talcum powder caked between her breasts. It was Mrs. Janesky who was a trove of "erotic folklore," a spout of "hoary hornyisms," who taught a young Lenny what a bidet was (*How to Talk Dirty* 1).

In 1959, *Time* magazine ran a feature article on "The Sickniks," a new school of "sick" comics who "joked about father and Freud, about mother and masochism, about sister and sadism. . . . They attacked motherhood, childhood, adulthood, and parenthood" ("Nightclubs: The Sickniks"). Yet it was a profile of an all-male crew of comics—including Sahl, Bruce, and Jonathan Winters—whose "social criticism laced with cyanide" was a "symptom of the 20th century's own sickness." Barth and Williams (or any other woman, for that matter) went unmentioned, even though they were practicing their own brand of sickness—perhaps too heavy on the vulgar, too light on the cerebral for *Time*—that was offering an explicitly gendered after-hours social criticism of Jewish life and identity. Jews were having sex but not talking about it. "Square broads" were being cheated on by Jewish husbands with a rolodex of prostitutes, the same Jewish husbands who only talk to their wives during sex "if there's a telephone handy" (Williams, *Bagels and Lox*). It's a brand of comedy that contemporary comics like Joan Rivers and Sarah Silverman are as clearly the inheritors of, as Barth and Williams were of the legacy left by early 20th century greats like Fanny Brice, Belle Baker, and Sophie Tucker. Together their work points us toward a deeper, more nuanced understanding of what Barry Sanders might call a "subversive history" of Jewish-American laughter, only here the rebel fools and clever clowns are women, and it's their jokes and their songs—and their laughter—that are doing the humiliating.

2. LISTENING FOR GENDER, LISTENING FOR RACE

It might seem surprising to find Barth and Williams included in a volume dedicated to Jews and popular music. Yet their comedy was based in piano-driven songs and comic ditties as much as sit-down joke telling, which makes their recorded output equally crucial to what Nichole T. Rustin and Sherrie Tucker have called "listening for gender," a theoretical and critical invitation they apply to jazz but that works equally well here (208). What does it mean to "listen for gender" in the history of Jewish-American musical performance? Both Barth and Williams began their careers as singers, not comics, and neither performed without piano-players by their side. In the case of Barth, her most frequent piano accompanist was Margie Sherwin, who was often a featured part of her live act as both a protagonist and the butt of many of her jokes. Barth claimed to have been the first singer to popularize Russ Morgan's 1944 song "You're Nobody 'til Somebody Loves You" and both women filled their live routines with snippets of songs, be it Williams' renditions of "Hava Nagila," "Great Balls of Fire," and "Joe and Paul," or Barth's takes on "Won't You Come Home Bill Bailey," "Birth of the Blues," and "Hello, Dolly." Of the latter she said, "My words don't sound like this," before adding her own line to the song: "Take her empty laps fellas." On her album *Belle Barth at Las Vegas: The Fabulous 5AM Show*, she does a full performance of Gene Austin and Roy Bergere's 1924 vaudeville staple "How Come You Do Me Like You Do" (delivered in a boogie-woogie barrelhouse growl with winking emphasis on the words "come" and "do"), as well as musical impressions of George Jessel, Al Jolson, and Sophie Tucker.

It is perhaps Tucker—the celebrated Russian-Jewish immigrant singing star and self-declared "Last of the Red Hot Mamas," who was not afraid of comic detours and who famously pushed the limits of female sexuality, sexual discourse, and corpulent Jewish female body politics throughout the first six decades of the twentieth century—who comes the closest to being the most obvious aesthetic forbearer of both Barth and Williams. Her song "Nobody Loves a Fat Girl But Oh How a Fat Girl Could Love" was an early precursor of much of Barth and Williams's material, and as early as 1911's "That Last Soul

Kiss," she pushed sex past innuendo: "Sip the honey divine, for a long time/ One, two, and three/Now, longer/Four, five, and six/Still longer, honey/Seven, eight, nine/Oh, oh, babe." Tucker is the unofficial "unkosher" godmother of the women Sarah Blacher Cohen has described as "brazen offenders of the faith," singers and comics who broke with prescriptions of modesty and kosher cleanliness and expectations of how Jewish women should sound—that is if they should make a sound at all (in the Talmud, "a woman's voice is a sexual enticement," and is therefore something that, like the woman's body, is dangerous and disruptive when not controlled) (Cohen 105). Barth and Williams had voices like Tucker: big, brassy, deep, loud, and thanks to too many cigarettes, gruff and gravelly. If "the Jew's voice" was a marker of racial difference for Jewish men in the Gentile imaginary, the Jewish *woman's* voice also became a marker of gendered difference as Jewish men imagined them. In this respect, Tucker was one of the first successful twentieth century entertainers to use the Jewish female voice as a transgressive tool (Gilman). As Barth and Williams would do in her wake, Tucker sang about and celebrated her weight ("I Don't Want To Get Thin"), her sexual prowess ("There's more shmaltz to sizzle when I turn the heat on"), and on songs like "Mister Segal, Make It Legal," spoke openly about extramarital affairs and sexual promiscuity.[3]

Tucker began her career in burlesque and vaudeville, alongside a cadre of fellow Jewish women singers and comics—Fanny Brice, Rhoda Bernard, Anna Held, Nora Bayes, Belle Baker, among them—who were likewise re-scripting the rules of performing in regard to race, ethnicity, and gender on the American popular stage. These women belonged to the tribe of "rank ladies" that M. Alison Kiebler has written about, women who helped vaudeville disrupt "19th century doctrines of domesticity, passivity, and passionlessness" (12–13). Vaudeville stages, in the midst of blurring hierarchies of class and taste, gave voice to a crew of "wild women" who operated beyond the bounds of accepted ideals of feminine behavior and beauty by expressing their sexual desires, mocking male authority, bragging about being divorced from their husbands, or celebrating themselves as fat, dark-skinned or "too mannish" (Kiebler 14). Jewish women in vaudeville added ethnic otherness and immigrant ghetto pasts to this equation of wildness. One critic called Belle Baker "a raven-haired, big-eyed, Jewish 'Momma', who used to sell lemonade at a penny a drink in New York's Delancey Street" (Merwin 31).

This performance tradition perhaps received its best unofficial anthem in Fanny Brice's 1909 performance of the Irving Berlin number "Sadie Salome, Go Home," which she sang in a thick, put-on Yiddish accent. Written in the spirit of the racy turn-of-the-century Salome dance craze (inspired by Oscar Wilde's 1893 play), the song introduced the world to Sadie Cohen who wants to make it on the stage as a Salome dancer, much to the chagrin of her husband Mose:

> Sadie Cohen left her happy home/ To become an actress lady/ On the stage she soon became the rage/ As the only real Salomy baby/ When she came to town, her sweetheart Mose/ Brought for her around a pretty rose/ But he got an awful fright/ When his Sadie came to sight/ He stood up and yelled with all his might:/Don't do that dance, I tell you Sadie/ That's not a bus'ness for a lady!/ Most ev'rybody knows/ That I'm your loving Mose/ Oy, Oy, Oy, Oy/ Where is your clothes?

In previous work, I have attempted to outline a tradition of Jewish performance and masquerade (or better, a history of Jewish performance *as* masquerade) through the vaudeville type of "Abie Cohen," a Jewish mask that Jewish performers have taken on and off throughout twentieth century entertainment ("'Abie the Fishman'"). But it wasn't just the Abie Cohens who were negotiating Jewishness through the popular arts, it was the Sadie Cohens as well—the Sadie Cohens who brought their Yiddish accents and Lower East Side mannerisms into vaudeville and burlesque houses, leaving their husbands behind while seeking stardom on the stage as exotic-Semitic Salomes. When Brice sang "Sadie Salome," she said it was a tribute to all the women she knew growing up. "I saw Loscha of the Coney Island popcorn counter and Marta of the Cheeses at Brodskey's Delicatessen," she said. "And the Sadie's and 'the Rachels and the Birdies with the turnover heels at the Second Avenue dance halls. They all wielded together and came out staggeringly true to type in one big authentic outline" (Merwin 33). Barth and Williams are direct descendents of this Sadie Cohen lineage, working-class women born in the same kinds of neighborhoods as Brice, though they were, proudly and defiantly, not the Salome type. Proof that Tucker was not the last of the red-hot mammas, they were latter-day Sadie Cohens who wanted to be on stage as Sadie Cohen. They divorced their fair share of Moses and in middle age were not about to give up the freedoms of the nightclub.

By inserting Barth and Williams into the historical record of Jewish American music, my hope is to also highlight their participation in what I've written about previously as "the audio-racial imagination"—the extent to which racial and ethnic meanings are embedded in sonic and musical performance—or what Ron Radano and Philip V. Bohlman have similarly explored as music's role in the "racial imagination" of modernity. As they put it, "The imagination of race not only informs perceptions of musical practice but is at once constituted within and projected into the social through sound" (Kun, *Audiotopia*; Radano and Bohlman 5). The musical comedy of Barth and Williams converts the social contexts of post-World War II Jewish life—lingering notions of Jewish difference and otherness, the continuing pull of assimilation and the desire for invisibility into American whiteness—into a very particular set of sounds that merge the aesthetics of Yiddish theater, vaudeville, and burlesque with those of African-American blues and cabaret culture.

In some sense, Barth and Williams had more in common with blues singers like Ma Rainey and Bessie Smith and Black "chitlin' circuit" comics like Moms Mabley than they did with any other of their Jewish contemporaries. Their singing styles borrowed heavily from early twentieth century African-American blues shouters and barrelhouse singers, while they both were also fluent in the stylistic vocabularies of the Jewish blackface songbook of plantation lullabies (both could easily slip into hyperbolic minstrel dialects). Daphne Brooks has rightly criticized the racialized "masculinism" in rock music criticism that devotes extensive attention to the investments of white male artists into the innovations of black male artists, while ignoring similar patterns among white and black women, "at the expense of producing more nuanced, heterogeneous tales of racial and gender collaboration and identification in popular music culture" (Brooks 55). Barth worked closely for a time with veteran black jazz trumpeter Cootie Williams, who served as her musical director, and often joked that she was once a member of the well-known black group, the Clara Ward Singers. Barth's resonance within black comic and musical aesthetics was so much a part of her persona that when a play about Barth's life debuted last year in Chicago, she was played by an African-American actress.[4]

As was always the case throughout the twentieth century, blackness was a way for Jews to negotiate their relationship to whiteness (which Barth clearly understood when she would sing "I Wish I Was in Dixie" in Yiddish or "The Birth of the Blues" in mock Al Jolson plantation vocalese). Pamela Brown Lavitt has argued that "coon shouting" was an effective mode of performance for many early twentieth century Jewish American women singers who instead of outwardly performing as Jews, could perform through the masks of black cultural types; and similarly, Kiebler has argued that vaudeville women used racial dialect comedy and blackface singing as a kind of "comic license" to adopt "uninhibited physical styles" (the black Mammy was often a favorite mask for large Jewish women who could not be "themselves" without it)

(Lavitt; Kiebler 112). Tucker is again the classic example here. In an oft-cited passage from her autobiography, she recounts having to black up in order to be seen and being told by the promoter at the 125th Street Theater that she was "too big and ugly" to perform without blackface: "The crowd out front will razz her. Better get some cork and black her up" (*Some of These Days* 33). While Barth and Williams were not blackface singers—in fact, they were more like Jolson's Jewish mother in the *Jazz Singer* (assuming she had walked out on the family, looking for a new husband) than his fantasy black Mammy—they did carry on the tradition of "unruly" Jewish women, portraying both black stereotypes and actual black cultural aesthetics. They performed what Maria Damon has called "Yidditude" in her work on Lenny Bruce, Mezz Mezzrow, and other male Jewish figures who used blackness as a home for alternative Jewishness, "a perceived opportunity for self-regeneration for Jews as creative non-participants in mainstream culture." For Bruce, she writes, "the jazz world offered a model of masculinity for Jewish men that enabled difference without weakness." I would further suggest that in the 50s and 60s, Barth and Williams were engaging with black culture and black comic aesthetics alongside their Borscht Belt training in order to enable their own difference to be perceived without weakness (Damon 167).

Off the Record

The careers of Barth and Williams—as well as those of Abbott and Warren—have been virtually erased from most histories of Jewish entertainment and popular culture. As Paula E. Hyman, Joyce Antler, Riv-Ellen Prell, and Miriam Peskowitz have all pointed out, the "master narrative" of modern Jewish identity has been one rooted in the experience of Jewish men and in an accepted masculinism that has gone unmarked and too infrequently analyzed as the source of Jewish history's "engendering." Barth and Williams tackled that masculinism and called attention to just how "engendered" Jewish history has been through their embrace of the vulgar, their celebration of a Jewish femininity based on *dreck*, and a reluctance to give Jewish men too much credit in the bed or in the boardroom. If the "Jewess" already represents "womanhood gone awry," as Carol Okman has written, a counter-figure to idealized American femininity, then Barth and Williams only add to the representational "gender trouble" that Jewish-American stage women pose by being *awry gone awry*—loud-mouthed and brash Jewesses eager to flaunt their Jewishness and their mockery of feminine gentility.⁵ Amy-Jill Levine has drawn a distinction between "the Jewess" and "the Jewish woman," the latter being domesticated and socially safe, the former historically a transgressive figure that represents a sexual threat—from the New Testament up through the films of Woody Allen—who is both more and less than "woman" and more and less than "Jew." For Levine, this makes the Jewess an "ideal sign for conveying cultural anxieties" and, I would add, an ideal target for marginalization in dominant histories of cultural production and performance.

The entire era of Jewish female performance they represent (the transition from early twentieth century vaudeville and 1930s and 1940s Catskills performance to the glory days of stand-up in the 1970s) and the entire tradition of Jewish female performance they embody (one that stretches from saucy vaudevillians and burlesque queens up through Barbra Streisand and Sarah Silverman) has been left as a barely acknowledged footnote in many leading histories of American and Jewish comedy.⁶ Even a recent documentary on Jewish women comedians, 2007's *Making Trouble: Three Generations of Funny Jewish Women*, skipped over them entirely, never even mentioning them as forerunners and trailblazers for better-known comics like Rivers and Silverman. While some of Wallis's material has been compiled on a greatest hits CD by her family, not a single LP by Barth, Williams, or Abbott has been made available in any digital format, a circumstance which, if not remedied, will virtually guarantee their gradual erasure from the living, historical record.

The songs and comedy of Barth and Williams fit squarely in the tradition of "klezmerical" creativity and innovation that Jonathan Freedman has argued is a driving force behind modern Jewish-American culture. For Freedman, there are three principal ways in which Jewish artists, intellectuals, and entertainers in the twentieth century have responded to their various social constructions and representation in American life: they contest images created by others, they internalize images created by others, and they project those images created by others onto others. In pursuing one or all of these routes, Jews have transformed "the ways in which Americans imagined otherness itself . . . the specific contours that other Others took in the unfolding ethnoracial drama of the 20th century U.S" (6). Barth and Williams certainly engaged all three of these strategies and their comic songs and after-hours one-liners can be read as parody-performances of otherness, stage shows that turned the othering of the Jew and the othering of the Jewish woman into an othering of America writ large. Like their 1950s contemporary Mickey Katz, they refracted America's othering of the Jew into a Jewish othering of America. "Oh give me a home, where the buffalo roam," Barth liked to sing, "And I'll give you a home full of *pishartz*" (*My Next Story Is A Little Risque*). The double move here is important. On the one hand, there is a playful Jewish refusal of the mythic Western frontier that is so central to the shaping of Anglo-American identity and patriotic citizenship and on the other there is a playful refusal of gendered Jewish domestic norms, with Barth defying the expectations of the traditional *balabusta*, the good Jewish home-maker who runs a good, clean household. Like Roy Rogers and Gene Autry, like Cary Grant and Myrna Loy, Barth also has a home on the range, only hers is Jewish and it's full of piss. This is just one example of how in the space of their LPs and in the space of their nightclubs, the dominant values, mores and customs of middle-class American citizenship—and the lengths to which so many upwardly mobile Jews would go to pursue them—were lampooned rather than celebrated. Once you took a seat at the foot of their stages, the world of images and representations you belonged to and the drama of ethno-racial otherness you were laughing along with, was one that Barth and Williams were controlling and staging themselves.

So much of that laughter was about public shame—comedy as embarrassment. The affective power of Barth and Williams came not only in their explicit embrace of sexual discourse but also in their use of jokes and songs as weapons of public shaming (after all, Barth called her first album *If I Embarrass You Tell Your Friends*). For Barth, there was *power* in embarrassment, in revealing that sex was not just about silence or speech, but also about an entire psychology of affect and identity, one that she could pass on to women in her audience. "Write it down, honey," she'd tell women at her shows after delivering a good put-down or piece of sexual advice. "I'll wait." It makes their work an important addition to the history that Donald Weber has charted as "the genealogy of Jewish affect," a genealogy he uses to measure the extent to which Jewish life in America is always haunted by ethnic and racial ghosts of the past and has always entailed negotiation with civility (4–5). Revelations about sex and desire, of course, were always linked to revelations about ethnicity and race, about Jews laughing about other Jews, laughing about themselves as Jews. Their shows were musical comedy as a kind of public bio-politics—routines that were all in some way about "coming out," something that could be done more easily in the safe shadows of an after-hours club. In this environment they could depict themselves and the women in their audience as open Jews who could also be desirous (and desired) women.

While Rusty Warren made the expression of sexual desire and agency the crux of her routines, most notably in her hit song "Bounce Your Boobies," and frequently told interviewers that she existed because she was saying things about sex that women were afraid to talk about, Barth and Williams took it further, or in Warren's own words, they were "vile" and "they always went for the gut" (Interview). For them the point was not simply to talk about sex or say the unsaid, but to re-think sex through affect and shame, through embarrassment and disgust. It was precisely this kind of thinking that was being pursued in the mid-1950s by the psychologist and personality theorist Silvan Tomkins in his four volume work *Affect Imagery Consciousness*. In their recuperation of his work for postmodernist and queer theory, Eve Sedgwick and Adam Frank write that for Tompkins—and I would add for Barth and Williams—"sexuality is no longer an on off matter whose two possibilities are labeled express or repress . . . its link to attention, to motivation, to action, occurs only through coassembly with an affect system described as encompassing several more, and more qualitatively different possibilities, than on/off" (Sedgwick and Frank 504). Weber's work on Jewish affect and Tomkins' work on shame are crystallized in the work of Barth and Williams, who use comedy and music to explore the coassemblies of Jewishness, affect, and shame, a performative system that is as much about personality drives as it is about ethnic and cultural identity formations.

3. JEWISHNESS AT 5 A.M.

Unlike so many of their contemporaries in mid-century Jewish entertainment, who made various negotiations with the assimilationist demands of mainstream television, radio, and popular music, Barth and Williams engaged in constant "antic-Semitism." That is, they made their Jewishness and their connections to Yiddish and immigrant pasts central parts of their routines. Much like the musical parodies of Mickey Katz that transformed the pop charts of the 1950s into a Yinglish wonderland of Jewish misadventures, their LPs and live performances are models of "out" Jewish performance, or what David Marc has dubbed "Jewing-out" (36). I see Barth and Williams in alliance with a definition of Jewishness that Joseph Litvak, inspired by Hanna Arendt's writings on parvenus and pariahs, has described as "a signifier for the pleasure of the pariah amid the deadly seriousness of nations and races: the comic pleasure of relinquishing or refusing the dubious privilege of national and racial dignity and belonging, by 'losing oneself in identification with the Other'" (31). In his work on testimonies before the House Un-American Activities Committee, Litvak identifies sycophancy as an unfortunate tradition of mid-century Jewish performance: the stool-pigeon, the informer, as the model of how Jews become upstanding citizens. "Hollywood's purge of Jewish communists, and its parade of Jewish informers," he writes, "taught every Jew in America how to become a model citizen, the cooperative witness. Starting with the blacklist, and continuing to this day, the Jewish-controlled media in the United States stage nothing less than the Jew's disappearance: the Jew's disappearance, that is, into just another American" (224). And yet at the very moment that Jerome Robbins named names and at the very moment that Marjorie Morningstar, on the page in 1955 and the big screen in 1958, was America's greatest proof that nice Jewish girls could become nice American girls, Barth and Williams were refusing sycophancy, refusing disappearance. Barth told the women in her audience "there are only two words you need to know in the Yiddish language: *gelt* and *shmuck*. If a man doesn't have any, he is" and Williams called herself a "lusty mammele" before closing her show with straight renditions of "Hava Nagila," "Sholem Aleichem," and "Dayenu."

For Barth and Williams, the nightclub was not just the site for their performance of Jewishness, it was the performance itself, the space that made their music and comedy possible. Nowhere else could a Jewish woman in her forties and fifties insult upwardly mobile Jewish men, joke about her piano being older than her vagina ("this box is older than mine" Barth would say while dusting off the piano), sing about the virtues of douching with Sprite over 7-Up, and generally claim the club as a safe space for frank and explicit female sexual discourse that she controlled and managed. Barth and Williams had axes to grind with both men and women—the men who held them down, the women who let them, the men who pretended not to cheat, the women who pretended to be prudes, the pathetic men with all the power, the pathetic women who hadn't realized that it was they who actually had the power—and the clubs were the only places they could have their say. The lounges and ballrooms of The Catskills—so crucial to the evolution of twentieth century Jewish entertainment and creativity—was ultimately too family-oriented to play completely blue; and while Milton Berle and Sid Caesar were able to get in a few off-color Yiddishims here and there, TV and radio were ultimately training grounds for mass cultural morality and suburban domesticity. Broadcast media were not a venue where Barth could joke, "You show me an Italian who isn't talented and I'll show you a Jewish broad who hasn't got a diamond"; or for Williams to answer the question "Who's the father?" with "How do I know? You think I got eyes in the back of my head?"

The after-hours club as a site of feminist dreck-performance was crucial as a space for "unruly women" like Barth and Williams. In Kathleen Rowe's definition, the "unruly woman" is "an ambivalent figure of female outrageousness and transgression with roots in the narrative forms of comedy and the social practices of carnival" (30). Unlike the *femme fatale* or the madonna, the unruly woman traffics in the grotesque and the excessively parodistic and is happy to offend anyone in her path. They are not permitted a "proper place," either due to an excessive body, excessive speech, excessive self-mockery, excessive sexuality, or above all, due to an association with the "dirt" of bodily life. Yet the after hours night club became the place for women not in their proper place; improper places for improper women that became the stages for the performance of unruliness, where their laughter and their bodies and their sharp tongues were the star of the show, offering up, in Rowe's words, "new ways of thinking about visibility as power" (30). While most of the clubs were owned by men, Barth eventually bought her own, Belle's Pub, in the lobby of the Coronet Hotel in Miami Beach. Patsy Abbott did the same, opening Patsy's Place just down the road. Belle's Pub became not just Barth's home base, a guarantee of her control over her own material and her own profits, but a place where she could manipulate the crowd at will. Most famously, she installed microphones in the men's bathrooms so while male audience members left her show to use the toilet, their private business was made public in the club.

While the Jewish after-hours club circuit had its roots in the Jewish world—vaudeville, the Yiddish theater, the Catskills—it also had much in common with various club circuits in African-American history: the hush-harbors, places where black could retreat to conduct their own forms of religion on antebellum plantations, the "chitlin' circuit" of black performance venues that prospered during the first half of the twentieth century, the buffet flat parties of the Harlem Renaissance where big and bawdy blues singers like Bessie Smith provided the soundtracks to private "AC/DC" worlds of poly-sexual freedom and "deep sea diving," and the inter-racial brothels and speakeasies that Kevin Mumford has written about as "interzones," spaces of vice that became vital spaces of cultural imagination and sexual, racial performance. Similarly, late night piano bars like New York's The Roundtable (where Barth recorded *My Next Story Is A Little Risque* in 1961) became the secret chambers of female Jewish performance, essential cultural laboratories, at a time when, as Leslie Fiedler famously quipped, Zion had become Main Street, and Jews were among the most visible protagonists of American pop culture. *Fiddler on the Roof* was a national hit on Broadway, Saul Bellow and Philip Roth were on the best-sellers list, *Exodus* won an Oscar, and, as a result, there were limits to the types of Jewishness that could be marketed and sold. Barth and Williams were a tough fit for the era of philo-Semitism, Old World *shtetl* nostalgia and Jewish heroism; their acts made jokes about Tevye's daughters as town sluts, they went to Israel to listen to groups called The Fourskins, and when they joked about knishes, it was their own, not the ones that Alexander Portnoy practiced on.

In terms of musical comedy, they were also a far cry from the middle-class normativity that Allan Sherman so frequently parodied throughout much of his best-selling recorded output in the 1960s. Marc Cohen has convincingly argued that Sherman's parodies of Broadway songs "exposed the ethnic nakedness of Broadway's Jewish creators, expelled them from the eden of pure Americanness, and led them back into the exile of Jewishness" (54). While this may be true, many of his songs' leading protagonists, especially the women, were plucked straight from the limiting middle-class dramas of suburban life. Sherman's Zelda might have run off with the money and the tailor, but Yetta was happy right next to Al watching TV: "Al n Yetta couldn't have it betta/ Their TV set has remote control/ So they both can stay in bed/ With Frankenstein and Mr. Ed." Barth and Williams made fun of the Als who came to their shows and they were themselves more like Zelda than a TV-addicted Yetta. You can bet that, if Barth and Williams were in bed, they weren't watching *Mr. Ed*. The inherent celebration of Jewish upward mobility in Sherman's music was mocked in the routines of Barth and Williams who instead reveled in an embrace of downward mobility, exploiting the pleasures and fears of not making it in America.[7] The dreck circuit was not where sex happened, but it was where sex was talked about, where sex was freed from the ascendant middle-class mores of post-World War II suburbia and allowed to get vulgar again, and in doing so, through the laughter and jokes and songs of the piano bar grotesque, it re-ethnicized, even re-racialized, these women as other than white—too Jewish, too black.

That Barth and Williams sang songs and told jokes full of sexually suggestive, often explicit, content as divorced women with no children, flew in the face of dominant notions and representations of Jewish women as domestic goddesses who maintained the order and civility of middle-class suburban life. As Giovanna Del Negro, one of the few scholars to write about their legacy, has argued, Barth and Williams not only aired the dirty laundry of Jewish gender politics in public, but by releasing their live shows on LPs that could be played back on living room hi-fi stereos in New Rochelle, they "pierced the boundaries of ethnic privacy by bringing the decidedly public setting of stand-up comedy performance into the living room" and thereby "created a semi-public context of performance in the heart of the domestic sphere" (188). In that sense, Barth and Williams might be seen as the black sheep antitheses of Molly Goldberg, the iconic Jewish mother made famous by Gertrude Berg on radio, television, and on LP from the 1930s through the 1960s. If Molly was the "delibinized Jewish mother," to use Roberta Mock's phrase, who protected and ran the assimilating nuclear family, then Barth and Williams were familial threats, vulgar interlopers who refused the norms of post-World War II domestic order and American civility (101). If Berg was, in the words of Donald Weber, "the symbol of the emerging Jewish middle-class," then Barth and Williams represented a turning-back to the working-class repressed; they were thus living reminders of Jewish blue-collar, immigrant pasts. Berg wouldn't have been caught dead at a Barth or Williams show, where "the sober sociology of suburban Jewish life" was put on comic trial every night (Weber 143).

Paula E. Hyman has shown how historically Jewish women have been used as tools of Jewish acculturation, in particular behavior, etiquette, and comportment as "central markers of the successful adaptation of Jews to bourgeois culture" (155). In their roles as homemakers, mothers, and wives, Jewish women kept the domestic order through performances of "bourgeois prescriptions of appropriate female behavior"; and as such, they were key participants in Jewish assimilation into the mores of mainstream civility. When Jewish male anxiety over assimilation reached a fever pitch, the stereotypes of the Jewish American princess and the Jewish Mother took over, which as Roberta Mock and Riv-Ellen Prell have argued, were projections of male fear of failed acculturation and civility. George Segal tried to kill his Jewish mother in the 1970 film *Where's Poppa* and Mel Brooks suggested that all Jewish mothers secretly wanted to sleep with their sons when he appeared on *The David Susskind Show* ("How to be a Jewish Son"). Enough people bought Dan Greenburg's manual on Jewish male suffering, *How To Be a Jewish Mother*, that it became the top non-fiction book of 1965, and in 1969 Philip Roth created in *Portnoy's Complaint* a whole novel around a son's complaint about his sexual neuroses that all lead back to his mother.[8] By calling themselves "mothers" on two separate LPs, *Battle of the Mothers* and *Return of The Mothers*, Barth and Williams were clearly referencing these portrayals but they were also turning them on their heads—they were mothers without children who turned the idea of being powerful, castrating monsters into a new comic subjectivities of empowerment.

Their routines are remarkable for just how far outside they were of these tropes and contexts that have become synonymous with American Jewish entertainment. And yet their anomalous characteristics only serve to remind us of the representational strangleholds of Jewish femininity in the US, a history of policed behaviors, policed language, and policed bodies, both from within the doctrines and codes of Judaism and Jewish culture, and within the rules of an America that all too often exercised its anti-Semitism on the bodies of Jewish women-from the Jewish American Princess in the 1960s and 1970s (after all, a man actually used the "Jewish Princess defense" in court as a rationale for murdering his wife [Frondorf]) or the teens and '20s when working class immigrant Jewish girls on the lower east side were either meant to be the demure, sexless, and quiet vessels of assimilation or were turned into the vulgar, humiliating scapegoats that made male assimilation possible. "The old women are hags; the young, houris," Jacob Riis famously wrote of the women of "Jewtown" in 1890's *How The Other Half Lives*, "Wives and mothers at sixteen, at thirty they are old."

Barth and Williams made careers out of parodying and rejecting both of these options. In many ways, their mix of piano-bar song and shtick echoed back to the "ghetto girls," as Prell has dubbed them, of the early twentieth century Jewish press, those uncouth working-class Jewish girls whose alleged loud voices, bodily vulgarities, and sexual and stylistic excesses made them impossible—even dangerous—ingredients in the American melting pot and thereby sources of shame for fellow Jews eager to move up the social ladder of American taste and culture. Instead of rejecting the ghetto girl, Barth and Williams resurrected her in order to celebrate her, flaunting their excesses, flaunting their differences, and finding their strength and pleasure in just how far they were from the mannered and genteel aspirations of vanilla middle-class Jewishness (Prell 21–57).

4. MRS. STRAKOSH WAS WRONG

In 1964, just three years after Pearl Williams made her recording debut and the same year that Belle Barth released *Live at Las Vegas*, Barbra Streisand starred as Fanny Brice on Broadway. As I have alluded to above, Brice's story was a key part of the story of Barth and Williams, but where they liked to shame others as part of their act, Brice liked to shame herself to please others—playing up what Stacy Wolf has called "her difference from other women" (253). Her relentless self-ridicule over her big nose, her Semitic face, and her bad looks, guaranteed her a kind of mainstream success in the Ziegfield Follies that would never become part of Barth and Williams' plans. In a sense, they were less Fanny and more Mrs. Strakosh, one of the portly, older Jewish women who always hangs around the saloon run by Fanny's mother. In the film version of *Funny Girl*, Mrs. Strakosh was played by Mae Questel, who was also the voice of two characters on extreme ends of female representation: the cartoon vamp, not only Betty Boop but also Mrs. Portnoy, the vengeful fictitious Jewish mother of Philip Roth's Alexander Portnoy. On the cover of the 1969 album *Mrs. Portnoy's Retort (A Mother Strikes Back),* she brings castration fears to life as she cuts through a round of salami with glee. Mrs. Strakosh is part of the film's first musical number, "If A Girl Isn't Pretty," in which she and the other women tell Fanny to give up her stage dreams because she isn't pretty enough, that to be on stage you have to be something for men to look at and with her looks and her nose, she had no shot. Fanny of course proved them wrong, and so did Belle Barth and Pearl Williams, but in a different way. Mrs. Strakosh was wrong. The choice for girls who aren't pretty—for Jewish girls with Jewish noses, for Jewish women who are forty or fifty, not thirty or twenty, who speak with accents and use Yiddish—the choice was not between being a housewife or a Broadway star, between expressing Jewishness and repressing Jewishness, between expressing sexuality and repressing sexuality. There was a *third* way, the way of the risque and the grotesque, the way of the nightclub and the piano lounge, where freaky Jewish broads could stop trying to be red white and blue American stars and just play it blue—telling the truth, hurling insults, and laughing at the world in front of a room full of strangers until five in the morning.

Notes

1. For a sampling of Wallis's songs, see Ruth Wallis, *Boobs: Ruth Wallis' Greatest Hits*.
2. Barth recordings include: *The Book of Knowledge; I Don't Mean to be Vulgar, but it's Profitable; If I Embarrass You Tell Your Friends; In Person; My Next Story Is a Little Risque; Wild, Wild, Wild, Wild World!*
3. For an excellent introduction to Tucker's recordings, see the recently released Sophie Tucker, *Origins of the Red Hot Mama 1910-1922*. Tucker recorded up through the 1950s, including her 1956 LP *Bigger and Better Than Ever*.
4. Joanne Koch's musical about Barth, *If I Embarrass You Tell Your Friends*, debuted in Chicago in 2008 with African-American actress Bethany Thomas in the role of Barth.
5. Both Barth and Williams were also long rumored to be lesbians and bi-sexual and both made frequent allusions in their acts to having sex with women. Regardless of their off-stage lives, on-stage they were certainly "queer" Jewish women in that their acts were constantly de-naturalizing heterosexuality, critiquing the assumed superiority of the nuclear family, and gleefully referencing and advocating a host of sexual desires and acts that go beyond the bounds of sanctioned straight behavior. "Did I ask you if you're sitting with your wife?" Barth asked an audience member on her *At Las Vegas* album. "She's great, I balled her before you did. In fact, I'm gonna be on the Dyke Van Dick show."
6. Barth and Williams figure marginally, or not at all, in the following: Nachman; Berger; Epstein; Adams; Unterbrink; Horowitz; and Collier and Becket.
7. I thank Gayle Wald for this insight.
8. Dan Greenburg's book *How To Be A Jewish Mother* became an LP of the same title featuring *The Goldbergs* star Gertrude Berg as "the Jewish mother."

Works Cited

Abbott, Patsy. *Have I Had You Before?* Chess, 1961.

———. *Suck Up, You're Behind*. Abbott, 1962.

Adams, Joey. *The Borsht Belt*. Indianapolis: Bobbs-Merrill, 1966.

Antler, Joyce. *Talking Back: Images of Jewish Women in American Popular Culture*. Hanover, NH: Brandeis UP, 1998.

Bakhtin, Mikhail. *Rabelais and His World*. Bloomington: Indiana UP, 1984.

Barth, Belle. *Belle Barth at Las Vegas: The Fabulous 5AM Show*. Record Productions, 1964.

———. *The Book of Knowledge*. Laff, 1966.

———. *I Don't Mean To Be Vulgar, But It's Profitable*. Surprise, 1961.

———. *If I Embarrass You Tell Your Friends*. After Hours, 1960.

———. *In Person*. Laugh Time, 1961.

———. *Belle Barth at Las Vegas*. 1964.

———. *My Next Story Is A Little Risque*. After Hours, 1962.

———. *Wild, Wild, Wild, Wild World!* Record Productions, 1963.

Barth, Belle and Pearl Williams. *The Battle of the Mothers*. Riot Records, 1967.

———. *Return of the Mothers*. Riot Records, 1968.

The Barton Brothers. "Joe and Paul, Parts 1 & 2." *Jewish Comedy Varieties*. Apollo Records, 1949.

Berger, Phil. *The Last Laugh: The World of Stand-Up Comedy*. Lanham, MD: Cooper Square, 2000.

Bruce, Lenny. *How To Talk Dirty and Influence People*. New York: Simon & Schuster, 1992.

Cohen, Marc. "My Fair Sadie: Allan Sherman and A Paradox of American Jewish Culture." *American Jewish History* 93.1 (2007): 51–71.

Cohen, Sarah Blacher. "The Unkosher Comediennes." *Jewish Wry: Essays on Jewish Humor*. Ed. Sarah Blacher Cohen. Wayne State UP, 1987.

Brooks, Daphne. "The Write to Rock: Racial Mythologies, Feminist Theory, and the Pleasures of Rock Music Criticism." *Women and Music: A Journal of Gender and Culture* 12 (2008): 54–62.

Collier, Denise and Kathleen Becket. *Spare Ribs: Women in the Humor Biz*. New York: St. Martin's, 1980.

Damon, Maria. "Jazz-Jews, Jove, and Gender: The Ethnic Politics of Jazz Argot." *Jews and Other Differences: The New Jewish Cultural Studies*. Ed. Daniel Boyarin and Jonathan Boyarin. Minneapolis: U of Minnesota P, 1997.

Del Negro, Giovanna P. "From The Nightclub to the Living Room: Gender, Ethnicity, and Upward Mobility in the 1950s Party Records of Three Jewish Women Comics." *Jews at Home: Domestication of Identity*. Ed. Simon Bronner. Oxford: Littman, 2010.

Epstein, Lawrence J. *The Haunted Smile*. New York: Public Affairs, 2002.

Freedman, Jonathan. *Klezmer America: Jewishness, Ethnicity, Modernity.* New York: Columbia UP, 2007.

Frondorf, Shirley. *Death of a "Jewish American Princess": The True Story of a Victim on Trial.* New York: Villard, 1988.

Gilman, Sander. *The Jew's Body.* Taylor & Francis, 1992.

Greenburg, Dan. *How To Be A Jewish Mother.* Los Angeles: Price Stern Sloan, 1965.

———. *How To Be A Jewish Mother.* Perf. Gertrude Berg. Amy Records, 1965.

Horowitz, Susan. *Queens of Comedy.* London: Routledge, 1997.

"How To Be A Jewish Son." *The David Susskind Show* (season 12, episode 7). Perf. Mel Brooks, David Steinberg, George Segal, Stan Herman, Dan Greenburg and Larry Goldberg. 1970.

Hyman, Paula E. "Gender and the Shaping of Modern Jewish Identities." *Jewish Social Studies* 8.2/3 (Winter–Spring, 2002): 153–61.

Kiebler, M. Allison. *Rank Ladies: Gender and Cultural Hierarchy in American Vaudeville.* Chapel Hill: U of North Carolina P, 1999.

Koch, Joanne. *If I Embarrass You Tell Your Friends.* Perf. Bethany Thomas. Theo Ubique Theatre, Chicago, 2008.

Kun, Josh. "'Abie the Fishman': On Masks, Birthmarks, and Hunchbacks." *Listen Again: A Momentary History of Pop Music.* Ed. Eric Weisbard. Durham, NC: Duke UP, 2007. 50–68.

———. *Audiotopia: Music, Race, and America.* Berkeley and Los Angeles: U of California P, 2005.

Lavitt, Pamela Brown. "First of the Red Hot Mamas: 'Coon Shouting' and the Jewish Ziegfeld Girl." *American Jewish History* 87.4 (1999): 253–90.

Levine, Amy-Jill. "A Jewess, More and/or Less." *Judaism Since Gender.* Eds. Miriam Peskowitz and Laura Levitt. Routledge, 1997. 149–57.

Litvak, Joseph. *The Un-Americans: Jews, The Blacklist, and Stoolpigeon Culture.* Durham, NC: Duke UP, 2009.

Making Trouble: Three Generations of Funny Jewish Women. Dir. Rachel Talbot. Jewish Women's Archive, 2007.

Marc, David. *Comic Visions: Television Comedy and American Culture.* Oxford: Blackwell, 1997.

Merrill, Bob and Jule Styne. "If A Girl Isn't Pretty." *Funny Girl (1964 Original Broadway Cast).* Angel, 1964.

Merwin, Ted. *In Their Own Image: New York Jews in Jazz Age Popular Culture.* Piscatway, NJ: Rutgers UP, 2006.

Mock, Roberta. "Female Jewish Comedians: Grotesque Mimesis and Transgressing Stereotypes." *New Theatre Quarterly* 15 (1999): 99–108.

Mumford, Kevin. *Interzones: Black/White Sex Districts in Chicago and New York in the early Twentieth Century.* New York: Columbia UP, 1997.

Nachman, Gerald. *Seriously Funny: Rebel Comedians of the 1950s and 1960s*. San Anselmo, CA: Backstage, 2004.
"Nightclub Reviews." *Billboard* 24 Aug. 1947.
"Nightclubs: The Sickniks." *Time* 13 July 1959.
Ockman, Carol. "When is a Jewish Star Just a Star? Interpreting Images of Sarah Bernhardt." *The Jew in the Text: Modernity and the Construction of Identity*. Ed. Linda Nochlin and Tamar Garb. New York: Thames & Hudson, 1996.
Peskowitz, Miriam. "Engendering Jewish Religious History." *Judaism Since Gender*. Ed. Miriam Peskowitz and Laura Levitt. New York and London: Routledge, 1997.
Prell, Riv-Ellen. *Fighting To Become Americans: Jews, Gender, and the Anxiety of Assimilation*. Boston: Beacon, 1999.
Questel, Mae. *Mrs. Portnoy's Retort (A Mother Strikes Back)*. UA, 1969.
Radano, Ronald and Philip V. Bohlman, eds. *Music and The Racial Imagination*. Chicago: U of Chicago P, 2000.
Riis, Jacob. *How The Other Half Lives: Studies Among the Tenements of New York*. New York: Dover, 1971.
Rolondtz, Bob. "Belle Barth Discards Her Sting." *Billboard* 27 March 1961.
Rowe, Kathleen. *The Unruly Woman: Gender and the Genres of Laughter*. Austin: U of Texas P, 1995.
Rustin, Nichole T. and Sherrie Tucker. *Big Ears: Listening for Gender in Jazz Studies*. Durham, NC: Duke UP, 2008.
Sanders, Barry. *Sudden Glory: Laughter as Subversive History*. Boston: Beacon, 1995.
Sedgwick, Eve Kosofsky and Adam Frank. "Shame in the Cybernetic Fold: Reading Silvan Tomkins." *Critical Inquiry* 21.2 (Winter 1995): 496–522.
Tomkins, Silvan S. *Affect Imagery Consciousness: Volume I, The Positive Affects*. London: Tavistock, 1962.
———. *Affect Imagery Consciousness: Volume II, The Negative Affects*. London: Tavistock, 1963.
———. *Affect Imagery Consciousness: Volume III, The Negative Affects: Anger and Fear*. New York: Springer, 1991.
Tomkins, Silvan S. and Bertram P. Karon. *Affect Imagery Consciousness: Volume IV, Cognition: Duplication and Transformation of Information*. New York: Springer, 1962–92.
Tucker, Sophie. *Bigger and Better Than Ever*. Mercury, 1956.
———. *Origins of the Red Hot Mama 1910–1922*. Archeophone, 2009.
———. *Some of These Days: The Autobiography of Sophie Tucker*. Garden City, NY: Doubleday, 1945.
Unterbrink, Mary. *Funny Women: American Comediennes 1860–1985*. Jefferson, NC: McFarland & Co, 1987.

Walker, Nancy A. and Zita Dresner. "Women's Humor in America." *What's So Funny? Humor in American Culture*. Ed. Nancy Walker. Wilmington: Scholarly Resources, 1998. 171–84.

Wallis, Ruth. "Boobs." *Boobs: Ruth Wallis' Greatest Hits*. Wallis Originals, 1998.

———. *Boobs: Ruth Wallis' Greatest Hits*. Wallis Originals, 1998.

———. "Drill 'Em All." *Boobs: Ruth Wallis' Greatest Hits*. Wallis Originals, 1998.

———. "He'd Rather Be A Girl." *Boobs: Ruth Wallis' Greatest Hits*. Wallis Originals, 1998.

———. *Here's Looking Up Your Hatch*. King, 1966.

———. "It's A Scream How Levine Does The Rhumba." *Rhumba Party*. Miltone, 1947.

Warren, Rusty. "Bounce Your Boobies." Jubilee, 1961.

———. *Knockers Up!* Jubilee, 1960.

———. Personal interview. 18 Jan. 2009.

———. *Songs for Sinners*. Jubilee, 1959.

Weber, Donald. *Haunted in the World: Jewish American Culture from Cahan to "The Goldbergs."* Indianapolos: Indiana UP, 2005.

Where's Poppa? Dir. Carl Reiner. MGM Repertory, 1970.

Williams, Pearl. *A Trip Around The World Is Not A Cruise*. After Hours, 1961.

———. *Bagels and Lox*. Laff, 1968.

Wolf, Stacy. "Barbra's 'Funny Girl' Body." *Queer Theory and the Jewish Question*. Ed. D. Boyarin, D. Itzkovitz, and A. Pellegrini. New York: Columbia UP, 2003. 246–65.

"Here's a Foreign Song I Learned in Utah": The Anxiety of Jewish Influence in the Music of Bob Dylan[1]

David Kaufman

Awarding the 2009 Kennedy Center Honor to his musical hero, Bruce Springsteen, comedian Jon Stewart began:

> I am not a music critic, nor historian, nor archivist. I cannot tell you where Bruce Springsteen falls in the pantheon of the American songbook. I cannot illuminate the context of his work, or its roots in the folk and oral history traditions of our great nation. But I am from New Jersey. So, I can tell you what I believe. And what I believe is that Bob Dylan and James Brown had a baby.[2]

It was a great line, wickedly funny, but it also made the serious point that to truly understand an artist we must see him as the continuation and combination of others who came before. Stewart's joke incisively pegged Springsteen as a conjoining of the songwriting genius of Dylan with the performative prowess of Brown, and moreover, as the crossroads of folk music and soul music, thus mixing musical genres generally thought of as white and black. Of course, such cultural hybridity has a long history in American popular music, from the blackface minstrelsy of Al Jolson, Eddie Cantor and Sophie Tucker to the cross-cultural appropriations of Irving Berlin, George Gershwin, Benny Goodman, Paul Simon, the Beastie Boys and Matisyahu (Melnick). The phenomenon, as illustrated by my chosen examples—all of them Jews—suggests that citing Dylan as a key influence on Springsteen may not only reflect a musical patrimony of whiteness, but of Jewishness as well. But Bob Dylan is not usually seen this way; he is not generally associated either with Jewish culture or with Jewish music. Tempting as it may be to read Stewart's comment as a suggestion of some Jewish influence on Springsteen, it is highly unlikely that anyone hearing Dylan's name in relation to "the Boss" would have thought, "Oh, so Springsteen has a little Jewish in him after all."

Indeed, the Jewish element in American music—referring not to the internal musical traditions of Judaism or Jewish culture, but rather to the broader influence of Jews in popular music, ranging from Berlin to Dylan to Ezra Koenig of Vampire Weekend[3]—is still largely unexplored. While it is often observed that Jews overpopulate the ranks of American composers and songwriters, rarely is any further analysis or explanation offered.[4] Few ask the most basic question: What in the collective Jewish experience accounts for the outsized contribution of Jews to American popular music? To see the anomaly more clearly, simply contrast the common assumption of the key role of Jewishness in American comedy with the relative lack of such a claim for pop music. Or compare Jon Stewart (and Lenny Bruce, Mel Brooks, Joan Rivers, Woody Allen et al.) to Bob Dylan. Whereas the former are unabashedly Jewish figures—often incorporating Jewish self-identification into their comedy and thus publicly marking themselves as members of the tribe—the latter most assuredly is not. That is, while we think of Stewart, for example, as a Jewish comedian, representing a tradition of Jewish comedy, Dylan is rarely if ever seen as a Jewish musician or part of an identifiably Jewish tradition of music. Yet the question of his Jewishness—and thus the Jewishness of his art—persists. For example, historian Michael Staub leaves Dylan out of his sourcebook of *The Jewish 1960s*, but does cite him in the introduction to illustrate the problem of Jewish definition (xxi). Staub wonders whether the artist formerly known as Zimmerman belongs to the Jewish narrative at all, pointedly asking, "Was Dylan a *Jewish* songwriter?"[5] That is to say, is there any relevance, anything *explanatory*, in the fact that Bob Dylan is a Jew?[6] Does his Jewish background—born to a Jewish family, raised in a Jewish home and community, associated with many other Jews by friendship and by love—have any meaningful influence on the adult and his art? As with so much else regarding Dylan, there is no easy answer, and in my own engagement with the subject I've experienced this confusion firsthand. While participating in a panel discussion on the historical legacy of Dylan held at the Skirball Center, a Jewish cultural institution in Los Angeles,[7] the moderator asked: would Dylan have been Dylan had he not been born a Jew? One of my fellow panelists, a renowned American musicologist and leading scholar of Bob Dylan, answered with absolute certainty that no, he could just as easily have been born Catholic, i.e., that Dylan's Jewishness is entirely arbitrary and has nothing to contribute to our understanding of his music and career. I respectfully disagreed, of course—not that my answer then was any more enlightening or compelling.

The question of influence in the music of Bob Dylan is especially salient insofar as he epitomizes the notion of musical assimilation, the artistry of weaving a new musical cloth out of disparate elements and multiple sources. Though it can be argued that all musical composition, like all great art, builds upon earlier musical forms and traditions, much of the recent literature on Dylan concerns the question of artistic originality (see, for example, Yaffe; DeCurtis; Jacobi). If, as internet searches have demonstrated, he "borrows" much of his material, then how original an artist can he be? Dylan himself acknowledged his indebtedness to others in the title of his 2001 album, *Love and Theft*, and then more expansively in his 2004 memoir, *Chronicles, Volume One*. But the controversy is moot, really, when we consider the range of influences in Dylan's music and therefore the extraordinary capacity he has for musical recombination. His remarkable capacity to serve as a nexus of musical and lyrical styles is captured memorably in a 1960s art poster entitled "Bob Dylan and his Musical Roots and Branches" by the children's book illustrator Michael Foreman. Inserted in the September 1968 *Eye* magazine, the poster portrays Dylan as a tree with two sets of roots—the musical roots, including Little Richard, Odetta, Dave Von Ronk, Woody Guthrie, Hank Williams and Buddy Holly; and the lyrical, including William Blake, Walt Whitman, Bertholt Brecht, Rimbaud, Allen Ginsberg, and again, Woody Guthrie. Many of these, it should be noted, were not only influences on Dylan's music, but models for his persona as a popular artist. The branches, those whom Dylan influenced, included Leonard Cohen, the Byrds, the Turtles, Sonny & Cher, David Blue, Phil Ochs, and again, Allen Ginsberg. At this still early stage of his career, it should occasion no surprise that the roots (twenty in all) outnumber the branches (eleven), yet some omissions are glaring. In fact, at least one oft-mentioned model is missing, as well as an entire genre of precedents. Thinking along the lines of Jon Stewart's comment on Springsteen, allow me to recommend two particular figures as the figurative "parents" of Bob Dylan—both seminal figures in American popular music, but neither, oddly enough, cited in the Foreman illustration. One was the first great star in the history of rock 'n' roll, Elvis Presley, and the other, the archetypal Jewish songwriter in America, Irving Berlin.

Though conventionally seen as the heir to Woody Guthrie's legacy of folk radicalism, the musical luminary to whom the young Dylan was most often compared was Elvis Presley. On one level the comparison was obvious as Presley had innovated the original fusion of (black) blues and (white) country music—and as such, was a key influence on the teenaged Robert Zimmerman and perhaps his most important idol growing up. In certain respects, Dylan did succeed in emulating Elvis. As early as 1962, one observer hailed Dylan as "the Elvis Presley of folk music" (Turner) and Robert Shelton, his longtime chronicler, wrote in 1965: "Many pop-music insiders regard Mr. Dylan as the most influential American performer to emerge since the rise of Elvis Presley ten years ago. Some think he is on the brink of superstardom." Dylan's star rose so rapidly in the early 1960s it seemed his celebrity would soon rival Presley's. While he never achieved quite the same degree of iconic fame as Elvis (if he had, we might be deluged with Dylan impersonators as well), Dylan is unquestionably an icon in his own right. Moreover, he succeeded Presley as the chief representative of both the outsider rebelliousness of rock 'n' roll, and, as noted above, the blending of black and white musical styles. Tim Riley writes: "*Bob Dylan* [title of his first album] was the sound of a young man trying to make sense of a black man's heritage, which made it a rock 'n' roll effort in the tradition of Dylan's idol Elvis Presley" (36). On the other hand, he transcended the King by expanding the art form of rock music into entirely new aesthetic and intellectual territory. Picking up on that distinction, Bruce Springsteen introduced Dylan at his induction into the Rock and Roll Hall of Fame thus: "Bob freed your mind the way Elvis freed your body" (Riley 30). In short, Bob Dylan was the Elvis for a new generation. In this regard, Michael Billig adds: "There is no denying Bob Dylan's iconic status. His face, with its expression of worry and loneliness, became as famous as Presley's. Dylan was the Presley for middle-class whites, born just after the second world war—the figure who symbolized their era, marking it off musically from that of the previous cohort. He was the outsider, when everyone wanted to be outsiders. To fulfill the role, Dylan had to be an ambiguous outsider—the outsider playing the insider-as-outsider" (118).

Billig's reference to Dylan's outsider status can be related to two features of the Dylan persona—first, and somewhat like Presley, he hails from a remote and sometimes derided part of the country, in his case the Upper Midwest; and second, unlike Elvis, he is a Jew.[8] Looking at the 1968 poster, one other anomaly jumps out at this observer. The musical roots include only one Jewish figure—Jack Elliott (born Elliott Adnopoz in Brooklyn)—whereas the highest branches are occupied by Jewish musicians Leonard Cohen, David

Blue (nee Cohen), and Phil Ochs. That is to say, the legacy of Jewish artists in American popular music is all but neglected in assessing influences on Bob Dylan. According to this prevailing view, he has nothing much to do with the grand tradition of American Jewish songwriters and composers such as Irving Berlin, George Gershwin, Aaron Copland, Harold Arlen, Yip Harburg, Richard Rodgers, Oscar Hammerstein, Leonard Bernstein, Stephen Sondheim, Burt Bacharach, Doc Pomus, Neil Sedaka, Neil Diamond, Carole King, etc. Yet it can be argued that Bob Dylan fits squarely within this tradition—especially when compared to the first name on the list: Irving Berlin. It is no exaggeration to claim that Dylan was to the second half of the twentieth century what Irving Berlin (1888–1989) was to the first—the greatest songwriter of his time, a creative genius whose classic compositions came to pervade the soundtrack of contemporary music, and a seminal figure whose achievement would inspire the popular musical careers of all to follow. Both were so prolific as composers that their very creativity has been called into question—Berlin was subject to nasty rumors that he kept "a little colored boy in the closet" who really wrote his songs (Melnick 114–19); and Dylan, as above, has been criticized for "stealing" others' music. And like Berlin (born Israel Baline), Dylan too was a "marrano" of a sort, a Jew in disguise. Unconsciously emulating Berlin and so many others, he changed his original Jewish-sounding name as he entered show business, and for the most part attempted to escape his origins. Though many know them to be Jews, many do not—and so they hide in plain sight. It is a familiar enough type in the modern Jewish experience, described by Isaac Deutscher as the "non-Jewish Jew"; by Ivan Kalmar as the "EJI" (Embarrassed Jewish Individual); and by Josh Kun, referring to pop music specifically, as the "audio-Zelig." Yet there are some important distinctions between the two: while Berlin belonged to a generation of highly assimilated Jews who actively rejected the foreignness of their immigrant parents, Dylan's evasion of Jewish identity took place in another era altogether, a time of racial consciousness and ethnic revival. Dylan's relationship to his Jewishness would follow a far more complex path than Berlin's (given his "born again" Christian period and the extreme social changes through which he lived); yet both were Jews fervently engaged in both the escape from Jewishness and the embrace of America. This, in a nutshell, is the Jewish factor in their music, placing Dylan in the modern Jewish tradition of cultural assimilation[9]—and the "assimilation" of musical influences, as suggested above, is the essence of Dylan. What makes him a great artist, of course, is his ability to transform and transmute those influences into something astonishingly fresh and entirely original.

Bob Dylan is a unique figure in the history of American music precisely because he is *both* Irving Berlin *and* Elvis Presley—just as surely as Bruce Springsteen is heir to both Dylan and James Brown. Imagine if Izzy Baline had grown up in the 1950s idolizing Elvis Presley—might he not have become Bob Dylan? In a memorable verse from one of Dylan's classic songs, "Desolation Row" (from the 1965 album, *Highway 61 Revisited*), he describes one alter-ego as "Einstein, disguised as Robin Hood"—that is, his true self behind the scenes is the archetypal Jewish genius, while his public persona is the dashing *goy* memorably played by Errol Flynn in the movies, the pop star as romantic renegade. Yet, as the next line continues, "with his memories in a trunk, [he] passed this way an hour ago." Though in disguise, he still retains memory of his former self. Neither the original nor the fake, he occupies the liminal space between, finding himself on "desolation row." According to some interpreters, his art flows from this very contradiction: "Dylan's relationship with himself has always been at the heart of his best work—the way the man who was born Robert Zimmerman communes with the songs, odyssey, and mystique of Bob Dylan" (Riley 271–272). It may well be this core conflict of Dylan's psyche, between the reality of his background and the image he created of himself, that infuses his music with its tension, its anger, its beauty.

Yet nevertheless, perhaps following Dylan's own lead, the voluminous commentary on his life and music offers relatively little insight into the Jewish side of the equation. The exceptions to this rule, the minority who do in fact stress Dylan's Jewishness, tend to be highly identified Jews who project their own experience of an intensive Jewish culture onto their idol, imagining him as their "rebbe," and thereby "Jewhooing" Bob Dylan. A term coined by historian Susan Glenn, "Jewhooing" refers to the proclivity of many Jews to emphasize the Jewishness of "their" celebrities, i.e., the habitual pointing out of famous Jews. In Dylan's case, the phenomenon may help elucidate the Jewish element in his art, sometimes operating as commentary on its absence. The Jewhooing of Dylan takes many forms, highlighted by the following:

1) From the start, his biographers have dutifully recorded Dylan's Jewish roots, family and upbringing. An early biography by Anthony Scaduto was especially careful to list all the Zimmermans and Edelsteins in his extended family, and also noted Dylan's flight from Jewishness during his brief college career. Scaduto quotes one early acquaintance saying: "I had a feeling he was rejecting a lot of things, running from his heritage, sort of traveling in disguise" (15). Later biographers such as Bob Spitz and Dave Engel would also play up the Jewish roots angle, but all biographical listings for Dylan include at the very

least the once controversial (and now iconic) information that his name was originally Robert Zimmerman.

2) Once "outed" as a Jew by *Newsweek* magazine in November 1963 (Schaap), Dylan's original family name would often be cited as a way to puncture his pretense. For instance, John Lennon called him "Zimmerman" in the 1970 song, "God"; a 1972 comic strip depicting Dylan as a super-hero in the satirical magazine *National Lampoon* was entitled, "Ventures of Zimmerman"; and many of the bootleg recordings of the 1970s and 80s would have "Zimmerman" as part of their titles. Dylan himself would include the line, "you may call me Zimmy" in his 1979 song, "Gotta Serve Somebody."[10]

3) A series of Jewish impersonations of Dylan have further "Judaized" his image. In the aftermath of the 1973 Yom Kippur War, singer-songwriter Yonatan Geffen built a career as an Israeli Bob Dylan, translating several of Dylan's songs into Hebrew and generally affecting a Dylanesque pose. In the United States, comedian Richard Belzer added a devastatingly funny impersonation of Dylan as both a bar-mitzvah boy and an old Jewish man. As A. J. Weberman (see below) put it, "Dylan was a folk rocka, but now he's an Alta Cocka." More recently, Cantor Jeff Klepper has performed a one-man show of Dylan parodies, including "Tangled Up in Jews" (take-off of "Tangled Up in Blue"), "Hockin' Me Til I'm Sore" ("Knockin' on Heaven's Door"), "Stuck Inside Of Monsey with the Brooklyn Blues Again" ("Stuck Inside Of Mobile with the Memphis Blues Again"), "Cantillation Row" ("Desolation Row"), and "Just Like a Chazzn" ("Just Like a Woman"). And whereas Elvis Presley inspired a legion of literal impersonators, Dylan has just one: a nice Jewish boy named Joel Gilbert, who looks and sounds enough like Dylan to make the illusion work. Gilbert also makes documentaries about Dylan's life, especially his religious phase.[11]

Beyond these, the most common form of Dylan Jewhooing is the Jewish interpretation of his music. Whether intended by the artist or not, Dylan's work can be, and often has been, read in the context of traditional Judaism. As J. J. Goldberg recalls: "Over the years, a cottage industry grew up to ferret out Judaic content—some genuine, some merely imagined—in his lyrics. Fans stalked him on his spiritual journeys the way other performers might be staked out during restaurant outings." Some of the most fervent interpreters of Dylan's oeuvre were Jewish hippies who began to treat his work "midrashically" in the countercultural 1960s. Beyond reading deeper meanings into every line of his songs, they saw the man himself as a religious symbol of transcendence and salvation. Mel Howard, producer of the 1975 tour film (that became *Renaldo & Clara*), explained it as follows:

> And, incidentally, Dylan's Jewish . . . and I'm heavily Jewish, I speak Yiddish, so there's that, the mythology of Dylan as a latter-day Hassid, as a Cabalistic kind of poet, all that, and as a kind of extension of the whole idea of the wandering Jew, wandering poet, the person who is inspired and goes amongst the community to carry the message of inspiration and renewed faith and renewed hope. (Sloman 330–331)

The principal exponent of this phenomenon has been Stephen Pickering, whom Scaduto called one of the few writers to "have recognized that . . . in all his songs since he waved farewell to protest almost ten years ago, Bob Dylan has been creating a body of work that is rooted in the Jewish mystical tradition" (287). And Michael Gray, in his *Bob Dylan Encyclopedia*, notes that "Pickering was the first to assert, not always convincingly but with an aggressive torrent of opaque argument, the centrality of the Jewish faith and Jewish teachings to Dylan's work. . . . He wrote from what he called the Center for the Study of Bob Dylan & Torah Judaism" (538). Pickering, an obsessed Dylan fan since 1962, devoted a decade of his life to what another uber-fan described as "Dylanology." That fan, a Jewish hippie as well, is A. J. Weberman. In Scaduto's description, Weberman is "the self-styled 'Dylanologist' who has made a career of interpreting Dylan's lyrics and going through his garbage to learn all he can of the man he both idolizes and hates" (277–278). In a later biography, Howard Sounes adds: "Born Alan Jules Weberman in Brooklyn in 1945, he became obsessed with Bob's music when he was at Michigan State University in the early sixties. Listening to the albums while stoned on marijuana or LSD he made what seemed to him a major discovery. 'I realized it was poetry and required interpretation,' he explains. 'I developed the Dylanological Method, which is looking at each word in the context in which it appears and looking for words that have a similar theme that cluster around it (concordance). I started to devote a lot of time to just sitting around interpreting Dylan's poetry'" (Sounes 263). Though Weberman did not obsess over the hidden Jewish significance of Dylan's work, his method was similar to Pickering's in that both purported to have discovered the "true" meaning of Dylan's enigmatic lyrics. Today's community of serious Dylan scholars tends to dismiss the Pickerings and Webermans as crackpots, and they understandably eschew the term "Dylanologist." Yet within the ever-growing industry of Dylan scholarship there continues to exist a minority who combine legitimate textual interpretation with the Jewhooing trend described above.

The main contemporary example is Seth Rogovoy, author of the recent *Bob Dylan: Prophet, Mystic, Poet*. An earlier subtitle considered by the author, "Prophet, Mystic, Jew," would have been more appropriate as the book is a prime instance of Jewhooing, claiming to have "delved extensively into Dylan's Jewish heritage and the influence of Judaism in his works" (blurb on dust jacket). Surpassing my assertion of Jewish patrimony for Dylan in Irving Berlin and other assimilated American Jewish composers, Rogovoy argues for a different kind of antecedent in the figure of Eliakum Zunser, a 19th century *badchen* (wedding emcee) and folksinger/poet. Rogovoy does more than draw the comparison, he opens his book with it, framing his study of Dylan with a portrait of a Yiddish-speaking Jew from the intensively Jewish world of Eastern Europe and thus a far more identifiably Jewish figure than someone like Berlin. According to Rogovoy, "Zunser was, in a sense, a proto-Dylan, or, conversely, Dylan was, in a sense, the Zunser of the second half of the twentieth century, albeit one . . . whose influence was more universal" (2). By claiming to see "something of Zunser in Dylan, as much as there is of the folksinger Woody Guthrie and the blues legend Robert Johnson" (8) Rogovoy commits the sin of essentializing, that is, seeing Jewishness as intrinsic and therefore essential to Dylan's being, or at least seeing Jewishness as being as deep-seated as his commitment to the music traditions of folk and blues. The Zunser analogy establishes the tone of the entire book, which has as its chief purpose to counter the image of Dylan as an assimilated Jew—as I characterized him earlier—and to replace it with the notion of Dylan as a fully identified Jew, from the start of his career and even through his Christian phase! Even if Dylan is a more committed Jew in private, we are more concerned here with his public image and popular art. Though we cannot fully know the private Dylan, it is the public Dylan in any event who affects us most deeply. Rogovoy contradicts himself on this very point when he writes: "This book sets out to make no claims about Bob Dylan's past or present religious beliefs or self-identification." Yet on the very same page he adds: "Dylan has never fully abandoned the faith of his forebears. Rather, he has apparently taken very seriously his relationship to Judaism, a relationship that, as this book sets out to demonstrate, so fully and completely informs his life and his work" (5).[12] The principal proof for this assertion, offered throughout the book, involves an effort to find biblical allusions in Dylan's lyrics, of which, to be sure, there are many. For example, he sees in the lyrics to "Blowin' in the Wind," "Masters of War," "Knockin' on Heaven's Door," and other Dylan classics direct influence from the biblical book of *Isaiah*; in "Love Minus Zero/No Limit" inspiration from the book of *Daniel*; and in "It's Alright, Ma (I'm Only Bleeding)" echoes of *Ecclesiastes* (7, 42, 50–52, 80–81, 84–86, etc.). The problem with this argument is that quoting from Scripture is no sure indication of Jewish identity—in fact, biblical citation is a religious practice far more characteristic of fundamentalist Christians than of traditional Jews, for whom the Torah, as sacred as it is, was long ago superseded by the Talmud and other post-biblical writings as the *sine qua non* of rabbinic literacy. Rather than providing evidence of Jewishness, Rogovoy merely demonstrates that Dylan has turned to the Bible for inspiration—but as sacred literature, the Bible is just as surely a foundational text for Christianity as it is for Judaism; and as a literary masterpiece, it is just as surely a foundational text in western civilization as it is for the Judeo-Christian religious tradition. Moreover, a touring musician like Dylan spends a good deal of time in hotel rooms, where a Bible is always right-at-hand and thus a ready source for such an absorptive lyricist in search of inspiration. Has Dylan often displayed a religious sensibility? Yes. Ought we see him therefore as an engaged Jew, self-consciously drawing upon the Jewish literary tradition? With apologies to Seth Rogovoy, no.

Yet as Rogovoy rehearses at length, there is certainly some Jewish element in Dylan's life and music. Dylan has on occasion employed explicit Jewish subject matter in his songs, and has made some notable excursions into the Jewish world; he has been reported to have visited synagogues, yeshivas, and Israel. This was evident especially following his "born again" Christian period in the early 1980s. His third of three Christian albums, *Shot of Love*, came out in 1981; it was followed by *Infidels* in 1983. In between, he had flown with his ex-wife Sara to Israel to celebrate their son Jesse's bar-mitzvah; and in addition, he began spending time in the Lubavitcher Hasidic enclave of Crown Heights, studying Judaism in an ultra-Orthodox setting. Did this exposure to Jewish culture find its way into his music? As Rogovoy and many others will note, Dylan's most explicitly Jewish composition is found on *Infidels*—"Neighborhood Bully," called "a thinly veiled paean to Israel and Jewish peoplehood" (Rogovoy 239). The song is often cited by Jewish Dylan fans as a source of ethnic pride—which is to say, it serves as fodder for the Jewhooing tendency. But most of Dylan's explicit references to Jewish themes occurred in the early 1960s, the very years he was most intent on obscuring his true background—both by changing his name and by concocting tall tales as to his origins. Contrary to his project of self-invention, he interpolated issues of Jewish concern into a number of his early folk compositions. In "With God on Our Side," for example, he originally included the verse:

> When the Second World War
> Came to an end,
> We forgave the Germans,
> And we were friends.
> Though they murdered six million,
> In the ovens they fried,
> The Germans now too
> Have God on their side.[13]

In "Talkin' John Birch Paranoid Blues," a scathing satire of right wing red-baiters, he referenced both the Holocaust:

> Now we all agree with Hitler's views,
> Although he killed six million Jews.
> It don't matter too much that he was a Fascist,
> At least you can't say he was a Communist!

and, in a later verse of the same song, he alluded to a well-known 1960 Hollywood film about Israel:

> Now Eisenhower, he's a Russian spy,
> Lincoln, Jefferson and that Roosevelt guy.
> To my knowledge there's just one man
> That's really a true American:
> George Lincoln Rockwell.
> I know for a fact he hates Commies cus
> He picketed the movie *Exodus*.

While indicating Dylan's awareness of the Holocaust and of antisemitism, none of these lines was exactly a ringing announcement of his "true" identity as a Jew.

Nor do they compare in blatant ethnic identification to another song he often sang for comic relief. With "Talkin' Havah Nagilah Blues," a staple of his early coffeehouse performances,[14] Dylan would signal both his true roots and his remove from them. Introducing his send-up of "Havah Nagilah" with the sly, "Here's a foreign song I learned in Utah," Dylan would launch into a ridiculously distorted and truncated version of the familiar Hebrew refrain—they were probably the first Hebrew words that had passed his lips since his bar mitzvah. More to the point, Israeli folk songs like "Havah Nagilah" were a staple of 1950s folk music, led by the Weavers ("Tzena, Tzena"), Theodore Bikel, and Harry Belafonte. Belafonte was one of those who popularized "Havah Nagilah" (and from whose 1959 Carnegie Hall concert recording the present writer first learned the words to the song—so perfectly did he enunciate the Hebrew), and who had been an early influence on the young Dylan. In fact, Dylan was no doubt titillated to play harmonica on the established star's latest album in June 1961.[15] By lampooning the song, Dylan was not only poking fun at his own bar mitzvah background, but also at the commercial folk revival—whose multicultural pretensions enabled a black Calypso singer to adopt this standard of contemporary Jewish music. Though adapting the song himself, Dylan stood just as far removed from Jewish life as Belafonte. Hence most critics tend to overlook the Jewish significance of "Talkin' Havah Nagilah," e.g., Gil Turner: "Dylan's flare for the comic is usually put to use in the talking blues form . . . 'Talkin' Havah Nagilah' was made up especially for members of the audience that shout out requests for songs way out of his line" (Turner). Likewise, the song was noted in the very first newspaper account of a Dylan performance. In his *New York Times* review of September 29, 1961, music critic Robert Shelton interprets "Talking Havah Nagilah" as "burlesque[ing] the folk-music craze and *the singer himself*" [emphasis mine]. The latter comment suggests some knowledge of Dylan's Jewish origins, yet Shelton (née Shapiro) concludes by honoring the young folksinger's obfuscations and protecting his true background: "Mr. Dylan is vague about his antecedents and birthplace, but it matters less where he has been than where he is going, and that would seem to be straight up" (*No Direction Home* 111). Much later, Shelton would describe "Talkin' Hava Negila Blues" as Dylan's "little jape of international 'stylists' like Harry Belafonte and Theo Bikel" (*No Direction Home* 109). But some commentators did note a Jewish issue at play. Larry Yudelson, writing in 1991 for the *Washington Jewish Week*, suggested that by mocking "the quintessential American Jewish tune," Dylan was:

> . . . going after an establishment—a Jewish establishment, for that matter. "Here's a foreign song I learned out in Utah," he twangs into the microphone. He strums his guitar, and continues tunelessly: "Ha! Va! Ha-va! Ha-va-na! Hava Nagila. Yodeleihoo!" With the yodel and a finishing harmonica flourish, Dylan had outlined an epitaph for the Hebrew folk songs sung by folksingers like Theodore Bikel and the Weavers as part of a vaguely leftist, working-man's ethnic repertoire. The mockery was prescient: The left would not be strumming love songs about Israeli soldiers much longer. Dylan, with his inspired instinct for the authentic, was first to smell the phoniness.

Though it is possible Dylan was thinking along such lines, and intended to critique the 1950s' romanticization of Israel, it seems far more likely he was unconsciously reflecting his own experience of the shallowness of American Jewish culture. Not surprisingly, Seth Rogovoy similarly overstates the Jewish relevance of Dylan's "Havah Nagilah" take-off. First agreeing that it was "a parody and mockery of the "ethnic" trend in folk music at the time" (35), he shortly adds that with this song, Dylan was making "his relationship with Jewishness and Jewish history quite clear." He further argues:

> Of all ethnic folk songs he could have chosen, why else did Dylan choose the best-known Hebrew song (a modern Israeli dance tune, really) for his material to mock? Were Dylan to have been seriously intent upon distancing himself from his cultural heritage, wouldn't he have put ten feet between himself and the kitsch of "Hava Nagila"? Didn't singing "Talkin' Hava Negeilah Blues" merely draw attention to his ethnic background? Even if read as a *mockery* of that background, it *still* served to draw attention to his Jewish origins. Far from distancing himself from his family and his Judaism, Dylan was planting hints right from the outset about who he really was, from where he was coming, and perhaps even where he was headed. (37)

Rogovoy might have a point that Dylan's choice of the song drew attention to his Jewishness had it not been Harry Belafonte who had previously turned it into a generic folk revival standard. But the truly strange part of Rogovoy's analysis is his contention that "Dylan was planting hints" that he was Jewish. But why merely plant hints at a time when other entertainers ranging from Lenny Bruce to Allan Sherman to Barbra Streisand were saying out loud, and in no uncertain terms, that they were Jews? Allan Sherman, in particular, boldly announced his ethnicity on his first two hit albums, *My Son, The Folk Singer*, and *My Son, The Celebrity*, released in October and December of 1962 respectively. Like Dylan, Sherman had also chosen to spoof "Havah Nagila," turning it into a satire of American middle class life called "Harvey and Sheila" (*My Son, The Celebrity*). Dylan's "Talkin' Havah Nagila Blues" was recorded during the *Freewheelin'* sessions in March 1962, making it a near contemporary with Sherman's offering. But "Harvey and Sheila," like many of the song parodies on Sherman's albums, reveled in its patent Jewishness. Bob Dylan would do nothing of the sort. When the 19-year-old arrived in New York City in 1961 he met many other young Jews, most of whom were, like him, eager to escape their ethnic origins. These included many of his fellow performers, such as two of the three Greenbriar Boys, the bluegrass band he opened for on the night of Shelton's review, as well as a goodly percentage of his New York audience. Playing his comic version of "Hava Nagilah" may certainly have indicated to some that he was a fellow Jew, but most would have only heard it as the good-natured joke he clearly intended it to be—or as Josh Kun calls it, "a knowing folk blues goof." Of all the commentators on the "Havah Nagilah" take-off, Kun is perhaps the most insightful in reading it as a performance of "Dylan's 'hidden' identity" (66). That is, rather than taking it as evidence of Dylan's "true" Jewishness or alternatively viewing it outside of a Jewish context altogether, Kun fully grasps the enigmatic nature of Dylan's assimilated Jewishness. Making reference to a character in the Marx Brothers' 1930 film *Animal Crackers* (Roscoe Chandler, outed by Harpo and Chico as "Abie the Fishman"), Kun writes:

> "Talkin' Hava Nageilah Blues" [may be] the best Abie song of all. In this performance, Dylan is both Roscoe and Abie, the hidden identity and the new identity, the father and the son. On the one hand, the song is foreign, he can't pronounce it, it's not his. Yet Dylan winks at us. It is his, he just chooses to not perform it as it should be performed. The chorus is strained, torturous, and stuttered, because Dylan knew who he was and he knew who he was pretending to be. Which leaves "Talkin' Hava Negeilah Blues" as a song about not singing "Hava Nagila," a performance about the refusal to perform. (66)[16]

Brilliant—Dylan's performance of a Jewish song demonstrates his own refusal to perform Jewishness. In classic Jewish fashion, the artist responded to the anxiety provoked by his own background—by the "Jewish influence" in his own life—by cracking wise. The sheer funniness of "Talkin' Hava Nagilah" is critical here, linking Dylan to Allan Sherman and Jon Stewart and so many other Jewish comedians who similarly have conjured humor out of the complexities and contradictions of being a Jew in late twentieth-century America. One of the few authors to treat Dylan in this vein is James Bloom. In *Gravity Fails: The Comic Jewish Shaping of Modern America*, Bloom highlights Dylan as a representative "funny Jew" and cites "Talkin' Hava Nagilah" (which he calls "Havanagila Rag") as a comic device working "to deny that traditions and similar utterances separating 'foreign' from native, the distinction Dylan's spoken introduction confounds, hold any intrinsic identity-setting authority" (38).[17] In this view, Dylan's opening, "Here's a foreign song I learned in Utah," *is* the joke, deftly dissolving boundaries between foreign/native, Jewish/American, Minnesota home/Utah desert exile, all at once. The comedic performance might be seen, therefore, as a response to the anxiety Dylan experienced as an alienated young Jew in the all "too Jewish" environment of New York City. It solved the problem of Jewish identity by joking about it—and though we have no record of the audience reaction, we can only assume that Dylan's comic number produced a more general catharsis, resolving the anxiety for all. In the end, however, the important point is neither Dylan's intention nor the audience's reception, but rather the way in which we today, by recalling a momentary flash of ethnic identification, tend to project Jewishness onto Bob Dylan. The Jewhooing tendency exhibited by Dylanologists from Pickering to Rogovoy is merely the tip of the iceberg.

This is further revealed in the recent burst of commentary on Dylan's 2009 Christmas album, *Christmas in the Heart*. The album caused a minor uproar, split between those concerned that Dylan was selling out to American commercialism, and those fearful that he was backsliding toward Christianity. Others thought (or hoped) it might all be a joke, a tongue-in-cheek ironic take on the popular holiday. But Dylan himself pooh-poohed such objections, insisting that "these songs are part of my life, just like folk songs" (Flanagan). Many observed that Dylan was merely joining a long music industry tradition of Christmas albums made by icons such as Sinatra and Presley, as well as by Jewish icons such as Barbra Streisand and Neil Diamond. Also commonly noted is the fact that some of the most popular Christmas songs were written by Jews, most famously Irving Berlin's "White Christmas." Others focused on Dylan's apparent revivalist interest in American music history, as evidenced on his radio show and in much of his own recent musical output.[18] That is to say, it wasn't the Christian content of the music that engaged him so much as the *American* cultural tradition it represented. While all this may be true, it does not begin to explain the sheer anxiety elicited by Bob Dylan, American Jewish icon, once again producing an album of patently Christian music. If he is so emotionally resonant to such music, the thinking goes, then he must still be Christian at heart and the longstanding hope for his Jewish "return" is dashed. If he is a Christian, then he is no longer Jewish; and if he is really a Jew, then how could he be celebrating Christmas so enthusiastically and so publicly? But such thinking misses the essential point regarding Bob Dylan—contrary to all those who seek to label him or to pin him down to a given category, "he's just not there" (to paraphrase the title of the recent Todd Haynes film about Dylan, *I'm Not There*). From the very beginning, Dylan constructed an image as a radical individualist, member of no group, adherent of no faith; instead, he created his own anti-category of neither/nor (reminiscent of comedian Al Franken's *Saturday Night Live* sketch, "Jew/Not a Jew"). As cultural historian

Stephen Whitfield writes: "Adjusting his yarmulke at the Western Wall one year, then claiming to have found Jesus, Dylan never has broken stride, for he seems to know instinctively that here it is possible to be a white Negro, a non-Jewish Jew, a Jew for Jesus, even an observant Jew" (*Voices of Jacob* 68). And he further adds: "He inevitably flummoxed the essentialism long entwined in Jewish identity" (*In Search* 113). By defining himself as a blank slate, however, Dylan inadvertently invited others to project identity onto him, to essentialize the very artist who taught us not to. In the end, Bob Dylan may be said to personify a central paradox of the modern Jewish experience: the further Jews run away from their Jewishness, the more they may be perceived to be particularly "Jewish" after all. In the case of Dylan and so many others, this Gordian knot of assimilation and identity is often revealed by the anxiety it provokes—the anxiety of Jewish influence.

Notes

1. Sections of this article are adapted from a chapter on Bob Dylan in my forthcoming book on American Jewish celebrity in the early 1960s (UPNE). Special thanks to Eric Greene, Josh Kun, and David Schulman for their incisive comments on an early draft.
2. "'32nd Annual Kennedy Center Honors' Salutes Mel Brooks, Dave Brubeck, Grace Bumbry, Robert De Niro and Bruce Springsteen." The speech continued: "Yes! And they abandoned this child, as you can imagine at the time . . . interracial, same sex relationships being what they were . . . they abandoned this baby by the side of the road between the exit interchanges 8A and 9 on the Jersey Turnpike . . . that child was Bruce Springsteen. . . ."
3. On Koenig and others, see for example: Shinefeld 11.
4. There are exceptions of course. See esp. Josh Kun's excellent review of "hidden Jews" in popular music, "Abie the Fishman: On Masks, Birthmarks, and Hunchbacks." Michael Billig's *Rock 'n' Roll Jews*, while a fine survey of the subject, does not move much beyond a cliched statement of outsider status to explain the influence being Jewish might have on American Jewish musicians.
5. Staub has explained to me that he did in fact plan to include an excerpt from Dylan, but had difficulty obtaining the rights.
6. By calling Dylan a "Jew," my intent is not to ascribe Jewishness to him as an essential part of his being, but simply to note that he was born to Jewish parents—this is, after all, the standard definition of Jewish identity according to traditional Judaism (not to mention modern antisemitism). Yet the significance of such descent, and thus the meaning of being a "Jew," is highly contested and has therefore given rise to a vast literature devoted to the problem of "Jewish identity." For further discussion in this context, see my forthcoming book.
7. Bob Dylan symposium, held at the Skirball Cultural Center, Los Angeles CA, 30 March 2008.
8. Though it should be noted, Jewish roots have been claimed for Elvis Presley as well; see: Goldstein and Wallace.
9. In a classic study, sociologist Milton Gordon distinguished between two types of assimilation: "structural" assimilation, referring to the abandonment of one's ethnic community and rejection of ethnic identity; and "cultural" assimilation, referring to the absorption of the majority culture without necessarily abandoning/rejecting one's original culture. Neither Berlin nor Dylan were assimilated Jews in the first sense (that is, neither would have stated, "I am no longer a Jew"); but given the high degree of their cultural assimilation, neither retained any meaningful ties to the Jewish community in structural terms. Thus, although "assimilation" is used here primarily in its cultural sense, synonymous with "acculturation," one does imply some degree of the other. See: Gordon.

10. For extensive information on Dylan bootlegs, see the website *bobsboots.com*.
11. Note: the content of numbers 1–3 is explored in much greater depth in my book chapter.
12. Two pages later he further elaborates: ". . . evidence from his lyrics, his public statements, and some undisputed biographical items add up to a convincing portrait of a mind profoundly shaped by Jewish influence, study, and belief, and a life lived largely as a committed Jew."
13. In later performance, Dylan would delete the verse—perhaps it seemed "too Jewish."
14. A version of the song, recorded on April 25, 1962, is included on the 1991 release "Bob Dylan: The bootleg series, volume 1" (Columbia Records).
15. Dylan is credited in the liner notes for doing a harmonica solo on Belafonte's *Midnight Special* album, produced by RCA in 1961 and released in 1962.
16. Kun follows the spelling of the song title as listed on the bootleg series recording.
17. The phrase "gravity fails" is a line from Dylan's song "Just Like Tom Thumb's Blues," off the album, *Highway 61 Revisited*.
18. The radio show is "Bob Dylan's Theme Time Radio Hour," available on Sirius Satellite Radio; and prior to that, Dylan's career resurgence of the 1990s commenced with two albums of "old-timey" cover songs, *Good As I Been To You* and *World Gone Wrong*. Much of his songwriting since has been steeped in the history of American music, including folk, blues, and country.

Works Cited

"'32nd Annual Kennedy Center Honors' Salutes Mel Brooks, Dave Brubeck, Grace Bumbry, Robert De Niro and Bruce Springsteen." 7 Dec. 2009. <http://www.poptower.com/news-10514/32nd-annual-kennedy-center-honors.htm>.

Belafonte, Harry. *Midnight Special*. RCA, 1962.

Billig, Michael. *Rock 'n' Roll Jews*. Syracuse: Syracuse UP, 2000.

Bloom, James. *Gravity Fails: The Comic Jewish Shaping of Modern America*. Westport, CT: Praeger, 2003.

Bobsboots.com: *The Bob Dylan Bootleg Museum*. 6 Nov. 2010 <http://www.bobsboots.com>.

DeCurtis, Anthony. "Bob Dylan as Songwriter." *The Cambridge Companion to Bob Dylan*. Ed. Kevin Dettmar. New York: Cambridge UP, 2009. 42–54.

Deutscher, Isaac. *The Non-Jewish Jew and Other Essays*. London: Oxford UP, 1968.

Dylan, Bob. "Blowin' in the Wind." *The Freewheelin' Bob Dylan*. Columbia, 1963.

———. *Christmas in the Heart*. Sony, 2009.

———. *Chronicles, Volume I*. New York: Simon & Schuster, 2004.

———. "Desolation Row." *Highway 61 Revisited*. Columbia, 1965.

———. *The Freewheelin' Bob Dylan*. 1962. Columbia, 1963.

———. *Good As I Been To You*. Columbia, 1992.

———. "Gotta Serve Somebody." *Slow Train Coming*. Columbia, 1979.

———. *Infidels*. Columbia, 1983.

———. Interview with Bill Flanagan. *NASNA (North American Street Newspaper Association)* 23 Nov. 2009. <http://bob-dylan-in-peru.blogspot.com/2009/11/christmas-in-heart-interview.html>.

———. "It's Alright, Ma (I'm Only Bleeding)." *Bringing It All Back Home*. Columbia, 1965.

———. "Just Like a Woman." *Blonde on Blonde*. Columbia, 1966.

———. "Just Like Tom Thumb's Blues." *Highway 61 Revisited*. Columbia, 1965.

———. "Knockin' on Heaven's Door." Soundtrack. *Pat Garrett & Billy the Kid*. Columbia, 1973.

———. *Love and Theft*. Columbia, 2001.

———. "Love Minus Zero/No Limit." *Bringing It All Back Home*. Columbia, 1965.

———. "Masters of War." *The Freewheelin' Bob Dylan*. Columbia, 1963.

———. *Shot of Love*. Columbia, 1981.

———. "Stuck Inside Of Mobile with the Memphis Blues Again." *Blonde on Blonde*. Columbia, 1966.

———. "Talkin' Havah Nagilah Blues." 1962. *Bob Dylan: The Bootleg Series, Volume 1*. Columbia, 1991.

———. "Talkin' John Birch Paranoid Blues." *Bob Dylan: The Bootleg Series, Volume 1*. Columbia, 1991.

———. "Tangled Up in Blue." *Blood on the Tracks*. Columbia, 1975.
———. "With God on Our Side." *The Times They are A-Changin'*. Columbia, 1964.
———. *World Gone Wrong*. Columbia, 1993.
Engel, Dave. *Just Like Bob Zimmerman's Blues: Dylan in Minnesota*. Rudolph, WI: River City Memoirs-Mesabi, 1997.
Foreman, Michael. "Bob Dylan and his Musical Roots and Branches." *Eye* 1968.
Franken, Al, perf. "Jew/Not a Jew." *Saturday Night Live*. 8 Oct. 1988.
Glenn, Susan. "In the Blood? Consent, Descent, and the Ironies of Jewish Identity." *Jewish Social Studies* 8.2–3 (Winter/Spring 2002): 139–52.
Goldberg, J. J. "Bob Dylan at 60: 'We Used To Be Young Together'; A Musical Seer Who Disdained Role of Prophet." *Forward* 18 May 2001.
Goldstein, Jonathan and Max Wallace. *Schmelvis: In Search of Elvis Presley's Jewish Roots*. Toronto: ECW, 2002.
Gordon, Milton. *Assimilation in American Life: The Role of Race, Religion, and National Origins*. New York: Oxford UP, 1964.
Gray, M. *The Bob Dylan Encyclopedia*. New York: Continuum, 2006.
Haynes, Todd, dir. *I'm Not There*. Perf. Christian Bale, Cate Blanchett and Heath Ledger. 2007.
Jacobi, Martin. "Bob Dylan and Collaboration." *The Cambridge Companion to Bob Dylan*. Ed. Kevin Dettmar. New York: Cambridge UP, 2009. 68–79.
Kalmar, Ivan. *The Trotskys, Freuds and Woody Allens: Portrait of a Culture*. Toronto: Viking, 1993.
Kun, Josh. "Abie the Fishman: On Masks, Birthmarks, and Hunchbacks." *Listen Again: A Momentary History of Pop Music*. Ed. Eric Weisbard. Durham, NC: Duke UP, 2007. 50–68.
Lennon, John. "God." *Plastic Ono Band*. Capitol, 1970.
Marx Brothers, perf. *Animal Crackers*. Paramount, 1930.
Melnick, Jeffrey. *A Right to Sing the Blues: African Americans, Jews, and American Popular Song*. Cambridge, MA: Harvard UP, 1999.
Renaldo and Clara. Dir. Bob Dylan. Perf. Bob Dylan, Sara Dylan and Joan Baez. Lombard Street Films, 1978.
Riley, Tim. *Hard Rain: A Dylan Commentary*. New York: Da Capo, 1999.
Rogovoy, Seth. *Bob Dylan: Prophet, Mystic, Poet*. New York: Scribners, 2009.
Scaduto, Anthony. *Bob Dylan*. New York: Abacus, 1972.
Schaap, Dick. "I Am My Words." *Newsweek* 4 Nov. 1963.
Shelton, Robert. *No Direction Home: The Life and Music of Bob Dylan*. New York: Da Capo, 1997.
———. "Pop Singers and Song Writers Racing Down Dylan's Road." *New York Times* 27 Aug. 1965; repr. *Bob Dylan: A Retrospective*. Ed. Craig McGregor. New York: Da Capo, 1972.
———. Rev. of Bob Dylan. *New York Times* 29 Sept. 1961.

Sherman, Allan. *My Son, The Celebrity.* Warner Bros., 1962.

———. *My Son, The Folk Singer.* Warner Bros., 1962.

Shinefeld, Mordechai. "Afropoptastic: American Jewish Musicians Entranced by Rhythms From Morocco to South Africa." *Forward* 12 Feb. 2010.

Sloman, Larry. *On the Road With Bob Dylan.* New York: Three Rivers, 1978; repr., 2002.

Sounes, Howard. *Down the Highway: The Life of Bob Dylan.* New York: Grove, 2002.

Spitz, Bob. *Dylan: A Biography.* New York: Norton, 1989.

Staub, Michael, ed. *The Jewish 1960s: An American Sourcebook.* Waltham, MA: Brandeis UP, 2004.

Turner, Gil. "Bob Dylan—A New Voice Singing New Songs." *Sing Out!* Oct.–Nov. 1962; repr. *Bob Dylan: A Retrospective.* Ed. Craig McGregor. New York: Da Capo, 1972.

"The Ventures of Zimmerman." *National Lampoon* Oct. 1972; repr. *Guilt & Pleasure* 6 (Fall 2007): 64–74.

Whitfield, Stephen J. *In Search of American Jewish Culture.* Waltham, MA: Brandeis UP, 2001.

———. *Voices of Jacob, Hands of Esau: Jews in American Life and Thought.* North Haven, CT: Shoe String, 1984.

Yaffe, David. "Bob Dylan and the Anglo-American Tradition." *The Cambridge Companion to Bob Dylan.* Ed. Kevin Dettmar. New York: Cambridge UP, 2009. 15–27.

Yudelson, Larry. "Dylan: Tangled Up in Jews." *Washington Jewish News* 1991.

Negotiating Boundaries: Musical Hybridity in Tzadik's Radical Jewish Culture Series

Jeff Janeczko

[Strangers] are that "third element" which should not be. The true hybrids, the monsters: not just unclassified, but unclassifiable. They therefore do not question this one opposition here and now: they question oppositions as such, the very principle of opposition, the plausibility of dichotomy it suggests. (Bauman 148)

To represent "I'm part American, part Jewish" by music containing Klezmer and Rock influences does no more to deconstruct either "Jewish" or "American" than saying "I'm part Jewish, that's why I'm good with money, but part American, cause I like to party . . . ." It accepts pre-existing hegemonic belief. (Ribot 27)

On New York's Lower East Side in the 1990s, a flurry of musical activity erupted that has had a lasting affect on the nature and content of secular American Jewish music. The venues in which it unfolded were primarily nightclubs like Tonic (a former Jewish winery-cum-nightclub, now closed due to higher rents caused by the area's recent gentrification [Chinen, "Requiem"]) and The Knitting Factory (originally on East Houston Street, then in the Lower Downtown district, and now in Brooklyn). Jews who frequented these venues may have been partially motivated by questions about their own Jewish identities, but mostly they wanted to hear good music—and not just any music. They wanted to hear John Zorn's groundbreaking Masada Quartet riffing on Jewish musical motifs just as jazz greats John Coltrane and Ornette Coleman once riffed on the blues. They wanted to hear clarinetists David Krakauer and Don Byron play as though the continuum of American *klezmorim*[1] had never been broken. Hearing Krakauer and the Klezmatics play klezmer tunes and riffs to an avant-rock accompaniment must have seemed as though the music of klezmer icons Dave Tarras and Naftule Brandwein never faded into obscurity. From a contemporary perspective, artists like Zorn and Krakauer seem like a natural progression emerging from a tradition stretching back to Eastern Europe and the minstrel-like *klezmorim* who traveled Europe playing for Jewish weddings and celebrations, encountering non-Jewish musicians and, without really thinking twice about it, incorporating the sounds they heard into their own music.

The flurry of musical activity described above eventually coalesced into what has generally become known as Radical Jewish Culture. Radical Jewish Culture did not emerge *ex nihilo*, but rather was a kind confluence of two musical streams: one klezmer, the other the downtown avant-garde[2] (Gammel). Though it emerged from these streams, it eventually went beyond them, incorporating not only klezmer and avant-garde music, but also non-Ashkenazi Jewish folk music, Jewish liturgical music, jazz, folk, rock, and a host of other musical genres and traditions. However, the central feature of much of this music was a focus on hybridity—the mixing of various forms, styles, and elements within what is generally considered "Jewish music" with other non-specifically Jewish musical genres. This continuing emphasis on hybridity has remained a relatively stable aspect of Radical Jewish Culture over the past twenty years.

In the epigraphs above, Zygmunt Bauman describes hybrid people and practices as elements that from the perspective of the status quo "should not be," that is, as unclassifiable phenomena which threaten and destabilize distinctions between self and other. Marc Ribot posits a different view of hybridity. From his perspective, hybrid cultural practices can just as easily reproduce "pre-existing hegemonic beliefs" as they can challenge or subvert them. This essay focuses on what we might call the double-edged sword of hybridity these two perspectives represent. My central question is how the hybrid music of Radical Jewish Culture is related to the boundaries that exist around constructs like "Jewish" and "Jewish music," and binary oppositions such as Jewish/non-Jewish. Has this music lived up to its promise of redefining Jewish culture and identity? Or, has the hybridization of Jewish and non-Jewish served to reinscribe boundaries and reinforce binary oppositions. In this essay, my aim is to explore these questions through four musical examples, in conjunction with ethnographic information, from musical recordings released on a recording series devoted to documenting and disseminating this music. First, we can begin by gaining an overview of Radical Jewish Culture, and a discussion of the concept of hybridity.³

RADICAL JEWISH CULTURE

Radical Jewish Culture is the title of a recording series launched in 1995 by avant-garde musician, composer, and impresario John Zorn on his record label, Tzadik (Hebrew: righteous person). The moniker's origins date to 1992 when Zorn was commissioned to curate the Munich Art Projekt, an annual German music festival devoted to new music. Having recently become interested in both his own Jewish identity and the pervasiveness of Jewish musicians active in the New York "downtown scene," Zorn gave the festival a Jewish theme and titled it "Radical New Jewish Culture." The 1992 festival saw the world premier of Zorn's first Jewish-related work, *Kristallnacht*, and featured performances from the likes of Lou Reed, Marc Ribot, God Is My Co-Pilot, Gary Lucas, and Shelley Hirsch, among others. A series of festivals followed in New York, most of which were held at the Knitting Factory. "New" was eventually dropped and these multi-artist performances became known simply as Radical Jewish Culture festivals. Zorn related the phrase's inspiration to author Steven Beeber:

> I'd been reading a book that discussed the JDL [Jewish Defense League, both famous for its "radical," baseball bat-swinging responses to anti-Semitism and infamous for its terrorist attacks], and as much as I deplored their practices and attitudes, there was something about that word *radical* that I liked. I'd been thinking about calling the festival "New Jews" or "New Jewish Music," and Ribot had suggested the ironically comic "Loud and Obnoxious Music." But then I heard that word and I had it—"Radical Jewish Culture." That was it. (Zorn, quoted in Beeber 211, emphasis and bracketed interpolation Beeber's)

What exactly Radical Jewish Culture might mean is an open and ongoing—sometimes contentious—debate. On its website, Tzadik, an organization "dedicated to releasing the best in avant garde and experimental music," describes the series as "Jewish music beyond klezmer: adventurous recordings bringing Jewish identity and culture into the 21st century" (www.tzadik. com). But individuals I consulted during the course of my fieldwork gave varied and divergent responses to questions about its meaning. Some pointed to Jews' historic involvement in leftist politics, labor unions, and the Civil Rights Movement as evidence that Jewish culture had, in some senses, always been radical. Others, like Zorn, conceived it in purely musical terms, associating it with avant-garde and experimental musical practices, or as Jewish music that was innovative, new, and would not be disseminated through more traditionally oriented channels. In this sense, "radical" connotes being at odds with tradition. Some equated radical with the foregrounding of their Jewish identities, with explicitly calling their music Jewish and putting their Jewishness up-front—something few felt comfortable doing prior to Radical Jewish Culture.[4] Others thought Radical Jewish Culture was nothing more than a marketing catch-phrase meant to spur record sales.

The perhaps inevitable controversy over both the phrase and its associated music has not gone unnoticed. To cite one example, *New York Times* critic Adam Shatz has accused Zorn of disingenuously exploiting his Jewish identity, calling his focus on Jewish identity an "atavistic form of identity politics," and his music "little more than radical kitsch" (Shatz). Shatz's criticism took particular aim at the Great Jewish Music sub-series of recordings, which acknowledges and celebrates notable ethnically Jewish composers and songwriters such as Burt Bacharach and Serge Gainsbourgh, "musicians whose Jewish ancestry is incidental, if not irrelevant, to their work." Still, beyond the polemical tone and biased nature of Shatz's editorial, he raises some important and valid points. The ethnically oriented question of whether or not there was an inherent "Jewish" quality to all music made by Jews surfaced in several of my interviews, and Zorn argues this point precisely in his liner notes to the Serge Gainsbourg album. However, in some senses, Shatz's focus on this point misses the forest for the trees. Zorn's *modus operandi* is not to provide simple and comprehensive answers to complex questions. In his view, the artist's job is to raise questions, however complex or uncomfortable they might be.[5]

More than ten years after the series' inception, Zorn published a manifesto on the label's website in which he both explained and defended his impetus behind the project. The following excerpt from that manifesto posits the series as an ongoing dialectic:

> The series is an ongoing project. A challenge posed to adventurous musical thinkers. What is jewish [sic] music? What is its future? If asked to make a contribution to jewish culture, what would you do?

> Can jewish music exist without a connection to klezmer, cantorial or yiddish theatre? All of the cds on the RJC series address these issues through the vision and imagination of individual musical minds. ("Radical Jewish Culture")

He closes the manifesto with a specific reference to the Great Jewish Music series Shatz critiqued:

> The Great Jewish Music series is as much about jewish contribution to world culture . . . as about an exposition of jewish culture. If I had titled the series accordingly perhaps we all would have been spared much of the polemical discussions and arguments—and I might have been spared a few vituperative attacks. But as several good friends have said—"if people are still arguing over these issues after 15 years, you must be doing something right"—and I am content with that.

The music of the Radical Jewish Culture series is not only about the question of what constitutes Jewish music. It is about the nature, meaning, and significance of Jewish identity in the current historical-cultural moment, and about how constructs like Jewish music and Jewish identity are circumscribed, and how they shape and are shaped by the thoughts and actions of those to whom they apply. At this point it is necessary to discuss some research on Radical Jewish Culture that predates or has more or less occurred simultaneously with my own.

In this realm, there are two important works to mention. The first major work to appear on the topic of Radical Jewish Culture was Tamar Barzel's 2004 doctoral dissertation. Based on research carried out in the late 1990s and early 2000s, Barzel's work deals with the emergence of Jewish-identified musical activity in New York's downtown music scene in the late 1980s and early 1990s, artists' coalescence around the Radical Jewish Culture idea, and the eventual fragmentation that occurred due in part to disagreements that arose concerning Radical Jewish Culture's nature and purpose.[6] The "downtown" scene in which Radical Jewish Culture emerged, she points out, was already highly eclectic, and experimentation with different musical genres and traditions was its hallmark. But it was not until the 1980s and early 1990s that "Jewish music" began to appear. Barzel locates the emergence of this music in what she calls "the Radical Jewish Culture idea," essentially the notion that the prevalence of Jewish musicians in this avant-garde and experimental music scene was more than coincidental; that is, that there might be something inherently Jewish in the inclination toward this type of fringe music (2–4). She focuses on how the ethos of the downtown scene was manifested in Radical Jewish Culture projects, how musicians musically addressed issues of race and ethnicity, and how their music related to issues of Jewish and musical identity with respect to lived experience. A key contribution of her work has been to point out that, while Radical Jewish Culture is most often thought of as an extension of the klezmer revival (because of its Jewish focus), ethically and musically it bears a much closer relationship to the "downtown" scene in which it emerged and was nurtured. To be sure, there are overlapping themes in her research and mine, but my dissertation ("'Beyond Klezmer'") focused on two issues largely absent from hers: the construct of Jewish music, and the significance of the kind of hybrid musical practices that are the topic of this essay.

The issue of hybridity, however, is central to the work of Jonathan Freedman, incidentally one of Barzel's dissertation advisors. Freedman's 2008 book, *Klezmer America: Jewishness, Ethnicity, Modernity,* focuses on how American Jews have, over the past several decades, transformed their status from a marginalized other to a model minority, and how in doing so they have challenged and restructured America's dominant black/white conception of race. Freedman discusses more than music in this book, though when he does discuss music he focuses primarily on music from the Radical Jewish Culture domain. But his guiding trope, "klezmer," functions mostly as a metaphor for interpreting how contemporary American Jews have redefined Jewishness and ethnicity. Analyzing examples from theater, literature, and music, Freedman finds a common element in much of the Jewish cultural expression of the late twentieth and early twenty-first centuries: hybridity. He argues that this is neither new nor exceptional, but rather a return to a trope that has been central to and has defined Jewish culture for centuries. The significance of these hybrid cultural forms has, in his view, been revolutionary:

> Precisely by returning to the syncretic, heterogeneous practices that characterized Jewish cultures in the Diaspora from the assimilating project that marked American Jewish culture of the past forty years, klezmer revivalists and postklezmer Radical Jewish Culture makers alike have not only redefined "Jewishness"; they have created *new* configurations from categories (black/white, Jewish/gentile, Western/Eastern) that have long seemed perdurable, fixed. (22, emphasis mine)

From Freedman's perspective, practitioners of Radical Jewish Culture are remaking traditional constructions of Jewishness, race, and "American-ness."

Yet Freedman also views Radical Jewish Culture and post-klezmer music more generally as an intercultural/musical-suturing project. For instance, he points to the work of Radical Jewish Culture artist Steven Bernstein, and similar work by the Klezmatics and the Afro-Semitic Experience, as evidence of "a consistent and sustained attempt to suture these two always already intertwined musical traditions" (87). Freedman's interpretation of these practices is compelling and eloquently argued, but also slightly problematic. I can accept his argument with respect to the Afro-Semitic Experience—their name connotes this and their press materials all but state this outright. But Steven Bernstein had a successful career in jazz before he had any significant involvement in Jewish music. Why should the sudden presence of Jewish signifiers in his music indicate an attempt to "suture" Black and Jewish musical traditions? And even if it does, how are we to read the bulk of his work, in which there are no such Jewish signifiers? I agree that the music of the Radical Jewish Culture series has, via hybridity, transcended and redefined some boundaries. But, following Ribot, I am uncomfortable interpreting this vast range of music in a monolithic or reductionist fashion. In the end, Freedman defines the revolutionizing practice of Radical Jewish Culture as "a move from klezmer beyond klezmer through Jewishness beyond Jewishness to an avant-garde modernity that is shaped by Jewishness but transcends any specific ethnic identification" (92). Again, I think Freedman has keyed into something compelling here but has perhaps over-generalized the phenomenon for the sake of argument. In contrast, the thrust and intent of this essay is to look at Radical Jewish Culture and its musical hybridity as a practice that both refigures *and* reproduces boundaries. But first, the concept of hybridity needs to be considered.

WHAT IS HYBRIDITY?

In this era of intense and rapid globalization, an era in which mixtures and borrowings are quickly becoming the norm rather than the exception, analyzing musical practices through the theoretical lens of hybridity might seem passé. Aren't most musical forms hybridized? American jazz emerged from the combination of European and African musical traditions and practices. Indian *bhangra* combines traditional South Asian music with electronic dance music. Debussy evoked the sounds of Indonesia in some of his music, and Mozart drew upon and imitated Turkish music. One of my favorite new bands, Dub

Trio, hybridizes Jamaican dub and reggae with heavy metal, and I recently attended a concert in which a work for symphony orchestra employed idioms from rap music in its choral sections. Not surprisingly, hybridity seems to be everywhere, especially in music (see Burke 3). In fact, a growing body of literature suggests that hybridity is the norm rather than the exception, a phenomenon common both to our own time and to the past (Burke; Kraidy; Pieterse). This being the case, it makes sense to study hybridity closely. In particular, there are three aspects of hybridity that deserve to be emphasized.

First, hybridity may be common, both in our time and throughout history in the long term but, as Peter Burke suggests, in the short term it happens in fits-and-starts. That is, there are periods of intense hybridization followed by periods of relative stability in which new hybrid forms become normalized (66). I believe that during those periods when hybridity rapidly develops, the processes that spur it on and the resulting hybrid cultural phenomena are experienced as new, different, and at times, threatening and unsettling. For example, consider the ambivalent opinion expressed a recent article by musicologist Marsha Bryan Edelman, in which she both acknowledges the historically hybrid nature of Jewish music, and at the same time expresses discomfort at the current pace at which this is happening:

> Yes, there is an inherent postmodern [read: hybrid] strand in most Jewish music, from synagogue *nusach* [musical style; usually refers to liturgical chant/song] (of all communities) to klezmer jams and Eastern ragas. . . . Klezmer has, indeed, been the province of cross-pollination between Jewish and non-Jewish musicians and cultures, but it was born in a closed, insulated, and incestuous community that was not challenged to accommodate radical changes from outside its familiar home base. There is no reason it should accommodate them now. (131).

Edelman's reaction underscores Burke's assertion that during periods of intense hybridization, "the traditional hybrid culture is defended against the new mix" (66). The musical recordings I discuss in this essay were all created between 1996 and 2003 and are arguably a part of just such a period of intense hybridization in Jewish music that, as Barzel documents, began in the late 1980s. That some greeted them with less than enthusiasm is to be expected.

Second, it is impossible to talk about or engage in musical and cultural hybridity without invoking boundaries. As Bauman reminds us, hybrids are not simply "others"; hybrids are mixtures comprised of multiple parts, each of which comes from a different source and has certain (if variable) signifying properties. To take an obvious example, John Zorn creates Jewish music in a variety of styles and genres. But he distinguishes (and thus draws a boundary around) his Jewish music from his non-Jewish music by employing musical scales historically associated with traditional Jewish liturgical and folk music.[7] This is not a uniform practice among artists associated with the Radical Jewish Culture series. Though they are in the minority, some artists in the series do not define Jewish music in musical terms, nor do they clearly delineate Jewish music and non-Jewish music.[8] The focus of this essay is precisely hybridity's relationship to boundaries, and how it can both transcend and reinforce them. For, as sociologist Jan Nederveen Pieterse points out, "in the end, the real problem is not hybridity—which is common throughout history—but boundaries and the social proclivity to boundary fetishism. . . . The importance of hybridity is that it problematizes boundaries" (220).

Of course, as a term often used to describe a wide variety of practices and phenomena involving mixture, hybridity has its own problems with boundaries. For Burke, "it is a slippery, ambiguous term, at once literal and metaphorical, descriptive and explanatory" (54); while for Marwan Kraidy it is "a concept whose definition is maddeningly elastic, whose analytical value is easily questionable, and whose ideological implications are hotly contested" (3). Kraidy alerts us to the fact that scholars are divided on the concept, "addressing hybridity alternately as a sign of empowerment or as a symptom of dominance" (5). My own view, which I will discuss at length below, is that it can be both, sometimes simultaneously, and to varying degrees. Thus, my third and final point is that hybrid musical practices, like all hybrid cultural practices, are multidimensional. That is, they take various forms and have divergent outcomes.

One of the most influential writers on the empowerment side of the equation has been Homi K. Bhabha, who argues that hybridity engenders a "third space" or in-between space that rejects both sides of binary oppositions:

> Strategies of hybridization reveal an estranging movement in the "authoritative," even authoritarian inscription of the cultural sign. . . . [T]he hybrid strategy or discourse opens up a space of negotiation. . . . Such negotiation is neither assimilation nor collaboration. It makes possible the emergence of an "interstitial" agency that refuses the binary representation of social antagonism. (Bhabha 58)

Lawrence Grossberg cites Bhabha's notion of hybridity as a type of "border existence," not unlike Bauman's conception. Importantly, however,

Grossberg distinguishes between three types of hybridity that are often conflated. Bhabha's "in-between" or third space existence is one. The second, liminality, is transitional and "collapse[s] the geography of the third space into the border itself." And the third, border-crossing, implies "an image of betweenness which does not construct a place or condition of its own other than the mobility, uncertainty and multiplicity of the fact of the constant border-crossing itself" (91–92). Hybridity can also be a means to, and expression of a diasporic identity, which I have explored elsewhere in relation to the Radical Jewish Culture series (Janeczko, "A Tale").

In their recent volume on hybridity and appropriation in Western music, Georgina Born and David Hesmondhalgh point out that academic perspectives on the consequences of musical hybridity have recently undergone a paradigm shift. Once seen as harbingers of inevitable homogenization and the loss of cultural distinctiveness (i.e., dominance), academics have become more sensitized to unique local responses to encroaching globalization. Born and Hesmondhalgh trace this paradigm shift to the early 1990s, and cite the work of George Lipsitz and Mark Slobin as examples of a shift to sub-cultural perspectives on hybrid musical practices. From a sub-cultural perspective, hybridity is a mode of opposition to the dominant cultural order (i.e., empowerment). Following Slobin and Lipsitz, Born and Hesmondhalgh argue for an interpretive model that recognizes the agency of the less powerful without assuming the dominating power of Western culture *a priori*. At the same time, they are reticent to grant musical hybridity, and those who practice it, too much subversive power:

> [I]n their desire to read these hybrid musics as embodiments of a new and effective cultural politics from the margins, as productive ways of "writing back" against the center, Lipsitz and Slobin perhaps overstate the relative cultural power and visibility of these musics, and neglect [to interrogate] the extent to which they are structured by an increasingly global and flexible industrial complex. (27)

It may be tempting to read this statement as a wholesale negation of hybridity's empowering, "third space" potential. But in positing this critique, the authors are not denying that music has subversive power, they are simply pointing out that such practices are not inherently subversive. As Christopher Waterman has observed in his study of Nigerian *jùjú*: "syncretic modes of expression may in fact uphold hegemonic ideological patterns" (9). Hybrid musical practices are influenced by a multitude of forces, be they the global marketplace, dominant cultural narratives, or the ethos of particular scenes. Mixing up the cultural order does not necessarily turn it on its head.

This argument has also been made by Ribot, a guitarist and bandleader who not only has contributed to the Radical Jewish Culture series, but also worked with Zorn on the 1992 Munich Art Projekt. In Ribot's opinion, a good deal of the so-called Radical Jewish music produced during this period of intense hybridization under our scrutiny shares a common feature: "... all [of it] followed a basic paradigm of creating a dichotomy between contemporary and Jewish with klezmer scales and gestures signifying Jewish." This is a problem for him, since relying on klezmer idioms and other traditional Jewish musical materials to represent the Jewish portion of the dichotomy occludes a more nuanced and elastic understanding of the concept of Jewish music, and therefore, Jewish identity. Like Waterman, he also argues that hybridity can uphold dominant ideologies:

> [While] contemporary postmodern critical concepts like "hybridity" and "multiple identity"... are fine in themselves, the idea that identity is complex can also be used to avoid looking at the construction of its component parts. A claim to embody a dichotomy may avoid the question of how these elements became constructed as dichotomous, or how the meaning of each was constructed, or how the elements are placed relative to one another on a grid of social power.

What I am arguing for here is a similarly nuanced perspective on hybridity that accounts for the complex relationship between hybrid musical practices and the boundaries upon which they depend. Hybridity can obscure and maybe erase musical and social boundaries, but it can also reproduce them. Or, as Evan Rapport has shown, they can do both simultaneously.

A Final Caveat: Most studies of hybridity focus primarily on globalization. That is, they examine hybrid cultural practices in contexts where a less powerful, developing nation or culture is adapting to encroaching forces of globalization over which it has little control, and how members of the dominating culture appropriate and represent aspects of the less powerful culture. This is clearly not the intent of this essay, as my focus is on a select few artists who belong to the Western world and are by-and-large not actively appropriating a less powerful foreign culture (though purists might argue they are appropriating traditional Jewish culture). Nonetheless, they still exist in a world largely defined by binary oppositions, where certain definitions of Jewish music, culture, and identity are more accepted than others; and where hybrid music branded as Jewish must vie for legitimation in a field of cultural production (Bourdieu).

THE MUSICAL EXAMPLES*

I. Jazzing Up the Liturgy: "We gotta do this."

When John Zorn asked Ben Perowsky to record an album for the Radical Jewish Culture series, Perowsky didn't give it much thought. As a professional jazz drummer and arranger, he was busy with a demanding performing and recording schedule and, feeling somewhat ambivalent about his Jewish identity, was a bit uncomfortable with the idea of making a Jewish record. Reflecting on the moment in 2007, he recalled: "I just thought: 'I wouldn't know what to do for that' [i.e., making a Jewish record]. And I was busy doing other things. So, it wasn't like I was saying I wouldn't do it. . . . I just didn't have an idea." Some time later, while traveling to a gig by train with pianist Uri Caine, the two discovered that they both attended Jewish summer camp as children and had learned many of the same songs. The trio arrived at the venue, set up their gear, and ran a sound check. Perowsky recalls:

> We went to the sound check and in the middle of some tune, [pianist] Uri [Caine] started playing one of those [summer camp] melodies. It was so funny. So, we started playing these [different] versions of those songs. And [bassist] Drew [Gress] didn't know what the fuck we were doing, but he was playing along and sounded great. We were at a café later, and I was like, "We gotta do this. Zorn wants me to do a [Jewish] record. This is the record."

The album that emerged from that serendipitous moment, appropriately titled *Camp Songs,* is Perowsky's only release on the Radical Jewish Culture series (though he has performed on other recordings). The songs Perowsky

---

* The musical descriptions I offer in this section are meant to give readers unfamiliar with these recordings a sense of what they sound like and the perspective I am coming from in my analyses. While they suffice for this purpose, they fall far short of doing justice to the music. Readers are encouraged to consult the recordings, excerpts of which are available on the Casden Institute's website at: http://casdeninstitute.usc.edu/annual.

learned at summer camp and included on *Camp Songs* were mostly prayer melodies from the Sabbath liturgy (e.g., "Adon Olam," "Yigdal," "Shema"). The musical approach involved adapting the melodies from those pieces into themes ("heads," in jazz parlance) for instrumental jazz performances. The use of traditional Jewish melodies for jazz performance is common on the Radical Jewish Culture series, and jazz influences could be detected in over half of the albums available at the time my research concluded.[9]

As rendered by Perowsky's trio, "Adon Olam" opens with a short introduction of simple, strummed guitar chords and a straightforward bass and drums pattern. After the short introduction, a statement of the "Adon Olam" theme follows. Played on the upright bass, bowed rather than plucked, the melody is presented in a clear and straightforward manner. This initial statement of the melody consists of eight measures and follows a simple rhythmic pattern. The bass and drums maintain a basic swing feel and walking tempo, and bassist Drew Gress offers a fairly strict interpretation of the minor-key theme. A second statement of the theme follows, this time played on the piano by the accomplished Uri Caine. Caine plays the melody virtually unharmonized, save for a couple of carefully placed accent chords toward the end of the last phrase.

Once the statement of the theme has been accomplished, the band proceeds into a series of improvisations over the established harmonic framework. They are improvisations validly read as deconstructive. Caine's piano lines are heavily ornamented with dissonance and chromaticism. In contrast to the head, here he achieves a very forceful swing feel as the rhythm section maintains the rhythmic and harmonic framework. A short bass solo follows, and the piano lays out as Gress plucks a series of melodies over two repetitions of the chord progression. The drums and guitar keep a simple, understated accompaniment, but effectively infuse a dynamic interplay to convey the phrasing. Caine returns with another piano solo, this one more densely harmonized and chromatic than the one before. The rhythm is freer here, too. At times, Caine's rubato (rhythmic freedom or variance) is so strong that it seems to work against the rhythm section. The solo lasts for six cycles of the chord progression, growing in intensity with each repetition. After the fourth, Caine begins to play fragments of the original theme, as if to suggest a recapitulation is on the horizon (as would normally happen in a conventional jazz performance). This never comes to fruition. Rather, Caine subtly brings back more and more fragments of the original theme as he cycles through the last two progressions, creating what amounts to a false recapitulation. The performance ends with a densely harmonized fragment from the end of the main theme and an ascending flourish of notes.

There is a strong stylistic consistency on *Camp Songs,* and "Adon Olam" is fairly representative of the album as a whole. Unlike many Radical Jewish Culture albums, there is very little stark juxtaposition of styles within or between the individual tracks. As with the majority of the album's performances, "Adon Olam" follows the standard jazz form of head—improvisations—recapitulation, and the album is firmly rooted in a traditional jazz aesthetic. When I noted this observation during my interview with Perowsky, he confirmed this. Before I even formulated my analysis into question-form, he answered, "Yeah, this is decidedly a jazz record."

As a genre, jazz is particularly well-suited to this type of iconic deconstruction. Its foundation in improvising on pre-existing or borrowed themes makes it a natural fit for this. Read iconically, this performance is a commentary, with the "Adon Olam" theme serving as the Jewish component of the hybrid and jazz as the medium through which the commentary is presented. We may come away from it thinking a bit differently about this particular piece (no doubt having enjoyed the stellar performance), but "Adon Olam" has not been irreversibly transformed. Nor, for that matter, has our understanding of jazz; which may be why jazz critic Nat Chinen observed: "Though released under John Zorn's Radical Jewish Culture banner, *Camp Songs* is less radical than reasonable: It underscores an affinity that always lurked beneath the surface." This rendition of "Adon Olam" is one part Jewish and one part jazz; the Jewish part gets played with a bit, but not redefined. So while hybridity has served the purpose of commentary, the dichotomy between the two entities has been preserved, reproduced.

From this perspective, "Adon Olam" represents a hybrid form that reinforces boundaries more than it crosses them. Recalling Grossberg's three varieties of hybridity, "Adon Olam" is neither a "third space" in which authority has been restructured, nor a "border-crossing." It most closely aligns with his notion of "liminality." "Adon Olam" lives *on* the border, even if it succeeds in deconstructing one side of it a bit.

II. Yiddishe Blues: "I don't feel these kinds of polka-mazurka, Eastern European things"

If there is one artist in the Radical Jewish Culture series that stands apart from the others, that artist is Wolf Krakowski. For starters, Krakowski has a particularly unique personal history. Born in a displaced-persons camp in Austria just after the Second World War, Krakowski grew up in a rough, working-class Toronto neighborhood, endured a brief stint in the circus, and spent a good deal of his early adult life traveling the United States on a shoestring before settling in his current home in Northampton, Massachusetts. He is one of very few artists in the series whose albums consist entirely of previously composed material. And, unlike most other series artists, Krakowski has no formal musical education—a fact he takes pride in. Finally, Krakowski has no connection to either the Jewish or downtown music scenes of New York, and John Zorn never asked him to record an album for the Radical Jewish Culture series. As Krakowski relates the story, he approached Zorn about releasing his independently recorded and produced album, *Transmigrations: Gilgul*, three separate times over the course of five years. Zorn rebuffed the first two requests but relented on the third.[10] Tzadik released the aforementioned album in 2001 and a second, *Goyrl: Destiny*, in 2002.

Krakowski's music has engendered some colorful descriptions. Tzadik describes it as "A unique fusion of traditional Yiddish song with country blues, rock, and reggae" and refers to Krakowski as "a Kerouac-inspired cult hero." Critics have variously described Krakowski's Radical Jewish Culture recordings as "[a] highly personal, striking modern idiom that successfully blends blues, R&B, folk-rock, country-rock, and more" (Review of *Goyrl: Destiny*); "*Fiddler on the Roof* laced with Bob Dylan, or *Yentl* as done by Leonard Cohen" (Rogovoy); and "the real Yiddishe Blues" (Review of *Transmigrations: Gilgul*). Krakowski refers to his music somewhat reluctantly as Yiddish world-beat, and relates that his intention behind these albums—which he feels he was destined to record—was to make a twofold statement: (1) that Jewish and American musical styles could by fused in a serious, artful way; and (2) in keeping with Tzadik's mantra, that Jewish music encompasses more than Eastern European-derived klezmer music. Speaking about *Transmigrations: Gilgul* in 2007, Krakowski noted:

> [T]here are musical cultures represented there that were never really fused—at least not seriously—with Yiddish and Jewish music. If

it ever happened, it usually happened as parody. And I actually did have an experience with that, and that in fact galvanized me to make *Transmigrations*. Because I saw someone perform essentially a parody, where he, accompanied by a band, brought together something Jewish with something black, blues. But it was done in a way that was a total send-up parody. I was in the audience, and I basically said, "Why is it that when these two cultures are brought together, why does it have to be a freakin' joke? Why?" I had already been around a little bit at that time. I'd been with black people. Why is this a joke? I just didn't accept that—that when these two cultures met it had to be a joke.

Contrary to what he observed at the aforementioned event, Krakowski finds a natural affinity between certain genres of (mostly African American-derived) American music and the Yiddish language in which his material was written: "There's something about American style that lends itself, I think very naturally, to Yiddish language. Rock and blues and country—these things carry Yiddish language very well." More to the point, Krakowski feels a certain dissonance between his individual identity and the music that for a time had become the *sine qua non* of contemporary secular Jewish music, klezmer. He explained:

> I knew I wanted to express myself, but I don't feel these kinds of polka-mazurka, Eastern European things. This is not the kind of stuff I gravitate to. I like Howlin' Wolf. I like Slim Harpo. I like Lead Belly. I like Hank Williams and this sort of thing. I didn't see why, if you were going to make a Jewish record, you were limited to klezmer, Eastern European music, and to clarinet, violin, and accordion. . . . There are a lot more colors in the palette.

Determined to avoid the musical gestures and instrumental timbres that characterize much Eastern European Jewish music, Krakowski went for what to him seemed more natural.

"Tate-mame," the opening performance on *Goyrl: Destiny*, tells a story of regret. The song's protagonist is a young person who longs for the safety and comfort of home and family and for the innocence of childhood, who questions life's struggles and laments the illusiveness of happiness. Following a short introductory flourish on the guitar, Krakowski jumps into the first verse abruptly. He sings the lyrics in their original Yiddish—Krakowski's first language—with a dry, Dylanesque timbre and restrained delivery, an aesthetic he maintains throughout the performance. Accompanying the simple strummed guitar chords and plaintive vocal line are a guitar, bass, and drums/percussion trio. While the drum and bass are slow and solid with slight syncopations, the guitar plays more freely. Its timbre is rich with reverb, and the chords and melodies are heavily ornamented with vibrato and bends. Short, dramatic guitar solos interject between the verses and choruses, offering a responsorial to the lead vocal part.

Setting aside the clever comparisons and descriptions, professional critics and educated listeners have taken Krakowski's music quite seriously.

For klezmershack.com contributor Mordechai Kamel, Krakowski's fusion of Yiddish song and American vernacular musical styles seems completely natural:

> What touched me, and in a way compelled me to write was, in fact, the rightness and naturalness of the CD. Krakowski is not only a musician deeply rooted in Yiddish, he understands the culture we lost in a way that few if any of the other modern Yiddish singers do. He sings the folk tunes and theater tunes with an understanding of "Before" that seems totally natural. It is important to say at this point that this is not a dry recycling of prewar material or stylings, but a complete *integration* of his Yiddish roots with his North American upbringing. [Emphasis mine.]

Shortly after *Transmigrations: Gilgul*'s 1996 release, Ari Davidow—owner and manager of klezmershack.com, moderator of the Jewish music listserv, and, by virtue of this, one of the more visible critics in the Jewish music world—published a review on klezmershack.com. While somewhat respectful, the review was unfavorable and questioned Krakowski's authenticity:

> I would be more excited [about *Transmigrations: Gilgul*], except that I am listening to this album after seeing Adrienne Cooper with the Flying Bulgars doing new Yiddish poetry to new klez/jazz/Afro-Carribean melodies. While Krakowski's album memorializes a one-sided perspective of a world that is now gone. And, although there is no rational reason why the existence of one should negate the other, I have problems thinking of this pleasant album as breaking new territory, and I find myself reacting as though Krakowski has changed some external trappings, but is presenting the same old one-sided view of Jewish culture in Europe before the war.
>
> . . . My problem is not with the music, which is okay, certainly not unpleasant, and occasionally delightful. It is with the essence of yet another album that, in my eyes, appears to romanticize, almost to

> appear nostalgic for, Jewish pain and longing, as though being victims (as individuals as well as a people) defined or defines Jewish existence. I further object to the presentation of such sentiments in a new skin as though that will speak to the memory of what was, or as if it represents something new, and especially, as if it represents something real. That is a dangerous, and, I believe, untrue place to live. ("Wolf Krakowski Transmigrations")

It is worth noting that this excerpt does not come from Davidow's original review. Krakowski felt that one was unfair and uninformed, and successfully lobbied to have it revised.

How are we to reconcile these divergent points of view? My concern is not that one person likes the music and the other does not, but rather with how passionately each person expresses his opinion. Kamel elevates Krakowski to the status of cultural hero while Davidow practically vilifies him. As this radical difference of opinion so clearly demonstrates, no music is uniformly received. There is no way to qualify these responses as correct or incorrect, nor is it desirable even to attempt to do so. But it does seem appropriate to explore these responses as articulations of each individual's relationship to Jewish culture and history.

Davidow's issue is not with the music's hybridity. He mentions how excited he was by the Yiddish-klezmer-jazz-Afro-Carribean hybrid he had just experienced. Yet, when hears Krakowski's music, he is unable to hear it as new, real, or true, and even objects to its purporting to be so. On the other hand, Krakowski's reworking of the material effects in Kamel an unflinching and beautifully authentic representation of "Before." Clearly, Kamel is not referring to historical authenticity. Krakowski's music bears little if any stylistic resemblance to inter-war Yiddish music. The authenticity Kamel is invoking is more artistic and personal, more in the sense of truth—and hence diametrically opposed to Davidow's reaction. For Davidow, Krakowski's music is ideological. That is, it presents itself as new while reinforcing what he sees as a hegemonic narrative. In contrast, for Kamel, Krakowski's music engenders a kind of third space that looks back on the pre-Holocaust lost world with 20/20 hindsight. It therefore follows that conceptions of history influence perceptions of the present and projections of the future.

It is this quality of "third-spaceness" that I think is the key to both the success of Krakowski's music and the source of Davidow's consternation. Commenting upon the ease with which the music came together and the albums were made, Krakowski sees them as reflections and manifestations of his life experiences: "This is who I am. It's not like I went out and made a study. This is who I am. It's not only who I am, but it's very real to me. It's not something I'm stepping into and doing for now. It's an accumulation, and representative of all the mileage." For Krakowski, then, the "real Yiddishe Blues" reflects the successful and natural hybridization of his inherited tradition and cultural identity with his individual and musical identity. The music succeeds precisely because it doesn't try to. It succeeds because is it an honest and heartfelt reflection of its creator's individual relationship to Jewish culture and history, a reflection that resonated strongly for Kamel. But it falls short for Davidow because it represents a view at odds with his own history. Hybrids that break down boundaries and challenge dichotomies threaten those who live by them; they call into question the notion that Jewish music, culture, or identity can be neatly or singularly defined.

III. Cantorial Death Metal: "... as long as there's a Jewish motive in the music"

If you have never heard the music of the Israeli-born, London-based Koby Israelite, just imagine a reality television show where several musicians of divergent tastes are forced to live and play together. Hoping for a huge ratings spike, the producers decide to pair up a speed metal band with a classical violinist, a cantor, and an accordion player. Then, they invite a host of the other contestants to sit in: a trumpeter, a clarinetist, maybe a jazz bassist. The producers, and probably most of the viewing public, expect a disaster of historical proportions. Instead, the combination proves a success and the group winds up winning the million-dollar record deal offered as the grand prize.

Hearing Koby Israelite's music can be a baffling experience. Tzadik's description of the album I discuss here draws comparisons to Frank Zappa and the Northern Californian experimental band, Mr. Bungle, and, seemingly at a loss for words, offers "Cantorial Death Metal, Nino Rota Klezmer, Balkan Surf, Catskills free improvisation," and concludes, "You've never heard such sounds" (www.tzadik.com). Israelite has released three albums on the Radical Jewish Culture series: *Dance of the Idiots* (2003), *Mood Swings* (2005), and *Is He Listening?* (2009).

"If That Makes Any Sense," from *Dance of the Idiots*, begins with slow, droning chords played on an accordion, and a deep, cantorial voice singing over top. The accordion plays a simple tonic–dominant chord progression, while the vocalist sings florid, improvisatory melismas, that is, a musical style that bridges and blends multiple musical tones across single syllables. This introduction lasts just over a minute, before abruptly segueing to a fast heavy metal section. Here, electric guitars play chunky, syncopated riffs over a driving drumbeat. The cantorial vocals return periodically throughout the performance, superimposed on the heavy metal pattern and interspersed with guitar and accordion solos. Israelite even inserts a classical-style piano and strings section at one point, but immediately returns to the heavy metal idiom to end the song.

In a 2003 interview with *Zeek* magazine, Israelite related how he became involved with the Radical Jewish Culture series:

> I always loved and respected [Tzadik owner and producer] John Zorn, so I sent him some demos of mine and one of the tracks had kind of a Jewish motive to it. He replied that if I wanted to release an album under the Jewish series, I should give him a ring. I was really happy but I freaked out because I never associated that strongly with Jewish music. I took the challenge with reassurance from Zorn that I can do whatever the fuck I want. I can go as crazy as I like, as long as there's a Jewish motive in the music. (Israelite, quoted in Roth)

In the sense that Koby Israelite utilizes a range of musical genres and styles, his musical orientation aligns most closely with other series artists I have elsewhere classified as "experimental" (see "'Beyond Klezmer'"). These artists often approach hybridity by starkly juxtaposing and superimposing different musical styles. But unlike most of those artists, atonality, extreme timbral experimentation, and free-improvisation do not figure prominently in Israelite's music. Israelite draws on a wide palette of musical styles, combining klezmer, Balkan, cantorial, and Middle Eastern melodies and rhythms with Western rock, metal, jazz, and classical idioms. But he does so in an unpredictable, often cut-and-paste-like manner, making it difficult to anticipate what might happen from one moment or track to the next. The most apposite analogy to the visual arts would be collage, where disparate, often seemingly unrelated, elements are juxtaposed or superimposed with no attempt to blend the boundaries between them.

Ari Davidow, whose lukewarm reaction to Wolf Krakowski I discussed in the previous section, takes quite a different view of Israelite's music. His review of *Dance of the Idiots,* avers, "Israelite creates not a new unified style, but instead a hip-hop pastiche of Jewish identity and incredible music." His response to the song "If That Makes Any Sense" is that it "makes much sense."

And he argues that, "Israel [sic] is staking a claim to the vast territory that defines 'Jewish,' or at least his musical world, some of which includes 'Jewish,' whatever that means." Finally, commenting on the album's brazen hybridity, he opines, "It is rare that this sort of mixture works. Here it does. The mixture of genres, of sacred and profane, from heavy metal to nusakh [cantorial art] shouldn't work, but it does, and the more one listens the deeper one goes" (Review of *Dance of the Idiots*).

Zeek magazine contributor and poet/author Matthue Roth shares Davidow's laudatory opinion of the album:

> Some of the tracks sound dangerously similar to that band that you begged your parents not to play at your Bar Mitzvah. The first song, "Saints and Dates," is a straightforward klezmer groove. But, by the third song ["If That Makes Any Sense"], when a straight-out-of-Detroit fuzz-guitar starts riffing over Marcel Mamaliga's violin and Koby singing the wordless melodies of Hasidic nigguns [i.e., wordless melodies which, in Hassidic tradition, are sung to induce an ecstatic spiritual experience], we realize that we are in the midst of something completely new.
>
> *Dance of the Idiots* is half a Sunday-morning brunch album and half a Saturday-night slam-your-friends-against-the-wall-dancing record. Sometimes, during the clarinet-and-accordion breakbeat groove of "Dance of the Idiots," it's both at once."

It is clear that both Roth and Davidow are moved by Israelite's music. But their discourse also suggests that they are hearing it as a jumbled mixture of divergent elements rather than an integrated whole (e.g., "half a Sunday-morning brunch album and half a Saturday-night slam-your-friends-against-the-wall-dancing record"; "not a new unified style, but instead a hip-hop pastiche of Jewish identity and incredible music"). Israelite's music, compelling and exciting as it is, seems to highlight rather than blur boundaries. By juxtaposing and superimposing Jewish motives over a pastiche-like musical framework, "Jewish" becomes one ingredient in a multi-musical stew rather than a musical melting pot in which the various elements have been blended into something new. Such juxtaposition and superimposition might complicate fixed notions of Jewishness, but it doesn't seem to have done so for Roth or Davidow. Rather, it seems to reflect their own conceptions of a modern American Jewish identity informed by (and accepting of) distinctions between Jewish and non-Jewish. It "makes sense" because, for all of its juxtaposition, it doesn't confuse anything.

After all, both pointed out which aspects of the music represented "Jewish" and which did not. Following Bhabha, Israelite's music represents a kind of "in-between-ness" that revels in difference, but its in-between-ness is dependent upon boundaries, which are so prevalent in the music. It evokes Grossberg's notion of a permanent liminality that collapses its "third space" potential and lives *on* the border rather than in spite of it.

IV. Avant-klez: "That's not my music!"

Given John Zorn's position as the curator of the Radical Jewish Series and his standing in the music world, it is easy to think of him as the godfather of Radical Jewish Culture. But while the extent of his influence and his role in furthering the cause should not be underestimated, the historical record suggests that Zorn was simply caught up in a *zeitgeist* already underway.[11] For example, artists like the Naftule's Dream ensemble and Andy Statman, began experimenting with klezmer/Jewish and avant-garde/experimental hybrids as early as the mid-1980s, not to mention Don Byron's work, which also predates the 1992 Munich Art Projekt and subsequent establishment of the Radical Jewish Culture series.[12] As a powerful figure in the world of music and the owner of a record label, Zorn had the clout and the infrastructure to give this new approach to Jewish music a global voice that could not be ignored. But in the estimation of Glenn Dickson, founder and leader of the Boston-based Naftule's Dream, the Radical Jewish Culture phenomenon was destiny: "As someone who was doing it before [Zorn] even started his thing, to me it was going to happen either way. This whole thing was going to happen. This music was going to happen."[13]

A five-piece ensemble consisting of clarinet, guitar, tuba, piano/accordion, and drum set (previously trombone as well), Naftule's Dream is the alter ego of the more conservative Shirim Klezmer Orchestra. And, like a significant number of the ensembles and projects on the Radical Jewish Culture series, its roots lie in Boston's New England Conservatory.[14] It was here that Dickson first heard and played klezmer music as a member of Hankus Netsky's Klezmer Conservatory Band, and decided to found the Shirim Klezmer Orchestra.

The difference between the two ensembles is purely musical, since the personnel for each group is identical. On the one hand, the Shirim Klezmer Orchestra plays more traditionally oriented material in a more conservative style, while, on the other, Naftule's Dream plays more original music in a more experimental style. Naftule's Dream has three recordings on the Radical Jewish Culture series (*Search for the Golden Dreydl*, 1997; *Smash, Clap!*, 1998; and *Job* 2001; plus *Pincus and the Pig*, a klezmer-style Jewish adaptation of Serge Prokofiev's children's suite, *Peter and the Wolf*, performed by the Shirim Klezmer Orchestra), but their aggregate recorded output comprises significantly more. Dickson discussed the need for two ensembles in a 2007 interview:

> [F]or quite a while we were just doing traditional tunes, sort of in the same mold as the Klezmer Conservatory Band—Yiddish theater and traditional klezmer music. And then, eventually, some time in the late eighties— probably '86 or '87—I started writing tunes, just because it seemed like a fun thing to do. . . . I was trying to do something more developed. And then in the late 80s and going into the early 90s I was doing more and more of that and arranging traditional folk tunes in very different ways. And a lot of that's on the *Naftule's Dream* album [by Shirim]. There are a lot of traditional tunes that I just wrote in more expansive ways. The arrangements just open up and go in different places. And that was the point that we really started having problems with the audiences, because the people who wanted to hear just traditional stuff, who were there for nostalgic reasons, basically, it was upsetting them . . . that we were messing with things. . . . Literally, we would have old folks come up to the stage while we were playing or in between songs yelling "That's not my music!"

Naftule's Dream incorporates klezmer scales and gestures into a musical framework informed by avant-garde jazz, and rock and metal music. "Free Klez 1 & 2" and "Free Klez 3 & 4" come from their 1998 release, *Smash, Clap!* "Free Klez 1 & 2" begins with a complex additive rhythm built on unpredictable beat groupings of two and three. The drummer accents the stressed beats with the kick-drum and tambourine, filling in the non-stressed pulses on the hi-hat. The clarinet, tuba, and accordion play a harmonized, angular melody that grows progressively more dissonant until it reaches its peak around thirty-five seconds into the track. The band abruptly transitions to a long improvised section that begins with a virtuosic, unaccompanied clarinet solo and progresses to a full-band free improvisation. The band eventually settles into a regular groove in which the tuba plays a repeating pattern while the other instruments improvise quasi-freely. Their parts become increasingly intense and erratic until the piece ends abruptly.

"Free Klez 3 & 4" follows a similar structure, beginning with a strong rhythmic theme and moving into an unmetered collective improvisation. Here, the clarinet and accordion improvise high-pitched, dissonant lines, eventually giving way to a guitar, tuba, and drum collective improvisation before the opening theme returns. Another unmetered, collective improvisation follows, replete with dissonances and ambient, unmetered percussion. This improvisation lasts nearly five minutes and the performance ends with a slow fade-out.

On the surface, the music of Naftule's Dream bears some resemblance to that of Koby Israelite (e.g., the experimental nature of the music, the incorporation of rock and metal influences). But while it is thoroughly hybrid, it lacks the pastiche, cut-and-paste quality that is so prevalent in Israelite's music. As noted by Davidow, Naftule's Dream stands apart from other artists on the Radical Jewish Culture series:

> Where many of the musicians recording for John Zorn's "Radical Jewish Culture" label are using the recordings as a place to explore what "Jewish" means, or might mean for them, looking inward. This does not appear to be Naftule's Dream's dream. Rather, having explored Yiddish culture and klezmer, they are looking out to see where it leads them.
>
> In this sense, the music is far more connected to the specific worlds of experimental music than many of the label's other recordings, and especially true to the sense of creating new music grounded in "Jewish" (whatever that means). Of course, if we follow that thought, we find ourselves right back at the "Haskalah," the age of Jewish enlightenment and the furor of experimentation created by Jewish creativity breaking beyond the pale. It's a fascinating turn of thought, and the sort of fascinating turn of thought that one feels whilst engrossed in music as involving and exciting as "Free Klez," or the urgency of "Speed Klez."
>
> That particular flowering was destroyed . . . But here's the thing about this particular dialogue and outpouring of passion and creative exploration of the avant-garde. It's [the *haskala*] back, and one listen to "Smash, Clap!" will make it clear why it couldn't be suppressed. (Review of *Smash, Clap!*)

In a laudatory and very colorful review, *Jazziz* critic Howard Mandel compared the group to the only Yiddish-language author to ever receive the Nobel Prize for literature, Isaac Bashevis Singer:

> Forsaking not the aromas of Sabbath breads and wine, embracing as well raucous laughter, delicate, quasi-minimalist vamps, and spectacular, horrifying blowouts, Naftule's Dream has a range actually akin to the late Yiddish writer I. B. Singer's . . . Singer's readers, and [early twentieth-century American klezmer clarinetist/composer] Naftule Brandwein's fans, too, knew that the old Jewish life was not one to pine for. Naftule's Dream plays so that the keen truths sounded in early Jewish American jazz are much more than mere nostalgic sighs for time that never was. (70)

I cite these reviews at such length to illustrate a point, one that allows me re-enter an important dialogue that we began in the opening pages of this essay. Both critics make reference to the music's hybrid quality, and both also place the band in a particular historical continuum. This brings us to a point where Freedman's view of Jewish hybrid cultural practices resonates forcefully. Of particular relevance is his notion that practitioners of Radical Jewish Culture have paved paths toward the future by returning to the hybrid past, have opened up new hybrid spaces by engaging old ones, and have created *new* hybrid categories out of existing monolithic ones. A view toward the future, accomplished in the present through looking to the past, provides a fresh perspective on history, which in turn influences perspectives on the present and future. Recalling Grossberg, this is neither a liminal, transitional space, nor border crossing for the sake of border crossing. In the music of Naftule's Dream, we can see (and hear) the traces of a true third space—one that lives *in spite of* the border rather than because of it, and exists in productive tension with the forces between which it lives.

CONCLUSION

In this essay, I have examined four fairly disparate musical examples loosely tied together by both their Jewish focus and their hybrid nature. My aim has been to show that hybrid cultural practices are not one-way streets to strangeness and subversiveness, but can also have an ideological dimension. Boundary crossing is risky business, not only because of the consequences, but also because boundaries themselves are tricky. We tend to think of them as fixed, but in reality it seems more likely that they are malleable and contextually defined. This might be why hybridity can be so effective at both problematizing and reifying them. Regardless of their orientation, hybrid cultural practices put boundaries in a new context. Ethnomusicologist Sarah Weiss argues that hybridity is always political, because, "the highlighting of cultural mixture . . . situates issues of authenticity, ownership, purity, difference, and power as unavoidable filters through which people of any culture process the aesthetic impact of the production" (209). The next logical step, one that Weiss takes as well, is that the success of a musical hybrid can be judged based on the degree to which it mediates these different filters.

What I am arguing here is that music that starkly juxtaposes different genres or cultural traditions, such as that by Perowsky and Israelite, highlights these "filters" more than it mediates them; whereas music that more fully integrates the different elements, such as that of Krakowski and Naftule's Dream, is more successful at mediating them. Music that lives in spite of borders rather than because of them can create the alternate spaces that are crucial to reimagining and remaking identities and the boundaries that circumscribe them. Some scholars (Kraidy; Weiss) have followed M. Bakhtin in distinguishing between "natural" and "intentional" hybrid cultural forms. In this perspective, natural hybrids emerge over time and are more likely to lead to distinctly new genres, whereas intentional hybrids are more dependent upon the highlighting of difference. In Kraidy's view, this latter approach "increases the possibility that it will become a process of othering" (152). So, does that mean that the intentional hybrids I've discussed here, Perowsky and Israelite, represent a kind of "othering" of the self or some sort of "exoticization" of Jewishness? Do natural hybrids represent empowerment and intentional hybrids domination?

In line with my contention that hybrid musical and cultural forms are neither *con*ceived nor *re*ceived unilaterally, I am uncomfortable making such an assertion. My intention here has not been to accuse Perowsky or Israelite of exoticizing Jewishness. However, I do think that the ethnographic evidence suggests that they are working with conceptions of Jewishness rooted in binary oppositions, and that these binary oppositions are present in their music. More broadly, as much as my research consultants expounded the view that Jewishness was flexible and multi-dimensional, they also often spoke it about in terms of dichotomies.

Pieterse points out that hybridity is important because it problematizes boundaries. But it seems reasonable, then, that some hybrid forms accomplish this more effectively than others. I believe that we live in a gray world, one so confounding that we are constantly trying to refigure it in black-and-white. Hybrid musical forms that highlight difference are empowering in that they can deconstruct the black-and-white view—but they don't achieve grayness.

Negotiating Boundaries

They may not construct third places of their own, but, through their intentional juxtaposition and superimposition of differences, they can put binary oppositions momentarily in flux, which, depending on the listener, just might open the door to something new. By contrast, hybrid musical forms that do not highlight difference exist in spite of boundaries rather than because of them, inhabiting a gray world ripe with the imagination and possibility necessary for refiguring identities and the categories that define them. So, rather than viewing Radical Jewish Culture as a wholesale reconstitution of Jewishness, Jewish identity, or Jewish music, I think it's important to look closely at how and to what degree its various hybrid forms problematize the boundaries from which they emerge. When we do this, Radical Jewish Culture appears less as a radical break from the dominant cultural order, and more as a complex, conflicted, and ongoing negotiation of boundaries.

Notes

1. Klezmorim is the plural of klezmer, the Yiddish word for "musician" (or, more specifically, "instrumental musician"), which is a contraction of the Hebrew phrase for musical instruments (k'li zemer, lit. instruments or vessels of song). Since the 1970s, klezmer has been used to describe the repertoire and practices of contemporary musicians who play Eastern European Jewish folk music or some derivative thereof (see Levin).
2. Marcus Gammel defines the "New York Downtown Avant-Garde" as "a fluid, hard-to-define conglomerate of musicians with some common aesthetic and political ideas, who [value] the refusal of any musical categorization and the interest in a vast number of musical styles that are sometimes pasted together within single concerts, albums or pieces." Tamar Barzel defines the "downtown scene" as "the network of jazz and improvisational musicians—and the clubs, rehearsal spaces, record stores, record labels, and audiences who support them (23).
3. This essay is based on ethnographic research conducted in 2006 and 2007, and my own musical analyses of the works discussed. Though many of the consultants I discuss have since read and commented upon my work (and, in some cases, edited their statements for clarity), the interpretations and analyses are wholly mine. I take full responsibility for any errors or misrepresentations.
4. For example, saxophonist Paul Shapiro related an anecdote from the 1980s, in which a bandleader introduced him to the audience as Paul Sergeant because he thought Shapiro sounded "too Jewish." Shapiro felt that the Radical Jewish Culture project had made it easier to publicly proclaim one's Jewishness.
5. German filmmaker Claudia Heuermann has produced several excellent films on Zorn and Radical Jewish Culture. For more on Zorn's view of the artist's role in society, see Heuermann, *Bookshelf*. For more on Zorn and Radical Jewish Culture, see Heuermann, *Sabbath* and *Following Eden*.
6. For more on the fragmentation and dissolution of Radical Jewish Culture, see Barzel 205–08.
7. Zorn's Masada project has involved writing "tunes" that can be arranged and performed by numerous ensemble arrangements. In his own work, this has ranged from classically oriented chamber music arrangements to an avant-garde jazz quartet and large rock ensemble. All of these tunes are based on "Jewish" musical scales.
8. I deal with the issue of defining Jewish music throughout my dissertation ("'Beyond Klezmer'"), but particularly in ch. 4, 233–77.
9. At the time my research concluded in December 2007 the Radical Jewish Culture series comprised 120 recordings. Chapter two of my dissertation ("'Beyond Klezmer'") surveys and categorizes those recordings according to a genre taxonomy of my own design.

10. The longer and more colorful version of this story involves several phone calls, two refusals, and a couple of heated exchanges between Krakowski and Zorn before Zorn finally agreed to release it.
11. Zorn has never claimed to be the inventor of the avant-garde approaches to Jewish music featured on the Radical Jewish Culture series.
12. Glenn Dickson related that his impetus for exploring klezmer through an avant-garde lens was inspired by seeing Andy Statman perform several times in the 1980s. For more on Don Byron's work, see Barzel.
13. Readers may be interested to know that while some members of Naftule's Dream are Jewish, several, including founder and bandleader Dickson, are not. Non-Jewish side-performers are common in the Radical Jewish Culture series; non-Jewish bandleaders are less common, but exist nonetheless.
14. A significant portion of Radical Jewish Culture artists attended the New England Conservatory, including Glenn Dickson, Jamie Saft, Alon Nechushtan, Oren Bloedow, and Frank London, as did Don Byron, whose Mickey Katz tribute album (1993) also predates the Radical Jewish Culture series. The New England Conservatory is home to both the Klezmer Conservatory Band and a number of avant-garde/new music advocates.

Works Cited

Barzel, Tamar. "Radical Jewish Culture: Composer/Improvisers on New York City's 1990s Downtown Scene." Diss. U of Michigan, 2004.

Bauman, Zigmunt. "Modernity and Ambivalence." *Theory, Culture, and Society* 7 (1990): 143–69.

Beeber, Steven Lee. *The Heebie-Jeebies at CBGB's: A Secret History of Jewish Punk*. Chicago: Chicago Review, 2006.

Bhabha, Homi. "Cultures In-Between." *Questions of Cultural Identity*. Ed. Stuart Hall and Paul du Gay. London: Sage, 1996. 53–60.

Born, Georgina and David Hesmondhalgh, eds. "Introduction: On Difference, Representation, and Appropriation in Music." *Western Music and Its Others: Difference, Representation, and Appropriation in Music*. Berkeley: U of California P, 2000. 1–58.

Bourdieu, Pierre. *The Field of Cultural Production*. New York: Columbia UP, 1993.

Burke, Peter. *Cultural Hybridty*. Cambridge: Polity, 2009.

Chinen, Nate. Rev. of *Camp Songs*, by Ben Perowsky. Tzadik 7175. *Jazz Times* Nov. 2003. 20 Nov. 2008 <http://jazztimes.com/articles/14258-camp-songs-ben-perowsky>.

———. "Requiem for a Club: Saxophone and Sighs." *New York Times* 16 April 2007.

Davidow, Ari. "Wolf Krakowski Transmigrations." *Klezmer Shack*. 1997. 22 Feb. 2007 <http://www.klezmershack.com/bands/krakowski/trans/krakowski.trans.html>.

———. Rev. of *Smash, Clap!*, by Naftule's Dream. *Klezmer Shack*. 2000. 23 June 2010 <http://www.klezmershack.com/bands/nd/smashclap/nd.smashclap.html>.

———. Rev. of *Dance of the Idiots*, by Koby Israelite. *Klezmer Shack*. 2003. 14 May 2007 <http://www.klezmershack.com/bands/israelite/dance/israelite.dance.html>.

Dickson, Glenn. Personal interview. 11 Feb. 2007. Digital audio recording. Boston, MA.

Edelman, Marsha Bryan. "Continuity, Creativity, and Conflict: The Ongoing Search for 'Jewish' Music." *You Should See Yourself: Jewish Identity in Postmodern American Culture*. Ed. Vincent Brook. New Brunswick: Rutgers UP, 2006. 119–33.

Freedman, Jonathan. *Klezmer America: Jewishness, Ethnicity, Modernity*. New York: Columbia UP, 2008.

Gammel, Marcus. "Migration and Identity Politics on New York's Jewish Downtown Scene." 1999. Unpublished paper. 1 Feb. 2007 <http://www2.hu-berlin.de/fpm/wip/gammel_01.htm>.

Grossberg, Lawrence. "Identity and Cultural Studies—Is That All There Is?" *Questions of Cultural Identity*. Ed. Stuart Hall and Paul du Gay. London: Sage, 1996. 87–107.

Heuerman, Claudia, dir. *A Bookshelf on Top of the Sky: 12 Stories about John Zorn*. Perf. Joey Baron, Greg Cohen, Dave Douglas, Fred Frith, and Ikue Mori. 2002. Tzadik, 2004.

———. *Sabbath in Paradise*. Perf. Roy Nathanson, Marc Ribot, John Zorn, Frank London, and David Krakauer. 1998. Tzadik, 2007.

———. *Following Eden.* 2004. *Sabbath in Paradise.* Tzadik, 2007.
Israelite, Koby. *Dance of the Idiots.* Tzadik, 2003.
———. *Is He Listening?* Tzadik, 2009.
———. *Mood Swings.* Tzadik, 2005.
Janeczko, Jeffrey. "'Beyond Klezmer': Redefining Jewish Music for the Twenty-first Century." Diss. U of California, Los Angeles, 2009.
———. "A Tale of Four Diasporas: Case Studies on the Relevance of 'Diaspora' in Contemporary American Jewish Music." *Perspectives on Jewish Music: Sacred and Secular.* Ed. Jonathan L. Friedmann. Lanham: Lexington, 2009. 9–40.
Kamel, Mordechai. "Wolf Krakowski's Goyrl: Destiny." *Klezmer Shack.* 2002. 22 Feb. 2007 <http://www.klezmershack.com/articles/2002.kamel.goyrl.html>.
Kraidy, Marwan. *Hybridity, or the Cultural Logic of Globalization.* Philadelphia: Temple UP, 2005.
Krakowski, Wolf. *Goyrl: Destiny.* Wolf Krakowski and the Lonesome Brothers. Tzadik, 2002.
———. Personal interview. 26 Feb. 2007. Digital audio recording. Northampton, MA.
———. *Transmigrations: Gilgul.* Wolf Krakowski and the Lonesome Brothers. Tzadik, 2001.
Levin, Neil W. "Introduction to Volume 05: Klezmer in the Concert Hall: Rebirth of a Folk Tradition." 1 Sept. 2010. 21 Oct. 2010 <http://www.milkenarchive.org/articles/view/introduction-to-volume-5>.
Lipsitz, George. *Dangerous Crossroads: Popular Music, Postmodernism, and the Poetics of Place.* New York: Verso, 1994.
Mandel, Howard. Rev. of *Search for the Golden Dreydl,* by Naftule's Dream. *Jazziz* 15.7 (1998): 69–70.
Naftule's Dream. *Job.* Tzadik, 2001.
———. *Search for the Golden Dreydl.* Tzadik, 1997.
———. *Smash, Clap!* Tzadik, 1998.
Perowsky, Ben. *Camp Songs.* Ben Perowsky Trio. Tzadik, 2003.
———. Telephone interview. 28 Feb. 2007. Digital audio recording. West New York, NJ.
Pieterse, Jan Nederveen. "Hybridty, So What? The Anti-hybridity Backlash and the Riddles of Recognition. *Theory, Culture, and Society* 18.2–3 (2001): 219–45.
Rapport, Evan. "Bill Finnegan's Gershwin Arrangements and the American Concept of Hybridity." *Journal of the Society for American Music* 2.4 (2008): 507–30.
Rev. of *Goyrl:Destiny,* by Wolf Krakowski. *Rainlore's World of Music.* 9 Jan. 2004. 14 May 2007 <http://rainloresworldofmusic.net/Reviews/Revws_E-K/Krakowski_Wolf-Goyrl_Destiny.html>.
Rev. of *Transmigrations: Gilgul,* by Wolf Krakowski. *Rainlore's World of Music.* 7 Jan 2004. 13 Nov. 2008 <http://www.rainloresworldofmusic.net/Reviews/Revws_E-K/Krakowski_Wolf-Transmigrations.html>.

Ribot, Marc. "The Representation of Jewish Identity in Downtown Music." Unpublished paper, courtesy Marc Ribot, 2002.

Rogovoy, Seth. Rev. of *Transmigrations: Gilgul. Sing Out* 45.4 (2002): 157.

Roth, Matthue. Rev. of *Dance of the Idiots,* by Koby Israelite. *Zeek.* Nov. 2003. 25 Nov. 2008 <http://www.zeek.net/music_0311.shtml>.

Shapiro, Paul. Personal interview. 22 Feb. 2007. New York, NY.

Shatz, Adam. "Music: Crossing Music's Borders in Search of Identity; Downtown, a Reach for Ethnicity." *New York Times* 3 Oct. 1999.

Shirim Klezmer Orchestra. *Pincus and the Pig.* Perf. Shirim Klezmer Orchestra and Maurice Sendak. Tzadik, 2004.

Slobin, Mark. *Subcultural Sounds: Micromusics of the West.* Hanover: Wesleyan UP, 1993.

Waterman, Christopher. *Jùjú: A Social History and Ethnography of an African Popular Music.* Chicago: U of Chicago P, 1990.

Weiss, Sarah. "Permeable Boundaries: Hybridity, Music, and the Reception of Robert Wilson's *I La Galigo.*" *Ethnomusicology* 52.2 (2008): 203–38.

Zorn, John. Liner notes to *Great Jewish Music: Serge Gainsbourg.* Tzadik, 1997.

———. "Radical Jewish Culture." *Tzadik.* 2006. 10 May 2006 <http://www.tzadik.com>.

About the Contributors

LISA ANSELL is Associate Director of the Casden Institute for the Study of the Jewish Role in American Life at the University of Southern California. She received her BA in French and Near East Studies from UCLA and her MA in Middle East Studies from Harvard University. She was the Chair of the World Language Department of New Community Jewish High School for five years before coming to USC in August, 2007.

JEFF JANECZCO holds a BA in music from the Metropolitan State College of Denver, and an MA and PhD in ethnomusicology from the University of California, Los Angeles. His essay "A Tale of Four Diasporas: Case Studies on the Relevance of 'Diaspora' in Contemporary American Jewish Music" appears in *Perspectives on Jewish Music: Sacred and Secular*, edited by Jonathan L. Friedmann (Lanham, MD: Lexington Books, 2009). He is currently Curator for the Milken Archive of Jewish Music, a non-profit, "living archive" dedicated to expanding the awareness and appreciation of Jewish music.

DAVID KAUFMAN is a scholar of American Jewish history and author of *Shul with a Pool: The "Synagogue-Center" in American Jewish History* (Hanover, NH: UPNE, 1999). Having taught at the Hebrew Union College and USC from 2000–2009, he currently holds the Robert & Florence Kaufman Chair in Jewish Studies at Hofstra University in Hempstead, NY. His second book, tentatively titled *Jewhooing the Sixties: American Celebrity and Jewish Identity*, is scheduled for publication in 2012.

JOSH KUN is Associate Professor in the Annenberg School for Communication & Journalism and the Department of American Studies & Ethnicity at USC, where he also directs The Popular Music Project of the Norman Lear Center. Kun's research focuses on the arts and politics of cultural connection, with an emphasis on popular music, the cultures of globalization, the US-Mexico border, and Jewish-American musical history. He is co-editor of the book series "Refiguring American Music" for Duke University Press and is a founding member of The Idelsohn Society for Musical Preservation.

PETER LA CHAPELLE is an Associate Professor of History at Nevada State College. A former journalist and Smithsonian Postdoctoral Fellow, he is author of *Proud to Be an Okie: Cultural Politics, Country Music, and Migration to Southern California* (Berkeley: University of California Press, 2007). When not listening to old records or trying to keep up with his sons, he is working on a new book about the connections between country music and political campaigns.

JONATHAN Z. S. POLLACK is Instructor in History and Chair of the Humanities Department at Madison Area Technical College. From 2008–2011, he has also held the MATC Fellowship at the Institute for Research in the Humanities at the University of Wisconsin-Madison. He holds a PhD in History from the University of Wisconsin-Madison and has recorded two CDs with Madison-based klezmer band Yid Vicious. His next project will examine Jewish scrap, second-hand, and surplus dealers in the industrial Midwest.

JODY ROSEN is a journalist and author. He is the music critic for the online magazine Slate, and the author of *White Christmas: The Story of an American Song* (New York: Scribner, 2002). In 2006, Rosen compiled *Jewface*, an anthology of early twentieth-century novelty songs about Jewish characters (Idelsohn Society). On March 27, 2008 Rosen's front page *New York Times* article reported the discovery by American audio historians of French inventor Édouard-Léon Scott de Martinville's 1860 phonautograph recording, the earliest known recording of the human voice to be played back.

GAYLE WALD is Professor and Chair of English at George Washington University. She is the author of "'Shout, Sister, Shout!': The Untold Story of Rock-and-Roll Trailblazer Sister Rosetta Tharpe" (Boston: Beacon, 2007). Her current book project explores the TV show "Soul!," a PBS production that brought black power sensibilities to a national audience between 1968 and 1973. In addition to her academic work, she works with Reboot, an organization devoted to the vitality of twenty-first century American Jewish culture.

BRUCE ZUCKERMAN is the Myron and Marian Casden Director of the Casden Institute and a Professor of Religion at USC, where he teaches courses in the Hebrew Bible, the Bible in western literature, the ancient Near East, and archaeology. A specialist in photographing and reconstructing ancient texts, he is involved in numerous projects related to the Dead Sea Scrolls. On ancient topics, his major publications are *Job the Silent: A Study in Biblical Counterpoint* and *The Leningrad Codex: A Facsimile Edition*, for which he and his brother Kenneth did the principal photography. Zuckerman also has a continuing interest in modern Jewish thought, often looking at modern issues from an ancient perspective. He most recently co-authored *Double Takes: Thinking and Rethinking Issues of Modern Judaism in Ancient Contexts* with Zev Garber and contributed a chapter to Garber's book, *Mel Gibson's Passion: The Film, the Controversy, and Its Implications*.

The USC Casden Institute for the Study of the Jewish Role in American Life

The American Jewish community has played a vital role in shaping the politics, culture, commerce and multiethnic character of Southern California and the American West. Beginning in the mid-nineteenth century, when entrepreneurs like Isaias Hellman, Levi Strauss and Adolph Sutro first ventured out West, American Jews became a major force in the establishment and development of the budding Western territories. Since 1970, the number of Jews in the West has more than tripled. This dramatic demographic shift has made California—specifically, Los Angeles—home to the second largest Jewish population in the United States. Paralleling this shifting pattern of migration, Jewish voices in the West are today among the most prominent anywhere in the United States. Largely migrating from Eastern Europe, the Middle East and the East Coast of the United States, Jews have invigorated the West, where they exert a considerable presence in every sector of the economy—most notably in the media and the arts. With the emergence of Los Angeles as a world capital in entertainment and communications, the Jewish perspective and experience in the region are being amplified further. From artists and activists to scholars and professionals, Jews are significantly influencing the shape of things to come in the West and across the United States. In recognition of these important demographic and societal changes, in 1998 the University of Southern California established a scholarly institute dedicated to studying contemporary Jewish life in America with special emphasis on the western United States. The Casden Institute explores issues related to the interface between the Jewish community and the broader, multifaceted cultures that form the nation—issues of relationship as much as of Jewishness itself. It is also enhancing the educational experience for students at USC and elsewhere by exposing them to the problems—and promise—of life in Los Angeles' ethnically, socially, culturally and economically diverse community. Scholars, students and community leaders examine the ongoing contributions of American Jews in the arts, business, media, literature, education, politics, law and social relations, as well as the relationships between Jewish Americans and other groups, including African Americans,

Latinos, Asian Americans and Arab Americans. The Casden Institute's scholarly orientation and contemporary focus, combined with its location on the West Coast, set it apart from—and makes it an important complement to—the many excellent Jewish Studies programs across the nation that center on Judaism from an historical or religious perspective.

For more information about the USC Casden Institute,
visit www.usc.edu/casdeninstitute, e-mail casden@usc.edu,
or call (213) 740-3405.

www.ingramcontent.com/pod-product-compliance
Lightning Source LLC
Chambersburg PA
CBHW051932160426
43198CB00012B/2119